MAP
OF THE
HARBOUR of DUNDEE
WITH THE
PROPOSED IMPROVEMENTS
August 1814
Reduced and Engraved from Mr Telford's Plan
by Thos. Ivory

Portrait of George Kinloch of that Ilk by an unknown artist — from
the collection of Sir John Kinloch Bart, of that Ilk.

The Radical Laird

A Biography of
George Kinloch
1775 – 1833

———

Charles Tennant

———

With a Foreword by
The Rt. Hon. George Thomson, LL.D., M.P.

Kineton: The Roundwood Press

1970

Copyright © Charles Tennant 1970

First published 1970 by The Roundwood Press (Publishers) Ltd.

SBN 900093 16 1

Set in 'Monotype' Bell, series 341 and printed by Gordon Norwood at
The Roundwood Press, Kineton, in the County of Warwick,
on paper made by the Guard Bridge Paper Mills, Leuchars, Fife.
Plates made by The Process Engraving Company Limited, Coventry.
End papers lithographed by Charles Hill of Warwick.

Made and printed in Great Britain

Dedicated to

my wife

Barbara Cecilia

who has inherited much of her great, great grandfather's sense of humour and made my life more enjoyable thereby.

Contents

Illustrations

Acknowledgments

The principle source of material for this biography is family letters, and so my thanks are due first and foremost to my brother-in-law Sir John Kinloch, Baronet of that Ilk, for giving me access to the 'Kinloch box'. His cousins Miss Kinloch Smyth and Mr Richard Linguard Guthrie have also contributed information, letters and papers which have helped to fill in the gaps in the life of their mutual ancestor.

I am also indepted to the Very Reverend Dr. John A. Fraser of Aberdalgie who helped me with the home & country life chapters and W. M. Roach of the Department of Extra Mural Studies at Glasgow University who helped with the historical chapters. These two people read my first script and advised in many ways. Besides these two individuals, I owe a debt of gratitude to the Principal of Dundee University, the Staff of his Historical Department, and to Professor Gordon Donaldson of Edinburgh University. I might never have completed the book had it not been for their encouragement in my belief that the story of George Kinloch was well worthy of the telling, and also that it would be a valuable contribution to the history of that period. I must also thank Hubert Fenwick, the author of Architect Royal, for introducing me to Gordon Norwood of The Roundwood Press who was the first publisher to take an interest in my work.

All the public libraries and public bodies whom I have pestered with questions have been unfailingly polite and helpful. To mention only The Dundee and Perth Public Libraries, the Signet Library, the Scottish Record Office, Hansard, the National Monuments Records and the Dundee Courier Library would not mean that I have forgotten the many other organisations and individuals with whom I have been in correspondence and to whom I am very grateful.

Lastly, and most sincerely, I thank my part-time Secretary Mrs Todd of Alyth for her meticulous care in transcribing the letters into typescript and, for the many hours of repetitive work.

Foreword

IREAD Mr Tennant's biography of George Kinloch for the first time during the week-end immediately after the General Election of June, 1970. In that election, one in four of the voters in the city of Dundee, where George Kinloch was the first Member of Parliament, failed to use the universal suffrage which he had suffered outlawry and persecution to win for them. I commend this book in the first place, therefore, as a reminder of the courage and the sacrifice that went into the cause of Parliamentary reform at the beginning of last century.

But the book is much more than that. It is a fresh and vivid study of the social life of the Scottish lowlands in that curious breathing-space — full of fears and hopes — before the full impact of the industrial revolution broke on city and countryside alike. It is also a touching human study of a man of nobility of character in the true sense of that word. He was a good husband and father, a progressive farmer and was inspired by a genuine love of his country and his fellow citizens. Mr. Tennant wisely lets George Kinloch speak for himself, for he was an inveterate diarist and letter-writer.

'What a glorious invention is that of writing,' he advised his son. 'It enables us to converse on matters of business or amusement however great the distance may be which separates us.'

Or again, when in exile:

'Cause Maggy to write in a small hand all the news of everything, however trifling it may appear to you . . . the weather, farm operations, windmill, etc.'

George Kinloch practised what he preached and we are the beneficiaries. He loved his family and his land, his work and his good causes, and his devotion to them all comes out in his letters and gives the reader a picture of his life and times as clear and as full of character as a period print.

He had his human foibles and frailties. He was an honest man, if ever there was one, but as a good pre-1832 radical, he hated all taxes and customs impositions, regarding them as the powerful robbing the people to pay for repressive and unnecessary armies and provide sinecures for placemen. (I wonder how he would regard modern radicalism with its belief in taxes as a means of redistributing wealth and welfare?) His detestation of customs duties leads him to much detailed advice to his family on the art of smuggling! His daughters are recommended to put silver forks inside the sleeves of their dresses, and his sons to wear two shirts and conceal the contraband between.

George Kinloch was not only an 'improving laird'; he was a pioneer of the application of science to industry. He was one of the creators of a modern harbour at Dundee. It was, in fact the clash between the advance Harbour Trustees and the reactionary self-appointed Town Council that led him into radical politics and to exile. He came back from exile in one of the early Cross-Channel steamboats, and immediately set about trying to harness steam to a railway from the rich farmlands of Strathmore where he lived, through the coastal hills to Dundee Harbour. His vision may be judged by the fact that the first meeting for this purpose was held in 1825, five years before the 'Rocket', the first steam locomotive, made its maiden trip. The 'Kinloch Railway', opened in 1831, was the first passenger railway in Scotland.

But George Kinloch's fame rests on his arrest and exile for advocating 'one man — one vote' and for denouncing the massacre at Peterloo in an address to a peaceful gathering of 10,000 people on Dundee's Magdalen Green. Such was the hysteria of the time that fashionable and famous Counsel in Edinburgh, briefed for the defence, refused to see him personally and saw their duty as being confined to convincing him of his guilt and the certainty of his punishment. He was forced to flee to France to escape transportation.

This was an ugly period whose characteristic figure was the informer or police spy — in Kinloch's case probably a Dundee clergyman. But luckily for Kinloch, the tyranny of the times was tempered by the incompetence of the tyrants and their lack of contemporary techniques of tyranny. At the Market Cross in Edinburgh, George Kinloch was denounced as an outlaw and fugitive and 'ordaned to be put to the horn'. But in an era before the invention of the telephone and with no full-time police forces, Kinloch was able to spend a week travelling by coach to London, obtain a passport in the metropolis and sail from Dover to Calais. Indeed, after three years of outlawry, he successfully risked coming back in secret to his Strathmore farmhouse before he was finally pardoned. Fortunate, inefficient times!

When Parliamentary reform was finally conceded it was appropriate that George Kinloch should become Dundee's first M.P. — but it also turned out to be an event of great poignance. There was time in his letters for only a few vivid pictures of the reformed Parliament before Kinloch was taken ill. In the travelling conditions of the times it was impossible for him to return home to be nursed by his wife. He died alone in London after attending for only a month the Parliament he had helped to reform.

Mr. Tennant has rescued from quite undeserved obscurity a significant figure in Scottish politics. Thanks to George Kinloch's own character and his quality as a letter-writer, he has also produced a minor masterpiece of social history.

GEORGE THOMSON

xiv

Author's Preface

I HAVE SPENT a lot of time in the past months in public libraries and attics trying to sort out the life of George Kinloch, the
Radical Laird of Strathmore whose statue stands in Albert
Square in Dundee. He was my wife's great, great-grandfather
and I have therefore had a personal interest in bringing this
unusual ancestor to life. I have collected as much information
as I can find about him from contemporary newspapers and the
writers of his time but, it is his own voluminous letters which
illustrate the character of this unorthodox man. These letters
are written informally to his wife and children, avoiding the
formal style of correspondence of the day and are therefore a
true commentary on the events of his life and illustrate how he
and his family lived.

To-day, from a viewpoint on the North slope of Kinpurnie
Hill, looking down on the valley of Strathmore, it is possible
to pick out the house in which he lived and to identify the land
which he farmed. Across the valley is the rising ground where
he hunted the roe buck, and, beyond Glamis, lie the more
distant glens of Glenshee, Glenisla and Glenogil where he went
to shoot the muirfowl. This is the land he loved and knew so
well. Looking down on the road which comes from Dundee to
Meigle, it is possible, in imagination, to see the Laird disap-
pearing round a corner, as he described himself passing by on a
hot summer's day one hundred and fifty years ago.

28th June, 1817.

I walked from Carnoustie on Sunday, and was completely
birsled, altho' I walked all the way without my coat. It was
liker the climate of Italy than of Scotland, the thermometer

standing at 80 degrees. The wheat is in the ear, and beginning to bloom. We had new potatoes twelve days ago, and pease as many as we chuse. In short the country presents a most beautiful prospect, with every appearance of happiness, if our *infamous* rulers would only allow us to enjoy our natural rights, instead of gagging the people of Great Britain in order that a base set of drivellers may continue in power. But it is impossible that their despotism can last long, and I most sincerely wish them all to the Devil.

With this extract from one of his letters, George Kinloch introduces himself as a man of extraordinary contrasts. On the one hand he is the laird, countryman, and farmer and, on the other, he is the Radical politician with intensely strong feelings for the lot of his less fortunate fellow men. This is the man whose life I shall try to describe.

October, 1970   CHARLES TENNANT

CHAPTER ONE

The Kinloch and Smyth Families in Strathmore

STRATHMORE IS RATHER off the beaten track of the conventional holiday-maker in Scotland so that many people may not know exactly where this valley lies. A motorist on his way North by the main road from Perth to Aberdeen enters Strathmore after passing through Coupar-Angus and, if it is a fine day in the spring, he will see the snow covered Grampian Mountains across the river Isla to the North and the Sidlaw Hills to the South. The Sidlaws divide Strathmore from the estuary of the Tay, Dundee, and the Angus coast.

It is an agricultural valley with some of the best farm land in Scotland and the names of the farms such as Islabank, Thorn, Newhouse of Glamis, Lindertis and many others have made history in the breeding of Pedigree Aberdeen-Angus and Shorthorn cattle. The second Statistical Account of the Parish of Meigle, the Parish in which George Kinloch lived reads: 'Few sheep are bred in this parish and the Leicestershire is generally most esteemed. Angus-shire cattle are the principal stock; but some are bred from a cross with the short-horned (Teeswater) bull and accounted good feeders and early fattened. It is pretty well known in Scotland, that the farmers in Strathmore are amongst the most intelligent and enterprising of their profession.' This description of the agriculture which was written by the Rev. James Mitchell, the Parish Minister in the year 1833, remains true of the farms and farmers

1

in Strathmore to-day. There are no factory chimneys or coal mines or power stations to disfigure the landscape and so, although the fields are larger to allow modern farm machinery to operate and many of the shelter belt hedges have disappeared, the countryside remains, to look at, much as it did one hundred and fifty years ago.

Traditionally it is the land of the Ogilvies, Wedderburns, Nairnes, Carnegies, Oliphants, Blairs and Kinlochs, and the descendants of these families are still to be found here. They have intermarried and dispersed and come back again, and their names are to be found in the telephone directory, often hyphenated, such as Ogilvy-Wedderburn, Blair-Oliphant, Kinloch-Smyth, etc. as a result of marriage or inheritance. These people are conscious of their roots belonging to the soil of Strathmore, and they return here to roost after service in other parts of the world in business or professional life, in the Services or in Industry, to enjoy their old age in retirement in the country of their origin.

The way of life of the people who make a living here is also not greatly changed. Their livelihood depends on the prosperity of farming, and the trades which go with farming. Their recreations and interests are the interests of all country people, the weather, the state of the crops, their gardens, the fishing and shooting. They notice the movement of birds, the arrival and departure of the geese and whooper swans which inhabit the Isla valley in great numbers in the winter, and all the other wild life around them.

The greatest change has come in the minds of the people, their ideas, their beliefs, their humour and their social conventions which make it difficult for the modern man to understand the mentality of the people who lived four or five generations ago, and so the man with the conventional ideas of 1800, if he came to live in a modern society would find it difficult to understand many things such as the attitude to crime and punishment, the absence of poverty, and particularly how the landed gentlemen are no longer more important than anyone else. Conversely a man having modern political ideas and social conventions and living in 1800 would be an oddity, so that he would be considered by his contemporaries to be

2

either a visionary or a revolutionary. Such a man was George Kinloch, a twentieth century man who was born five generations before his time.

The story of his life starts at the end of the 18th century when there were Smyths of Balhary living in the old house of that name on the North bank of the Isla, not far from Alyth, and Kinlochs in Kinloch house across the south bank of the river, near to the village of Meigle. Although there was no bridge over the river at that time, a rowing boat worked a ferry at the 'Boat Hole' and the families knew one another very well. These two families had lived face to face across the river for the past three centuries and five generations, but, in spite of being neighbours for so long, had retained very different characters and characteristics.

The Smyths[1] are first recorded in the 'Baronage of Scotland' compiled by Sir Robert Douglas of Glenbervie, as being in Polcalk, a farm about a mile east of Balhary, in 1520, when John Smyth, first of Polcalk, married Janet, daughter of Blair Drummond. Perhaps he married above himself, and so got admitted to the records of the landed gentry. By his wife Janet, he had one son John who married Marian daughter of John Blair of Ardblair, and their son John again married a Drummond of Atholl. John Smyth succeeded John Smyth with unfailing regularity, and nothing else in particular happened until the eighth generation of John Smyth who, for some unknown reason, made a break with tradition, and called his son James. This James, whose life span took him through the greater part of the eighteenth century, may have been the most interesting character of the Smyth dynasty. Besides inheriting the Balhary property, he became Clerk to the Signet in Edinburgh, and acted as legal, financial, and estate adviser to most of the families in Strathmore, conducting his legal business both from Balhary and from an office in Geddes Close, in Edinburgh. Unlike the Kinlochs, the Smyths seldom, if ever, put a foot wrong and were respected in Edinburgh as being reliable, respectable, and probably very conventional people. The only remarkable feature of their history is the formula of how they managed to restrict their family to one male child in each generation.

The first Kinloch to become a 'man of property' was a Dundee doctor, Doctor David Kinloch, who lived from 1559 to 1617. He dedicated a poem written in Latin 'De hominis Procreatione' to James VI in which he expounded some early theories about sexual intercourse, conception and advice to midwives as a result of which he became 'Medicinae Doctor Regius' or medical adviser to the King. He travelled widely on the Continent, was imprisoned in Spain during the Inquisition and acquired a sufficient fortune to purchase the estates of Aberbothrie and Balmyle astride the River Isla which he re-named Kinloch. Doctor David's grandson purchased a Nova Scotian Baronetcy and the next two generations of Baronets were sufficiently leisured to play golf on the links of St. Andrews using golf balls made out of seagulls feathers. The eighteenth century Kinlochs of Kinloch, however, became involved on the rebel side with the Jacobite risings of the '15 and the '45 which proved disastrous to the family fortunes. Sir James Kinloch, great great-grandson of Doctor David raised the second Batallion of the Angus Regiment to fight for Prince Charles Edward Stuart and, as a result, he forfeited his estate and title and was fortunate to escape hanging. During these generations the Kinlochs, in contrast with the Smyths, had been prolific and they had married within the close circle of landed families in Perthshire, Angus and Fife. Cousins were living on smaller estates in the neighbourhood and they all seem to have been liberal minded with strong political opinions very different from the Smyths.

Another great difference between the Smyths and the Kinlochs was their attitude to land and money. The Smyths had become professional people and got into the way of advising their clients about their land in terms of pounds, shillings, and pence, whereas the Kinlochs lived on their land, and thought of their land with the pride of possession. Money was not so important to them as land. It was the Kinloch's way of life,and they were jealous to acquire more and more land. James Smyth, who had married one of the Kinlochs, — George Kinloch's Aunt Cecilia, said of the Kinlochs, for whom he had acted professionally all his life, and whom he had helped in their many difficulties — 'I did not charge so much for all my trouble as would have paid my Horse Hyre, and acted for the family purely out of the regaird I had to Sir James who in my younger days of business had befriended me.' If one branch of the Kinloch family lost or squandered their inheritance, there was a good chance that another would make it up, and this is what had happened at the end of the eighteenth century, and how George, the subject of this life story, happened to become the Laird of the most coveted Kinloch land, and was able to call himself Kinloch of Kinloch.

George Kinloch and his branch of the family to which this biography relates was descended from a younger brother of the first baronet described above. His grandfather and great grandfather had both been doctors but his father was Commissioned into the 53rd Regiment of Foot and became Captain George Oliphant Kinloch. This was a strange break-away from the Jacobite tradition of the family as the Captain's own father had taken part in the rebellion of 1715 with his cousin Sir James, had been imprisoned in Stirling Castle, tried in Carlisle, and sentenced to death, although he escaped the extreme penalty. When the rebellion of '45 broke out, George Oliphant, then a Cornet in the 53rd Regiment serving in Ireland, wrote to a younger brother in Edinburgh in a letter dated 13th December 1745, saying—

'I was sorry to see in our news letters that Sir James Kinloch was apointed by the Pretender (who with the Divell had) to be Shyrif of Forfar and was reasing a Regt. for the Reables. I am afraid he will feel his fault when it is too late. I was in hopes his good sense would have dictated better to him and for my own part he was one of the last I should have suspected. God petty him and all those that have been so foolish. I am sure his going has given me a good deal of uneasiness, besides the misery of his learge family which God Almighty help.'

Captain Kinloch's military career was undistinguished. He was stationed for a long time in Gibraltar and after failing to raise sufficient money to purchase his promotion to Major, retired on half pay. He sold the family property of Clashbennie and settled down on the small estate of Rosemount near

Blairgowrie, not far from the well-known golf course of that name.

At last, when he was over fifty years old, his luck took a surprising turn for the better. His younger brother John, had gone out to Jamaica as a Sugar Planter where he accumulated a considerable fortune from rum and sugar grown on the Grange estate. He died out there in 1770 and left his entire estate to Captain George. A letter from Jamaica acquainting the Captain of this brother's death said that the planter bowed round to each of his weeping friends, and, with a placid smile on his face, departed into 'the world of Spirits.' The writer also said that Mr Kinloch had left two mulattoes and one quadroon child, but that these things happen to most people in Jamaica.

The Jamaican estate was not the whole extent of George Oliphant's surprising windfall. It so happened that the planter had intended to come home from the West Indies and retire and, with this prospect in view he had instructed James Smyth his lawyer brother-in-law to purchase the family property of Kinloch at Meigle from his cousins if this became available. This purchase had just been effected because, after Culloden, Sir James had been tried for High Treason, condemned to death and, although later reprieved was ordered to leave the country or reside in England. His son William had been unable to maintain the estate and found it necessary to sell. In consequence, by pure chance, George Oliphant Kinloch, who had said of his cousins that they would 'feel their fault when it was too late' became the Laird of Kinloch.

On the strength of his inheritance, the Captain, although well beyond middle age, proceeded to marry a county lady, Anne, the twenty-year old daughter of another penniless laird, Colonel John Balneavis of Cairnbeddie, an estate a few miles north of Perth. Anne and her sister were to be the last generation of the Balneavis family.

Anne, who suffered from tuberculosis and would not live long, bore her husband two sons in quick succession, John, born in 1773, called probably after his Jamaican uncle, and George, who was to become the Radical Laird, born on the thirtieth of April 1775. In October of this same year, Captain George became seriously ill, and James Smyth the family lawyer, was hastily summoned to prepare a Will suitable for the circumstances. 'By reason of his distress,' as the Will stated, the Captain was unable to sign, so that two Notaries were brought in and confirmed 'by getting full power from him by his touching of the pen,' as a result of which a most elaborate settlement of his estate was drawn up.

Needless to say, Captain George Oliphant Kinloch died very soon afterwards, and his widow Anne — herself not strong, was left with her two infant sons, John aged two, and George, a baby in arms. She was then living in a house called Belle Vue, later to be called Airlie Lodge in Dundee, because Kinloch House was in the course of re-building after a fire. By this accident of birth, George was able to claim that he had been born 'A native of Dundee,' and was proud to do so.

His statue, standing in Albert Square, Dundee, is not far from the site of the house in which he was born.

---

[1] Baronage of Scotland by Sir Robert Douglas of Glenbervie. Vol. 3 p. 542.

CHAPTER TWO

George Kinloch's Early Life: 1775-1796

GEORGE KINLOCH and his elder brother John were brought up in conditions which would be described to-day by psychologists as a 'disturbed' or 'insecure' childhood. World conditions of the time and their home life were both disturbing. In world affairs it was the time of the French Revolution and the Reign of Terror when the French Aristocrats were either being guillotined, or escaping from France with the help of the legendary Scarlet Pimpernel, or by similar means. In the boy's home life, the disturbance came from the early death of both parents, constant change of home surroundings and family illnesses, but the effect which this insecurity had on young George Kinloch was to produce a strong and independent character with a wide experience of life and world affairs at an early age.

To begin at the beginning, the baby George was born in Dundee on the 30th April 1775, and his father only survived long enough to be able to announce the arrival of his second son to old James Smyth at Balhary—

Dear Jame,

Yesterday, about six of the clock, Mrs. G. Kinloch was safely delivered of a son, a great stout child. She is as well as her situation will admit of.

I shall give you and my sister some days notice before the Christening in hopes of having the pleasure of both your companys and John if he is in the country.

I remain Dear Jame,
Yours sincerely, G. O. Kinloch.

The widowed mother Anne, who was now only twenty-two, was left with the two boys, the infant son George and elder son John not yet out of nappies or 'hippens,' as these garments were then called. Anne, being so much younger than her husband, was a contemporary of the next generation of Smyth, another John who had become the active partner of the law firm and lived in Edinburgh. Unlike other generations of Smyth, he and his second wife Joanna went in for children in a big way and so Anne turned to the Smyth cousins for family and financial advice. Although they were her late husband's nearest relations and her best friends, the formal style of letter-writing was customary and the following is how she wrote for advice.

Dundee,
18th March, 1776.

Mr. John Smyth,
Writer, Geddis Close,
Edinburgh.
Dear Sir,

I hope Mrs. Smyth and you are well, and that your little daughter has got the better of all her complaints; my little Georgie has quite recovered his little brash, and is grown the liveliest little fellow ever you saw, and Jock has got the use of his tongue so well, that it seldom lies. I am glad to hear that you are like to get so good a tenant for Airlie Lodge. I hear Jas. Wedderburn has made an offer, I had got the garden laboured, and am getting it sown, that can be no loss to anybodie. As the grass in the upper park will not cut, what would you think of ploughing it up; the crop would pay the feu duty; however, as it's only a thought of my own, its more than probable its not proper, but you may let me know your opinion. I am desired to draw on you for what money I want, I would not wish to do it if it were in the least inconvenient, so let me hear from you, and what you can spare. Have you heard of any Chaise that you think will answer me, I will need one by the time I go to

9

Kinloch, but a new one comes so terrible high, that I fear it will break me — that's true.

Mr. and Mrs. Nairne (of Drumkilbo) join me in offering best compliments to your wife, father, and all other enquiring friends.

And I remain, Dear Sir,
Your most humble servant,
Anne Oliphant Kinloch.

Her little Georgie and his cousin, the little Smyth daughter Helen, about whom she was enquiring were to become man and wife and will therefore become the principal characters of this story.

Anne Kinloch only survived until her little Georgie was seven years old and during these seven years she had married again and become a Mrs Calderwood — all very confusing for the children. She died in Plymouth on her way to the South of France to try to find a cure for the tuberculosis from which she suffered, and so the children had to find another home. Anne's sister, a Mrs Pringle, stepped into the breach and gave them a home, but she had the same tubercular affliction and died in Gibraltar five years later. Mr Pringle wrote telling of their Aunt's death and saying —

My Dear Boys,
Your aunt spoke of you and blessed you in her latest breath, prayed that you might be good men, as just and honourable as your father and that I would continue to regard you as my nephews. You may therefore depend on every advice and assistance I can give you in your journey through life.
Yours,
B. Pringle.

At least the boys had received love and affection during some of their formative years first from their mother and then from their aunt, but now they were out on their own again. Their nearest relatives, the Smyths, were living in St. James Square in the old town of Edinburgh and, by this time, John and Joanna Smyth had three boys and six girls of their own; it was a problem for them to accept two more Kinloch children into the family circle, and also, the fact that the elder Kinloch boy had shown obvious signs of inherited tuberculosis, did not make them any more welcome.

John Smyth therefore called a meeting of the other Tutors, who were Thomas Graham of Balgowan, later Lord Lynedoch, and Sir William Nairne, Baronet of Dunsinnan to decide what was best to be done for the boys.

They took advice from the famous Edinburgh medical specialist Alexander Munro Secundus[1] about the problem of the elder son's health, and this Doctor Munro with another Doctor Joseph Robertson, gave the following report of his case —

We have carefully considered Mr. Kinloch's constitution, and present state of health, and join entirely with his Tutors in the opinion that it will be of material service to him to go abroad for a considerable time, and to spend the summer in a Northern, and the winter in a Southern country, so as to live in as equable a temperature of climate as is possible.

For his summer residence we would recommend Nancy in Lorraine, in preference to any of the towns in the Netherlands, as having a very dry and airy situation, with every advantage of language, education in general, and company. For the shortness and mildness of the winter, no place seems to us preferable to Nice. He ought to move from Nancy about the end of September, when the cold begins; and from Nice about the beginning of April. Although we are well convinced that a Sea Voyage is of great use in a certain state of Breast complaints, yet, on account of the coldness of the East winds, the time that may be lost waiting for a change of wind, and, after all, the danger of a sudden change of life from a warm house to a ship, perhaps indifferently accomodated for passengers, we think he should travel to Nancy by land as much as is possible, or that he should take the shortest passage from Dover to Calais. The sooner he sets out, we think it will be the better, as, in the space of a single week, he will get into a much better climate; and during his journey his face is to the sun and the back of the carriage to the cold winds. We think he ought at all times to wear thin Spanish flannel next the skin, and to be otherwise well clothed.

His diet ought to consist of vegetables, milk, with the addition, at dinner only, of soup, calves feet jellies, and a sparing portion of white fowl, or of the lighter parts of fresh meat, plain drest; water, with a single glass of wine, will make the best drink at meals. Riding slowly on horseback is the kind of exercise best suited to his constitution, and he ought carefully to avoid not only cold and wet, but being overheated or fatigued with moderate exercise too long continued.

He ought to be as regular as possible with respect to the times of his meals and hours of sleep. He should go early to bed, sleep alone on a mattress and remain in bed eight or nine hours. The morning and evening dews are heavy, and dangerous in a greater degree in a warm than in a cold country, and therefore to be guarded against. If, notwithstanding the above precautions, he shall happen to be seized with pain and difficulty of breathing, cough, heat, thirst and quick pulse, it will be necessary for him to let Blood from the arm once, or oftener, if the symptoms are not relieved. To keep the belly open by taking occasionally a tea-spoonful or two of the cooling laxative electuarys. To take two or three times a day a table-spoonful of the cooling Pectoral Mixture B.

If after bleeding once or oftener, a fixed pain remains in the breast or much difficulty of breathing, a blistering Plaister C. is to be applied. Gentle sweating is to be promoted by the Pectoral mixture B. and lukewarm drink. Till all feverish symptoms are gone, his diet is to consist of vegetables, bread, milk, whey. The steams of hot water in which honey is dissolved, breathed from a tea-pot give some relief in cough and pains of the breast.

After the violence of an attack upon the breast is abated, he ought to be put on a course of asses milk.

EDINBURGH, May 4, 1788.   Alex. Munro.

Jos. Robertson.

A contemporary doctor who has read this advice describes it as 'amazingly sound.' He says that, of course, blistering and bleeding would do more harm than good, but that the climate, clothing, diet, and moderate exercise are all in accordance with modern practice. To-day there is no experience of asses milk owing to the difficulty of finding suitably lactating asses. The laxative electuaries had to be absorbed by licking instead of swallowing, like the 'salt lick' which is given to sheep and cows to-day.

The advice was accepted for both sons, which relieved the Smyth family of the responsibility of looking after the boys.

They were sent off to France in the autumn of 1788, with a tutor called John Stewart, who proved to be a most faithful friend and an excellent tutor. Instead of going to Nancy, as recommended by the doctors, they went to Dijon, and in the winter of this year John Stewart took John Kinloch down to the Mediterranean coast to Nice, to get the benefit of the better climate. This was of no avail, and John died on 2nd January 1789, and was buried there in the English Cemetery.

At this date George was thirteen years old, and had been left by himself to board with an old lady in Dijon. He wrote from there to Mr John Smyth the first of his beautifully hand-written letters with the same characteristic signature and the well-formed capital 'K' for Kinloch, which distinguished all his later writings.

Dijon, Feby. 15th.
1789.

Dear Sir,

I had the pleasure of receiving your letter, and am very happy to hear that you and all Friends in Scotland are well. I have passed the winter very agreeably here, I was lodged with an old lady who treated me very well, and with whom I was very comfortable, and if everybody I have lodged with, spoke as much as she, I have no doubt I should already speak French like a Frenchman. The winter was severer here than ever I saw it in Scotland, and at one time there was a great scarcity of water and bread, as it froze so hard that the mills could not grind. The Bishop (who has some small revenue from the water mills) with much charity and humanity would not allow them to erect windmills unless they consented to pay him the accustomed duties. You will no doubt have received accounts of poor

John's death before this time. I need not mention to you how much I have been afflicted by his loss, and how much I regret him. Mr. Stewart arrived here from Nice about ten days ago, after a long and tedious journey, for the roads are so very bad that it renders travelling almost impracticable; he received your letter three days ago, and desires me to tell you that he will write you as soon as he gets some accompts copied over for you. Please present my best compliments to my aunt, Mrs. Smith, to all your family, and to Mr. and Mrs. Fraser, and in short, to all my old acquaintances, and tell John that I shall be very much obliged to him for a letter as soon as possible. Mr. Stewart joins me in wishing you his best compliments and all happiness.

I am, Sir, with esteem and affect,

Your most obedient and humble servant,

George Kinloch.

Even at this early age, it is interesting to notice George Kinloch's independent mind criticising the vested interest of the Roman Catholic Bishop.

A letter of March 1789 from Captain Durham, a relation of the Balneavis family, to his mother and handed on to the Smyths gave a report on George's character—

Dijon, the 5th. March.

Dear Mother,

I received yours, I am very sorry to hear that you do not get rid of your lameness; you must bathe in the sea for it. Mr. Stewart has been returned from Nice about a month, and he is here with George; they have had no directions as yet from the Tutors; George is much improved in his manners since he was left here to take care of himself; he took a fancy to learn the Flute which I positively forbid him, and since he would seem homesick, I advised him to learn the fiddle which he does at present; he is pretty obstinate, and as avaricious as a Jew; when he came first here I thought him one of the stoutest healthy boys I ever saw; he is since grown astonishingly; I daresay he has grown four inches since October; he will be a very tall man. He looks more delicate than he did, but he certainly carries breadth with his growing, for 'the mournings' that he got

14

for his brother will not now button across his breast, if he was of any other family one would think him safe enough. He has an astonishing fine colour, which I think is the only bad symptom about him. I think he should drink asses milk in the spring, and go into Switzerland in the summer, spend the winter in Provence, and if any bad symptoms appear, he can easily get into Spain or Italy, as there must be danger from his violent growing. This place is very high, six hundred feet above the level of the sea.

James Durham.

This letter from Captain Durham was received at home and passed round the family, the tutors, and friends, and it was agreed by them that George should continue to stay abroad in the meantime.

George Kinloch's second letter written in October 1789, three months after the storming of the Bastille on the Quatorze Juillet described the condition in France at that time. It is not surprising that the relations at home were worried at not hearing from him, and they may have instructed Mr John Stewart to move off to Italy, if and when it could be arranged.

Dijon, 19 October, 1789.

Dear Sir,

I had the pleasure of receiving yours of the 12 Sept. a few days ago, and I am very sorry I neglected writing you so long, but I shall be more punctual for the future, and I hope you will have no reason to complain of me. We made a trip to Besancon some time ago where we staid a few weeks, but finding it much inferior to Dijon, we thought proper to return. We went to see the Citadel where we were shewn the place on the opposite hill, where (as the story goes there) Lewis the fourteenth was thrice unhorsed by a Capuchin monk who was afterwards hanged for his trouble. It is reckoned one of the strongest towns in France, but as I am no judge of fortifications I shall say nothing about the matter. Dijon has been very dull ever since the troubles commenced and this town where some months ago one hardly saw a soldier is now quite a warlike town. Every little village on the road has its militia, and we don't want ours; we have 6000, some of whom are instructed every day in their military exercises by a Capuchin, but I believe most of them would be more alert at presenting their back than their front, to the enemy, and that they know perfectly how to use their heels. You will perhaps find it extraordinary that a Capuchin should exercise them, but his history is shortly this; he was first a Capuchin, and not liking that sort of life, left his Convent, and enlisted in a regiment in which he continued seventeen years, but at last growing tired of that also he returned to his Convent, and is now Father Eugene Instructer of the Dijon militia. The Vintage is begun here and is almost finished already, for the last winter has so destroyed the vines that they only make one hogshead of wine where last year they made fifteen, in consequence of which the price of wine will soon be doubled. There has been a heavy fall of rain here a few days ago, which although the river is very little, has occasioned a great deal of damage; several bridges have been carried away, and many people have lost their lives. Captain Durham writes us from Lusanne that the concourse of strangers there is so great, that everything is at a most exhorbitant price, bread being 4½d. a pound, and other things in proportion, however, he intends to winter there, and return home in the Spring. I will be much obliged to you if you will let me know in what year and in what place I was born, for I absolutely don't know whether I was born at Johnny Grott's house, or at Portpatrick. Please present my best compliments to my aunt Mrs. Smith, to all your family and to Mr. & Mrs. Fraser, and tell them I am still alive and in good health.

I am, Dear Sir, Yours most affectionately,
George Kinloch.

Tell John that nothing will make me happier than a letter from him. Please direct to me A Monsieur, Monsieur Kinloch, Chez Donat Orsi et fils Banquiers Florence, Italie.

The address for forwarding letters show that he and John Stewart had made arrangements to move to Florence, and the next letter described their journey.

16

Dear Sir,

We arrived here all safe and sound the 16 November after a long and tedious journey of 22 days, of which 1 was over the Mount Jura, 7 among the Alps, and 2 over the Appennines, so that at present I know pretty well what mountains are. We crossed the Mount Cennis, which was entirely covered with snow, very merrily in company with 3 other gentlemen, without ever alighting from our Mules, except to eat trouts on the top of it, which, to be sure, after the cold we had suffered, were excellent. We passed through Turin which is one of the dirtiest and most unhealthy towns we have seen on our road; the streets are all well peirced, but they are in general so narrow, and the houses so high that tho' we were lodged on the 4th. story, we could hardly see to read at mid-day, however, there are 2 or 3 streets and severals hotels very magnificent, and the theatre is one of the prettiest we have seen. There was a vast number of French Nobility there most of whom have since passed this way, looking at everything and seeing nothing, which indeed is the way with most travellers, here they go 3 or 4 times to the Gallery, examine everything, at least think they do so, then take a Voiturin and set off for Rome, stay there a month, and then for Naples and so on; they then return as wise as ever, telling what they have seen, and what they have not seen, having bought a Parcel of new made antiquities at Rome and Naples, and when they go home they confirm the old Scotch Proverb, 'send a fool to France and he'll come home a fool.' People here have no great opinion of French Politicks, most of them think them 'foutus,' which in plain English is that they are gone to pot, nothing is more probable, but, if they are, they have themselves to blame. The Florentines are very polite to strangers, they are in general well made, and the women especially are beautiful; Every woman of Fashion has her cicisboe or galant, who waits in her antichamber in the morning, walks with her in the forenoon, dines with her wherever she goes, in the evening accompanys her to the Conversazione, while the husband is just playing the same part in another house, so

17

that few men here can call their children their own. We have
called upon Lord Hervey, the Envoy here, at whose house
we dine generally every Sunday, and who has very politely
offered to introduce us to the first people of the town. The
Carnaval is begun which promises to be a very gay one,
there are 7 theatres open every day except Saturday,
besides numberless private and public balls, concerts etc.
I am sorry to hear the harvest goes on so ill, here they have
had a plentiful crop of corn wine and oil, with which all the
neighbouring mountains are covered; myrtles and lavander
with all sorts of flowers grow also wild all around. I already
understand Italian, and I begin to speak it a little, and I hope
in a few months to be quite master of it. Our Prince Augustus[2]
passed here 10 or 12 days ago in his way to Pisa where he
is now lodged in the Grand Duke's Palace. Mr. Stewart
presents best compliments to you, and hopes you have
received his letter which he wrote you upon our arrival. I
hope you and your family are well. Mr. Stewart joins me in
wishing you, my aunt, and all your family a good New Year,
may you have many of them, and may they be happy.

I am, Dear Sir,
Yours most affectionately,
George Kinloch.

Lord Cowper died here, universally regretted the 22nd.
December. His body will be embalmed and sent to England
in a few days.

The adolescent George Kinloch, age 15, had arrived in
Florence after crossing the Alps on mule back, an experienced
traveller with considerable knowledge of men and affairs. His
next two letters from Florence in the summer and autumn of
1790 show him as a young man developing his interest in the
society of Florence and in the politics of Tuscany.

Florence, May 7th. 1790.

Dear Sir,
    The noise of your political motions reached us on
this side of the Alps some time before I received your last
letter, and as it is now full time to abolish the influence of
Clans and Highland Chieftains, I wish Mr. Drummond
success with all my heart; I am afraid, however, you will

lose the question; perhaps against next election I shall be able to assist you with a vote. These Political contests, tho' productive of confusion, keep up that spirit of independance which has long been and which I hope will always be the Character of the English nation. Here where the people have nothing to say in the Government, an Englishman is surprised to see what indifference all ranks shew to everything that concerns their country, or their liberties. Since the extinction of the Medicis Family in 1707, they have seen themselves transferred from one Power to another without shewing the least concern about the matter. The Nobility here are extremely proud, extremely poor, and extremely ignorant; they are all Counts, Marquisses etc. who would rather want their dinner 13 times a week than their horses and carriages. The farmers here make very little use of the plough, but dig most of the ground with spades, and except when there is a scarcity of rain raise excellent crops of wheat which is the principal grain they cultivate, yet they are so poor, they ask Charity from all the Passengers. After wheat, the most considerable articles of produce are oil, and silk which they generally export raw, as they are but indifferent manufacturers; the wine is in great plenty and very cheap, tho' by no means equal to the French wines in quality as far as I am a judge, it does not keep long, and a sea voyage generally destroys it. I have not been away from hence since I came as travelling in a country without knowing the language, besides being exposed to impositions of all sorts is very disagreeable; now as that difficulty is over I should like very much to see Italy before I return; for my part I should wish to pass next summer at Naples if it is agreeable to you and my other tutors, whom I hope one day to be able to convince of my gratitude for the care and trouble they have had with my affairs. I hope you will write me in your next, whether you think it proper we should come home next winter or not, as we would take our measures accordingly. The weather here has been very warm for some time past (I should like to know how it has been in Jamaica) but tho' I have been more accustomed to cold than heat, I hope to be able to resist it without much inconveniencey. There are a great number of English here, returning from Rome, and Naples to the Ascention at Venice. The Duke of Argyle and family are here; there are also the Mardgrave of Brunswick, an aunt of our King, Prince Augustus, who sets off today or tomorrow, Lord Titchfield a son of the Duke of Portland, Lord Montague, and a great many others all setting off for Venice. The Queen of Hungary, and all the Royal Family set off yesterday for Vienna where they hope to arrive in 12 days. The following curious accident happened here a few weeks ago. The wife of a Mr. Locwood, an English gentleman, was brought to bed without knowing she was with child till an hour before her delivery; she was come here for her health thinking herself consumptive, and expected to die in a few days.

Mr. Stewart begs his compliments to and will write you soon. Please offer my best compliments to my Aunt, Mrs. Smith, and all your family, and believe me ever to be,

Yours most affectionately,

George Kinloch.

Florence, July 24, 1790.

Dear Sir,

I received yours of the 20th. June a few days ago by which I see you think we are at Sienna, but we have not stirred from Florence where we intend to pass the rest of the summer, as the weather is by no means so disagreeable as we expected, on the contrary the heat has not been much greater than in England, but the dog-days are yet to come, and then I fear we shall know what heat is; my morning dress is a little jacket, and a pair of trowsers, and as there is no going out till 6 o'clock I fiddle or read in the morning, and in the evening go and play cricket with some English boys of my age who have been here some time. Sir John McPhearson who was some time Governor of India left this yesterday with his Secretary Mr. McAla (who knows Mr. McDonald very well); he gave balls and dinners and made us all merry during a month he stayed here. Since I wrote you last there have been some signs of a revolt in this city, and in all Tuscany. About 200 blackguards who had nothing in the world to lose complaining of the scarcity of money and of consequence of the high price of provisions went and pillaged 2 or 3 Noblemens houses, and as the Grand Duke[3] thinking he was more liked than he really was, had disbanded all his troops, they did what they pleased for one day, and after having marked out some houses for next days work, they got all drunk with the wine they had stole, and then fell fast asleep, and next day, by the activity of the sbirri (a kind of thief-catchers) they were all clapt up in Prison where they are yet; a Militia of Volunteers was immediately raised to the amount of 3 or 4000 men who are worse looking fellows (if possible) than the French Militia. It has since been discovered that they had a plot laid for St. John's Day which is a great Festival here. They intended to set fire to the theatre in the middle of the play to steal what they could with more conveniency. One party was to plunder the Grand Duke's Palace, another the Noblemen's houses, in short there was to be nothing but robberies, murders, and I don't know what all. Luckily it has all been prevented; everything is now quiet, and is like to continue so. If the Grand Duke, when he set off for Vienna had left his son Ferdinand here as Grand Duke, it is very probable none of this would have happened, they say he now means to do it, and in that case everything will go on well. One thing which has justly enraged the Florentines against the Grand Duke is the shocking way in which he causes them to be buried. When a person dies, he is immediately carried to a small Chapel where he never remains more than 24 hours; he is then tossed into a cart with half a dozen others stark naked, in which they are carried to the Campo Santo a place about 6 miles from town, where they are thrown into a great hole all together, they then throw quick lime upon them which consumes their bodies in a few days. Thus are all the Florentines buried, except the Royal Family, and the Archbishop only, the Prince and the beggar who were so far distant during life, must after death lie in the same hole, and what is very hard those that have a burying place of their own cannot make use of it; I have often thanked God I was not born at

21

Florence, and I believe anybody that had heard of their way of burying would do the same. Another complaint the people here have against the Grand Duke is his keeping spys, of which Tuscany is full. When anybody reproaches him with keeping spys, he answers he has no troops, but it is his own fault for it is certainly a more honourable way of keeping people in awe by troops, than by spys. The result of all this is that he has entirely spoilt the Tuscan character, for a Florentine dare never speak out what he thinks. Leopold is given to women, for not content with having 14 children of his own, he kept 4 or 5 mistresses, while he denied his subjects even one; he was very avaricious, for he has carried off with him 4 or 5 million sterling a greater loss than Tuscany can repair for some time. But passing from Leopold to myself, I desired Mr. Stewart in his last letter to you, to make my compliments to Dr. Robertson, and ask him what I should do to get rid of some small eruptions on my face, which go and come every week or so, and which, though very trifling, are very disagreeable, and I should like to know from him what I should do to get quit of them, for the physicians here are so stupid, there is no trusting them. In other respects, I enjoy perfect health. Please present my best compliments to my aunt, Mrs. Smith, and all your family, and believe me to be,

Yours most affectionately,

George Kinloch.

To James
Smyth, of
Balhary,
St. James Square,
New Town,
Edinburgh, Ingliterra.

In the early part of the year 1791 George Kinloch returned to Scotland. He was now heir to the Kinloch estates which he would inherit when he came of age in five years time.

By this time old James Smyth who had become 'the worse of wearing' was dead, his widow, George Kinloch's aunt Cecilia was living at Balhary, and their only son John Smyth with his large family was living in St. James Square, Edinburgh. This

Square, behind the newly built Register House, 'the most magnificent pigeon house in Europe' was at the eastern end of the New Town where the exclusive Bar Society of Edinburgh was coming to live. John Smyth and his second wife Joanna who, before she married had been a Gray, another family of Writers to the Signet, were on intimate terms with this Bar Society of Judges, Advocates and Writers, and their next door neighbour was Lord Dunsinnan, one of the Judges of the Court of Session.

George Kinloch took lodging near to his relations and enrolled at Edinburgh University which was then known as 'The College' for the session of 1791/1792. His signature can be seen in the Matriculation Album of the University as a student attending classes in Logic, Mathematics and Ethics, but he did not stay long enough to graduate. During this time he may also have been studying Law in the Writing Chambers of the Smyth family and so completed a good all-round education before settling down as a country gentleman on his estate in Perthshire. His later letters show that during this time in Edinburgh, he made many friends with the society and professional people of Edinburgh to many of whom he was related. Unfortunately, no letters have been found concerning the years 1791-1796 and so the story of his youth must end here. His life will continue after his marriage as described in the next Chapter.

[1] Alexander Munro Secundus (1733–1817.) Anatomist in Edinburgh. Portrait by J.T. Seaton in Royal College of Surgeons, Edinburgh.

[2] 'Our Prince Augustus' — 9th child of George III, born 1773 — living abroad at this time, he adopted liberal opinions including abolition of the slave trade, Catholic emancipation and Parliamentary reform.

[3] This Grand Duke was Leopold, second son of Maria Theresa who became Emperor Leopold II. He was grandfather of the Austrian Emperor Franz Joseph.

CHAPTER THREE

Beside the Watersyde

O N THE 5th September 1796, Helen, third daughter of John and Joanna Smyth married George Kinloch of Kinloch. They were first cousins once removed, as the bride's grandfather had married the bridegroom's aunt but, in spite of this difference in generations, they themselves were of the same age, she being 22 and he 21. They had been childhood friends as the Smyth house had been the only home which George Kinloch had known. It was a love match and a good choice for both of them.

George Kinloch was very much the dominant personality, but from Mrs Kinloch's diaries in later life, it is clear that although her main object in life was to carry out the wishes of her husband, she had the same tastes in the love of her garden and everything to do with outdoor life. It may have been that she was the Smyth daughter chosen to keep house for her father when he came to stay in his Perthshire country house at Balhary and that her mother, who was of Edinburgh stock, preferred to remain in the Edinburgh town house. In any case, by the time that she married her cousin, she had been well schooled in domestic responsibilities.

When George Kinloch came to live at Kinloch[1] as a young bachelor and began farming there, he must have been a frequent visitor to his cousin's house across the river. His route to Balhary would pass through his own fields by the path which starts at the doocot, through hedge-bordered fields with picturesque names such as Quarryley, Wellfield and Shovel-boards down to the low-lying pasture called the Horsehaugh.

This low ground had been so called after an incident in the Rebellion of '45 when Lady Kinloch had hidden the horses of the Angus Jacobite batallion here out of sight of the English troops. The path goes on beside the river through the Flooder-haugh, ground which floods when the Isla is in spate, to the Boat hole where George Kinloch would ferry across the river and walk up the slope of the hill through his cousin's land to breakfast or dine at Balhary.

No love letters have been preserved to describe their courting, but a regular happening which was recorded in Mrs Kinloch's diary showed that, against the background of jam-making and household chores, she kept a hidden corner of romantic memories of their courting days. In this diary, in June of every year, was recorded — 'Mr. K. and I walked beside the watersyde.' Even after her husband had died the annual pilgrimage down to the river through the fields and along the watersyde, usually in company with her grand-children continued and in the June months of these later years the diary entries were — 'with the children beside the watersyde.' It does not require a great deal of imagination therefore to see that this path beside the river in June of 1796 had been the setting of the love affair between George and Helen which lasted all their lives together.

They were such a suitable couple — he a fine tall man well-known to everyone in the district, a great walker, a magnificent shot, an amusing talker on every sort of subject, and she a more prosaic character, but house-proud and full of knowledge of cooking and domestic matters. One would almost expect the marriage to have ended any restless ideas which he may have had, and that the story would finish here by saying that 'they lived happily ever afterwards.' They did live happily, but it was not to be the quiet, domestic routine country life which Helen might have expected, and was certainly not the end of the story.

On the twenty-fifth anniversary of their wedding day on 5th September 1822, George, then an outlaw in France, wrote to his wife.

My Dearest Helen,

      Many, many happy returns of the day to you. It is

now a quarter of a century since you and I were made one and I can assure you that few have had more reason to be satisfied with their choice than I have had, and I would fain flatter myself that you also have not had much occasion to regret yours. I am not such a fool as to fancy that I am without faults but, among them all, I am certainly free of being capable of ill-using any woman, and much more so, one who has made herself entirely over to me. When we shall have seen as many more 'happy returns of the day' as we have already witnessed, I hope we shall still be a 'canty couple.'

When they started their married life, he was farming some 250 acres around Kinloch House and had an additional small income from two let farms of Blacklaws and Chapelhill, so that they could consider themselves to be comfortably well off. He had also bought another property where the Burgh of Carnoustie now stands but which at that time consisted of nothing but a few new houses on sandy grass land of no great agricultural value. He had to borrow £10,000 for this purpose but the loan did not worry him, as he was feuing the land for building development and considered it to be a good investment. Perhaps he thought that the new Regency fashion for sea bathing would bring people to live at Carnoustie as he could not have foreseen the popularity of this resort as a championship golf course.

At first they gave the impression of settling down and living in much the same way that all their neighbours lived, bringing up a family and having all the usual anxieties of health, education and expense. Helen, at least had no time during the first eight years of marriage for anything other than giving birth to children, and thereafter coping with their incessant ailments. In 1797 the first born, a daughter called Cecilia, arrived, in 1798 another daughter Margaret, in 1799 another daughter Helen. At last in 1800 the first born son George arrived, in 1801 another daughter Ann, in 1802 another son John, in 1804 a daughter Eliza, and lastly in 1805 a sixth daughter who died soon after birth. Luckily this seemed to have stopped the procession, but eight children in nine years must have needed all their mother's strong constitution. Her husband was a child-lover and adored them all — 'the little cheapies' as he called them in his letters.

George had more time than his wife for amusement, sport and travel. When he was away from home, he wrote regularly to her and told her everything that he had seen and done. Whether it was the influence of his early tutoring by John Stewart, or just a natural gift, he had the art of describing every-day details so as to make them both interesting and amusing.

Owing to the close connection with the Smyth family, there were frequent visits to Edinburgh and correspondence between the families and, piecing these together, it is possible to get a fairly realistic picture of how the Kinloch family lived in the countryside of Strathmore.

The first letter about a visit to Edinburgh was written from 1 Hart Street, Edinburgh, in February 1802, when Cecilia the eldest daughter was six, and she and her father had gone there by the mail coach—

We arrived here, all safe and in good health at a little after seven o'clock, and found all friends in good health. We had a very pleasant passage across the ferry without a breath of wind, in a yawl, and dined on a beef-steak at the south Ferry. Cecil was not at all wearied and in great spirits. When we got to Edinburgh I sent her into the dining-room without any warning, which astonished them not a little. She is, to do her justice, a most excellent travelling companion. It rained when we got to Coupar [Coupar-Angus], faired when we got to Perth, snowed about the Wicks of Baiglie, and was a fine day when we got to Kinross, which continued till we got to Edinburgh. Cecil has been skipping and dancing, and is now gone to bed. God bless you and all the rest of them. Write me how they all are.

and again, on the same visit—

My Dear Helen,

I received your letter of the 22nd. and was glad to have it confirmed that the little bodies are now quite recovered. I am afraid that you have had a great deal of fatigue with them, and that, in taking care of them, you have neglected yourself, as the Doctor mentioned that you was a good deal colded and complaining of your stomach. Cecilia has had a little cold and has been rather irregular in a certain respect [not surprising if she suffered from constipation after the long coach drive]. Your mother is alarmed about her wanting physick although I think there is no reason for it, and, as I am no friend to the Apothecarie's shop, I would rather endeavour to remedy it by diet than Physick.

George Kinloch and his mother-in-law usually disagreed on every subject and it gave some relief to his feelings to tell Helen all about it. Later, when his son was ill in Edinburgh, he wrote—

Your mother, although as good a woman as ever God made, yet has such an uneasy, fretful temper, so anxious and busy about trifles, that it is most distressing to an invalid. Then, the slightest alteration to her domestic economy, the displacing of a chair or a table, puts her all out of sorts.

However, he found 1 Hart Street very convenient and turned up there at any time of day or night without warning, which probably put his mother-in-law 'out of sorts' many a time.

The purpose of this visit to Edinburgh in 1802 had been two-fold, first to find out about the Will of his wife's uncle, one of the Gray family, who had died in Jamaica, but on this he reported—

The family have been a little disappointed in your Uncle's matters, as he has left all his property to his natural children [presumably coloured people] in Jamaica. It appears he had some strong cause of dislike to your father, as he never once mentioned his having such relations. What cause of dislike he had will probably remain a secret, but it must have been something which he had taken very much to heart. He had strong attachments there, and none here.

Perhaps the conservative Edinburgh W. S. family had been rude about mixed marriages.

The other business in Edinburgh was to have his portrait painted—

My Dear Helen,

I am afraid you will begin to think that I have forgotten you and your little bodies, but the truth is that I am very wearied of this good city, as I feel that there is only the half of me here, and I long to get back to the other half. It was some time before I could fall in with a miniature painter, and it seems he cannot finish my phizy before Tuesday next. Cecil has been in perfect health, tho' she has lost all relish for porie; she is a great favourite everywhere and has been very much amused, particularly with the shops, and she has been at two practisings, which she liked very much. John and I have been dining at Mr. Wedderburn's with a large party of young people, indeed, I have been very little at home since I came. I find I have still a great many acquaintances here, tho' there is in a manner a new generation sprung up since you was here. The public places have been remarkably well attended, and there are a great many private balls and routs. What I find the most change in, is the dress of the ladies, and the shape of the carriages. The former are as naked as summer, [this was before Victorian modesty], to the great annoyance of passengers, and the latter are like nothing I ever saw, unless it be an ill-shaped square pincushion with the corners taken off, and they are hung very low and canted up before; so that in the inside you see nothing but the clouds. If Cecil was not asleep she would have sent you her compliments. She has grown a fashionable lady, and sleeps till eight o'clock. God bless you, my dear Helen.

George Kinloch enjoyed these expeditions, but he never liked to be away from home for long. By March he would be anxious to get back from Edinburgh, not only to see how his wife and all the little bodies were, but to see whether the land was ready for ploughing and planting and to supervise all the work on the farm. He kept careful weather records with daily entries of temperature, wind direction, rainfall, snowfall, etc. and became an authority on farming matters to the extent of writing the monthly agricultural reports for the 'Dundee Advertiser.'

Although there was a cattle market at Coupar-Angus, the distance factor and the difficulty of transport prohibited the regular attendance of farmers at this and other markets. Instead of this, most of the buying and selling of stock took place at the private Roup Sales which were held half yearly near to the Whitsunday and Martinmas term days. The Roup day was a social occasion at which everyone came into the house for a 'dram' and a letter reported on one of these at Whitsunday in the year 1818—

David Nairne and Dr. Boyter came in to their dinner when the rest of the people were almost done with their punch, so just got the leavings.

The Parks let upon the whole better than I expected, and the cattle sold better than last year. The Ewes netted 10/- a head more than they cost me. I shall get my barley sown this week, and then for the turnips.

The Term day was also the occasion for paying wages, and engaging farm workers for the next half year;—

John Miller and Jamie Baxter are both going away at Whitsunday. John got drunk in Dundee, and nearly upset his cart in a ditch. John Irons is to be grieve in his place.

As always there were good and bad years in farming, and the post Napoleonic war years were badly affected by the poverty of the people and lack of purchasing power. In April 1816 he wrote—

The market is quite glutted with cattle and nobody has any money to buy beasts with, so that we must just make hay of the parks and, if nobody will buy it, we can bonfire it. Money seems to be growing scarcer and scarcer every day. Improvements stand still. The labourers are starving.

By August and September he had time to get away and enjoy the sport at which he excelled — shooting muirfowl, or what we call grouse to-day, in the glens, where there were always invitations to shoot. He wrote from Whitelay, Glen Ogle in Angus, in August, 1802—

My Dear Helen,

I received yours last night on my return from Easter Ogle where we dined by invitation from Capt. Simpson, who called on us yesterday forenoon. We found Gartmore there, a Mrs. Cunningham, Capt. Jamieson, Capt. & Miss Christie, and Capt. Simpson's mother, and were most hospitably received, and got as much excellent claret as was good for us; indeed Col. Sandeman says his head is 'weaving Dornoch' this morning, in consequence of it. I

30

came up there on Sunday evening, and found the Colonel who had arrived about an hour before me. Next morning it rained till 8, when we sallied out upon the muirfowl. I found them very scarce in this neighbourhood, and went a good way out where they were rather more plenty. I fired exactly 33 shots, one of which missed, two sent away feathered, and 30 came home on Rob's back, which was pretty well. The Col. killed only 4 brace. Yesterday it rained so heavily when we got to the hill that we were obliged to return; I, with one old cock, and the Col. not a dotterel. I had a line from Jamie Yeaman, who killed 16 brace the first day, and 9 brace yesterday morning, so they must be plentier where he is. Walter Gray killed 5 brace. Capt. Simpson & Gartmore 12 brace between them. I have sent down 16 brace, 2 brace to be left at Logie, 2 do. for Arthurstone, 3 birds for Sir John, 3 for Meigle, 2 for Wingate, 2 for Cronan, 2 for Mrs. Blair, 3 for Mrs. Phillips, and the rest for your Ladyship and Balhary. If the weather would keep fair, I think I would nab a few more, but it looks very ill this morning. We are pretty well lodged here, having the end of a house to ourselves, with a separate entry. I am glad to hear you are all well, and hope you will continue so.

I met Mr. Taylor on Monday; he had but poor sport. John Irons may get the cart to Dundee. Tell Robt. Baxter his barn is to be covered with Clunie slates, and to get Walter to bespeak them immediately.

In considering his ability as a shot, it must be remembered that he was shooting with a double-barrelled flint-lock, muzzle loading gun. This gun occasionally failed to flash in the pan and so mis-fired, but when it flashed, there was rarely a miss.

From the Spittal of Glenshee, which more people know to-day for the ski-ing and pony-trekking rather than shooting, he wrote in September 1802—

My Dear Helen,

I send you by Mr. Grubb's servant 16 brace of muirfowl, and am so wearied (it being ten o'clock at night), that I can only tell you that we find ourselves very comfortable as a tenant of Invercauld's house, close by the

Spittal. You will see by the number sent, that we have had tolerable sport for the two days, during both of which we have shot upon Mr. Macintosh's property, which is much better ground than I could have had any idea of; indeed for the beginning of the season, I would not desire better. I wrote to Invercauld and got a most polite answer with leave to shoot on his property, where we design to go tomorrow. Mr. Honey arrived yesterday forenoon, and we are no worse of his company, tho' he is a very bad shot. You can send 3 brace to Arthurstone (and if you think proper) the same with my compts. to Meigle; a brace to Dr. Crockett, and to Balhary and anywhere else what you please. You will send up upon Friday morning vegetables of all kinds, particularly peas, onions, carrots and turnips; a basket of gooseberries (if any), and two bottles of shrub by James Martin, who will beg, borrow, or steal a horse. Our Landlord's name is Fergie Ferguson. Good-night & God bless you and the little bodies all, and let me know how they are.

Like all good shots he was inclined to poke fun at his less successful friends. The shooting nearer home was for roe deer, grey hens and black-cock which he called heath-fowl, with occasional pheasants. This was a sport which he enjoyed enormously, but it was partly a sport and partly a source of food for the family; baskets of game and provisions from the garden were sent regularly to the relations in Edinburgh if there was any transport available.

George Kinloch's neighbour, young David Nairne of Drumkilbo, was George's usual shooting companion. This property of Drumkilbo now belongs to the Queen's cousin — Lord Elphinstone, and is shot over by the Duke of Edinburgh on the occasional visits of the Royal Party. One expedition is described as follows—

David Nairne and I went to Sir John Ogilvy's and tried Balbeuchly on our way, but found no deer. On Monday we went to Strathmartine and killed two fine deer in Lord Duncan's wood, in half an hour, with one shot each. We did not look for any more. On Thursday we went to Ingliston, where I killed a hare with one barrel and a roe

32

with the other, and a second roe crossed within 20 yards of me, which I could easily have killed if I had had a third *barrel*. As David Nairne was standing *Glowrin o'wr* a tree, a buck passed literally within six feet of him to his yeuter astonishment, and it would be difficult to say which of them was most *frightened*. David said he never was sae fleyed a' his days. He fired after the buck, but, as might be expected, without effect. We yesterday went to the Hunter's Hill, but were unsuccessful. David got a shot, but did no damage, except to the trees. I had a chance also, but my gun unluckily flashed in the pan.

David Nairne of Drumkilbo was a gay young spark, and when rather more merry than usual he was referred to as 'Kildrumbo,' or 'Drummie.'

Rabbits do not seem to have been popular on the table. They had only recently been introduced, and it is not clear whether the Kinloch rabbits were wild or tame. 'We had a most famous fricasse of the rabbits you killed and, although none of the Misses would taste them, Mr. Putland and I made shift to dine off them.'

The distances that shooters covered on foot make some of us nowadays feel rather weaklings. 'Dr. Boyter and I walked down to Sir John's [that is Ruthven House near Airlie] to breakfast; we then walked about five miles before dinner, and after partaking of Sir John's [Wedderburn] *hospitality*, we set off about seven p.m. for Carnoustie where we arrived about ten; making altogether about thirty miles, with which, the Doctor declared his walking propensity perfectly satisfied.' Again walking with Dr. Boyter's son, a Lieut. in the Army, he wrote—

We went to Tullyfergus on Wednesday last. We saw only one roe there, which Vixen [his dog] turned away when it was coming right upon me. We followed it over towards Drimmie, when Vicky again turned away another, so I take her no more to the deer shooting. We did not get any, but I shot a black-cock, a hare and muirfowl, all with Bulesto. We had to walk from near Craighall when it was near 5 o'clock, and the Lieut. says he has hardly yet got the better of it. Vixen accompanied me to-day to the Justice Court, and behaved with all due decorum.

The distance from Craighall to Kinloch as the crow flies is about ten miles, and this distance across country at the end of a day's shooting was quite a step.

Joking about other people's shooting exploits he wrote—

Graysum and Alex. Yeaman are gone on a wild goose expedition to the north side of the water. (Thousands of geese feed on this ground nowadays, but are always wary and difficult to get near to). I suppose they will kill a good many hares, tho' I don't think the geese run any risk from their *brethren*. There are two covies of partridges still come to be fed at the lime tree, ten and five. There is a slight covering of snow on the ground, which will give the poachers an opportunity of the hares. 3 o'clock I have just been out for a short time, and met the two shooters, who have killed six hares; two of which were sent to Balhary. Graysum has got the lend of a lurcher from Inches to make the business of hare shooting *easier*.

At this time there was no fishing for salmon and trout by rod and line but the Kinloch Estate had the right to the fishing on the Ericht and the Isla rivers. Netting the river was the normal method of fishing and the pool of Blacklaw on the Ericht was very productive of baskets of salmon, grilse and trout—

I had gone to try the fishing at Blacklaw with my new net. We got two grilses and some trout, but I don't think there were any salmon in the pool. The net completely commands the pool, and when it gets a bag added to it, I think nothing will escape it. I tried it one night in the Isla and got 25 trouts, one of them $3\frac{1}{4}$ lbs. and several about $1\frac{1}{2}$ lbs.

Everything about the countryside was of interest to him, and in the nesting season a careful watch was kept on all the game and other birds.

I believe I formerly mentioned that we had discovered a land rail's nest [corncrake] with eleven eggs to the east-ward of the house. She has abandoned it, but, to make up for it, there is a partridge nest within ten yards of it, with nineteen eggs. She was driven out of the nest by the scythe, and lost a good many feathers. The eggs too were scattered about; but, on replacing them, she returned and has continued on the nest ever since and, I hope, will bring up her numerous family. There is another nest on the red brae, which Gipp discovered and at the same time plucked some feathers out of the partridge. However, she likewise returned and I have since frequently seen her on the nest. I have not seen the *'Ephesian Fool'* lately, but I am in great hopes that she has a nest in the planting on the East side of the Cowshed. I don't know whether I told you that Gipp discovered the cat which showed such a *partiality* for rabbits and, as she had gone up an ash tree on which there were no leaves to conceal her, I *punished* her as I would all tyrannical *monsters*.

The 'Ephesian Fool' was a hen pheasant which nested near the house.

His son, George, kept a wood pigeon in his room (the house-proud Helen must have been forbearing), and his father wrote to him to say—

I don't know if you have heard of your pigeon having made it's escape. Being anxious to see the world, it chose to make a dash through a pane of the window, and set off on it's travels. As I am an enemy to all unnecessary confinement of animals, I am very glad it has gone; only I could have dispensed with it's breaking the window, as quite needless.

and again to his son—

Your room has been occupied lately as a *nursery* for some *partridges* which were cut over in the greens. Five of them came out, but I am sorry to say after living a week, they all took it into their heads to die.

The Kinlochs were a 'joky' family, and poked a lot of fun at their friends and relations. One of their cousins, Charles Graham, had built himself rather a magnificent modern house on rising ground outside Blairgowrie called 'Altamount,' and which the Kinloch family nick-named 'Mount Atlas'—

Charlie has taken possession at 'Mount Atlas' one day lately, and is very magnificent upon it.

and again—

Charlie is so *buzzy* he hardly knows which way to turn himself.

'Uncle John,' that was Mrs Kinloch's eldest brother John, was building a new house in front of the old one at Balhary. He was using his own trees for the wood-work and a stone quarry on the estate for the stone.

A great part of Uncle John's wood is come to Balhary, so that I expect to see the Castle begun to, soon,

and later—

Uncle John is busy laying lead pipes and talks confidently of beginning the Castle this year.

George Kinloch was not very respectful of the Church. The family were Episcopalians and his wife was a very devout church-goer. As a Heritor, he had to maintain the fabric of the Established Church of Scotland.

I am going down to Carnoustie on Wednesday for a day or two, as the Minister wants a larger Kirk to exercise his oratorical powers in. Your mother will probably accompany me.

but the Minister did not get his way, as he reported later—

I walked down to Barrie, where we had a meeting about the Kirk. The Minister was disappointed that we did not agree to give him a new one. However, we agreed to add a loft to the aisle and plaster the roofs, and make it comfortable so that the good fruits of the Gospel might not be intercepted by the cold.

About this same visit to Carnoustie he wrote—

I dined on that day at Major Hunter's where we had the accomplished Jeannettina for our Landlady. Affleck and Mrs. Yeaman [the owners of Affleck Castle nearby] went to wait upon her next day, and Roguey, the terrier who accompanied them, thought fit to show his attention to Miss Jenny by lifting up his leg and copiously sprinkling her gown, in the genteelest manner possible.

This Major Hunter and Alexander Yeaman of Affleck were quick-tempered people, as, later, George Kinloch reported that after a dispute between them over the right to shoot hares—

Major Hunter and he had like to have fought a duel in consequence of Alick telling him that, if he did so and so, he was anything of a gentleman. The *pustles* were brought when the Major, not relishing the thoughts of half an ounce of lead in his thorax, accepted of a very slim apology through James Yeaman, and the matter dropt.

Some of the humour was unkind, as George Kinloch believed in saying just what he thought and, on the occasion of one neighbour's death, he said—

You will have heard of Colonel M's. death. He was found dead in his dressing-room and was buried on Friday last. Everybody wishes it had been the wife in place of the husband.

So life went on at Kinloch—

James Pullar has bought a mare, a good deal like old Mary, and the Misses are all quite *vogie* about her. Uncle and Aunt dined with us at Arthurstone on Saturday, and got their feet wet coming through the Isla in the chaise. The young chestnut mare has got a foal of which she is vastly proud.

The Misses, his daughters, in their letters to one another were rather more 'gossipy' about people, books, etc. and the following letter from Ann to her brother in Edinburgh is typical of the social 'chit-chat'—

I must begin by wishing you many happy return of the year. I have sent you a New Year's gift which I think will make your bread and butter go down better in the morning, it is ready for eating, as it was boiled before we sent it away. Charles Kinloch has been here some days, he and Papa are going to Logie the week after next to try the roe shooting. Have you read Rob Roy yet? We have got a lend of it from Lady Ashburton, and Papa seems to think what he has read of it is great stuff. I suppose that you have heard that Bobby Graham has bought Kincaldrum, he paid 32 thousand 5 hundred for it, which everybody seems to think is a great deal more than the value of it, *except* Mr. Bower [presumably the seller]. How do you like your place of abode? and what sort of companions have you got? What sorts of stumps are the Miss Renwicks [his landlady's daughters], and how many are there? The rest join me in love to you.

P.S. Nelly bids me tell you that your cat is a wild devil for it was at the birds last night, and Vixen just follows Papa the same way she did you.

Margaret wrote—

Have you heard of David Millar's new purchase? It is said

he has bought the Laws, Effabeaton, and some other place for which he has paid forty-three thousand pounds. As it was generally understood that he was more in the way of selling than buying at present, people are a good deal surprised at it.

I suppose John will have told you that Nelly is going to take unto herself a man, and the happy youth whom she has honoured with her choice is no other than Tom Turnbull. I suppose he is ten years younger than she is. Mama is getting her sister Jenny in her place. As we have not been to Dundee this winter, I cannot give you any scandal, and I have only room to add that I am,

Ever your,
Affectionate sister, Margy Kinloch.

Mrs Kinloch did not keep a diary in her early married life, but she kept a housekeeping note-book which also acted as a sort of bank-book for wages paid or held on account of members fo the domestic staff. The term day cash entries read such as—

Money received to keep for Helen Porter   £1
Money received for Cecilia Carver   £1

This was the greater part of the half-yearly wages of these two trusting servants who used their mistress as their banker.

The same book recorded every year from 1809 until 1845 the amount of gooseberry or currant wine, laid down in cask and then bottled. The most popular Kinloch vintage of currant wine had as its basic ingredients:—

10 Pints Black Berries.
15   ,,   Red Berries.
 2   ,,   White Berries.
16 Pints of Juice in whole.
26 Pints Water.
60 lbs. Lump Sugar.

The method of preparation was to—

Put into the large Cask 42 pints and 9 into the small cask. This mixture had to be left in cask for 10 days or three weeks. When only a hissing noise remained, you drew off a pint for every 20 and added a pint of brandy and a quarter of an ounce of isinglass dissolved in water; stirred well, bunged up, and surrounded the bung with clay. A fortnight after, tasted, and if not sweet enough, sugar added. Left it six months in the cask, but, after it was quite fine, the sooner it was bottled the better.

The Wine-making was Mrs Kinloch's special responsibility, and it was only in 1824, the year before her daughter Margaret married that she risked one of her daughters taking charge This year she entered in her diary—

Margaret made the wine.

[1] Kinloch House, which is now an hotel, has been added to to such an extent that the original structure of 1797 is not recognisable from outside. The farm steading has the date 1782 on the entrance so that the Kinlochs probably lived in the farm house while the Mansion House was being built.

CHAPTER FOUR

How He Brought up his Children

(The extracts from family letters quoted in this Chapter are all dated 1816 to 1818, unless otherwise stated).

IN THE DAYS at the beginning of the 19th century when the Kinloch children were growing up, the word of the parents was law. The children spoke when they were spoken to, and did as they were bid. There was a standard of discipline which would be quite unacceptable to the young in this permissive age.

George Kinloch, by comparison with other Regency parents was a most lenient and liberal minded father but even so, everyone hung on his words, and his consent had to be obtained for everything that happened.

To-day, any young girl of fourteen who received a birthday present from her father wrapped up with a sermonising letter on good behaviour, would never speak to him again, but George Kinloch thought that it was a kind way of giving advice, and his duty to do so. This is the birthday letter which his eldest daughter received—

My Dear Cecilia,

You have now completed your fourteenth year, a period, at which, the manners of a girl are generally left off, and those of a woman are adopted. The watch I now give you, may serve for several purposes, besides being an expression of my affection for you; in the first place, when my head is laid in the grave and when you look at this watch, it will recall to your mind, a departed *friend*. In the next place, if you will examine how quickly the minutes and the hours pass away, it will put you in mind not to throw away time which, once lost, never returns. Again, if your watch goes too fast, by touching the regulator, you can temper it to your mind. What the regulator is in the watch, *reason* is in you. Your temper is too hasty, and you do not employ your reason to regulate it. If you neglect it just now, you will not be able to do it, when you grow older, however much you may be convinced of the necessity of doing so. Therefore attend to this, before it is too late. When you feel inclined to say or to do a violent thing, consult your reason whether it is proper or not. You will find that reason will almost always decide against you. Above all, do what you can to act according to your mother's wishes. She has borne and suffered a great deal for you; she is older and consequently more experienced than you, and whatever she directs you to do, is intended for your advantage; consequently, when you thwart her, you are acting against yourself. And not only against your own interest, but against the express commands of God, as you well know, in the fifth Commandment. Therefore, my dear Cecilia, attend particularly to this. Your example is now, of consequence to your brothers and sisters. Let it be one that it will be proper for them to follow — not to avoid. You have not, hitherto, made that progress in your studies, which you are very capable of doing. You will now be more aware of the value of time and will be more attentive to them. Live in peace with your brothers and sisters.

Recollect that it requires more spirit to forgive an injury than to resent it. Whenever at a loss, with respect to any part of your conduct, apply to me. I conclude this hasty epistle by wishing you many returns of this day and all the happiness this world affords — my dear Cecilia,

Your affectionate father,

Kinloch. 5th. Septr. 1811.   Geo. Kinloch.

It must be recorded that this early advice to his daughter had no effect whatever on her character. Cecilia became a quick-tempered lady of great presence, and when she came to live at Carnoustie House, in later life, she ruled the inhabitants of

Carnoustie with a rod of iron. She is reported to have commanded an untiring flow of strong language, and always referred to her brother as 'That damned devil George,' although she was on very affectionate terms with him, and visited him frequently. On these occasions she drove over to Kinloch in a coach, accompanied by two footmen and armed with a couple of holster pistols in red bags, fiercely disdaining the use of the Newtyle railway. In Church during the Litany which runs — 'that it shall please Thee to show thy pity on all prisoners and captives,' she invariably added in a very loud voice 'and Exiles,' referring to her father's time as an outlaw. At Carnoustie she claimed to have the first pick of the seaweed which was washed up on the shore after a storm, and which was used to manure fields and gardens and, when she had taken what she needed, the Town Crier was sent round with his bell calling out 'Miss Kinloch is sairved, ye can tak the sea waur noo.'

To go back to the children's schooling, the education of daughters was at that time considered to be of much less importance than the education of sons. Beyond teaching the girls to read and write and do some simple arithmetic, the next step was in the arts of domestic economy, with music and painting being desirable and, for anyone so inclined, the study of French. All this could be learnt at home and, as a whole, the daughters had a dull life and a bad deal all round as compared to the sons. It was recognised that the eldest son would fall heir to the heritable estate, which was the main asset of any landed family, and that the daughters must take their chance in a rather narrow marriage market, since any suitor had to have parental approval. In fact, only one, Margaret, of the six Kinloch daughters found a husband, and their mother, Helen, was the only one of six Smyth daughters to marry. The marriage of George Kinloch's aunt Helen to a man called Reoch who was in the 'mirror-making or glass-grinding business' was only just acceptable, because this was said to be a 'very genteel business,' and 'profitable.' Although the Reochs were not people of property, it made up for quite a lot if their business was profitable.

The Kinloch sons were brought up to understand this code of behaviour and would not think of introducing 'improper young men' to their sisters. A letter from father to son on this subject makes this matter quite clear—

I already told you that you was heartily welcome to ask any friends of yours to come here and to stay as long as you please, the very same as if the house was your own. You will, of course, not ask any improper person, for although some of your acquaintances may do well enough for companions at College, yet your *friends* should be nearly of the same rank in life with yourself; you have judgement enough not to chuse an improper friend.

The first and most important step in education in George Kinloch's estimation was to develop a good style of writing, and this is emphasised again and again in writing to his sons, with little effect. He was himself a most beautiful writer and excellent grammarian, so that he was well qualified to give advice in this much neglected art which was so important in the days of the quill pen, and before the typewriter. In his letters he usually underlined words and phrases intended as a joke, or requiring special emphasis, in case the point of his best jokes should be missed. He wrote to his son George—

Pray do pay some attention to your writing. I believe I already mentioned to you that it is of great importance to be able to write a good letter and, as this can be acquired only by practice, you should lose no opportunity of writing to me or to some of the rest of the family. It will give you the *habit*, so that you will acquire *facility* in it.

and again—

What a glorious invention is that of writing. It enables us to *converse* on matters of business or amusement however great the distance may be which separates us. Both your last letters, having been written in a hurry, are not so well penned as they ought to have been. Pray attend to this. It appears to me that you write with too hard a pen.

He suggested as an exercise—

When you write letters, use black lines under your paper, from which you will soon acquire the habit of writing straight without lines at all. Always keep in view that the end of writing is to be legible.

As regards grammar and punctuation, he said—

Your punctuation was very defective; you put a comma immediately after the verb which can very seldom be done with propriety. Punctuation is of the utmost importance to the proper understanding of writings and altho' the rules for it are simple, yet few understand them. When we meet, I shall point them out to you in a few minutes.

Parents writing to their children at boarding-school may have felt inclined to write as he wrote—

I have repeatedly asked you several questions which you have never answered such as, how is your time disposed of? Do you learn riding? What progress have you made in French? Do either of you learn the violin? Pray answer these questions, and any others that are put to you. When I answer a letter, I begin at the beginning and, as I answer each paragraph, I draw a score through it so that no part of it is omitted. You will find this useful in answering the letters you receive.

George Kinloch had a pigeon-hole brain which went with his imaginative mind, and could not understand how his children could be so un-methodical.

The sons, to whom he was writing, were living in Edinburgh, at this time lodging with their Smyth grandmother, and studying there for the profession of the Law which was their father's idea of the most suitable career for them. Their instruction included attending classes at College, and also tutorial instruction on various subjects over which father kept very close supervision. A letter on the subject of the ultimate career read—

I confess that, for you, the Law appears to be the best. It is the profession of a gentleman, is attended with no great outlay and almost immediately brings in some return and, if attended to with diligence, will, in a very few years, make you independent. Without flattering you, you have abilities which I have no doubt would enable you to make a respectable figure in it, and you do not want for application. It affords ample time for the enjoyment of all country sports, of which I shall always be glad to see you take your share; and, in short, it is the profession, which, had I been in your situation, I would have adopted. At the same time, though

44

I advise you, I shall not control you, in your choice. Many are disgusted at the Law, from the dryness of the study for it, but it appears to me that a person may be completely qualified for it, without wading through all the absurdities and nonsense which, like Cerberus, are placed at the entrance to prevent too many from going in. Besides, tho' it were a little disgusting at first, that, like a disagreeable operation, is soon over, and becomes pleasant as we advance. Reflect carefully on all I have said, and then form your opinion. If you are anywise at a loss, consult me, and I shall give you my best advice.

His son's reply was not quite satisfactory, so Papa went into more detail about the studies necessary—

I think you mention only fiddling and French, to neither of which I have any objection, but you know something more is requisite; if you mean to be an Advocate, then it is easy to point out what your studies ought to be, vizt. enough of Latin to understand the Law books which are written in that language; and this, I believe, is most easily learned from persons who make a practice of teaching it, privately. Then there are a certain number of Law books, which it is also necessary to read, and which somehow or other, are not half so agreeable as *Tom Jones*. These are all that are necessary for *you to study*; and all the rest is a matter of amusement; and, as to them, I leave you perfectly at liberty to chuse what you please, *knowing that you will not be idle*. Mathematics, French, writing, counting, drawing, fiddling, fencing, dancing, etc. etc.

Perhaps Father intended to allow his son perfect liberty to 'Chuse what you please,' but, as he was used to giving advice to everyone else from economists and politicians to friends, relations, and everyone else that he met, it is hardly likely that he would refrain from giving advice to his eldest son on the important matter of his education and consequent career, so that he continued in further letters—

With respect to your going to the dancing school, I shall be most happy that you do so. Not, that I would wish you to *cut capers* like a dancing master, for nothing can be more ungenteel. But, by being taught to dance, you will learn to use your limbs without the swagger of a ploughboy, and you will feel confidence while joining in a dance with your friends and companions, which you should never decline to do when you have an opportunity. As you will not need much of the dancing school, I would wish you to postpone going to it, till after the balls, which I believe take place soon, and after that, you may go when you please. I likewise wish that you should go to the fencing school, which will also strengthen your limbs, and besides will enable you to defend yourself, if attacked; for a weak person who has learned to fence, if provided with a sword or stick, will overcome a much stronger person who has not been taught, skill being more than a match for strength. It will be time enough for this, some time hence. If there is anything else you wish to be taught, mention it.

and again—

I hope you are both behaving well, paying proper respect to your grandmother, *and not quarrelling.*

I should wish you to attend a fencing school three times a week, dancing the same, and music an hour every day. In dancing, I would advise you to learn chiefly the minuet, which, altho' but a dull performance as a dance, is very useful to teach the graceful use of the arms and legs. You may learn what other dances you please, and two months of it (three times a week) should complete you, as far as is necessary. Fencing is a noble exercise and useful as a defence. You will seek out the cheapest school as some of them are dearer than others. The same as to the violin. You will go to the master, and if you wish to practise at home, use a mute, for fear your audience should be overpowered with *extasy* by your melodious tones. I have no objections to your learning landscape drawing, which is the only kind you can ever have use for. Three hours a week will be sufficient. Arrange all this as soon as you can and let me know when it is done.

Commenting on the wider aspects of education he said—

Music is an innocent amusement and I have often found it a useful resource to fill up the time. Your Aunt Margaret seems to think that I will disapprove of your going to the

46

Playhouse etc. I certainly think that going *often* to it is throwing away money. I would reckon once or twice in a season quite enough, unless it was to see Kemble or Kean, or some such actors. By all means, go once to the Circus, and also to see the wild beasts, and examine them minutely and attentively, without being *bothered* with the nonsensical description the showman will give you. I would wish you to see every object of *national* curiosity.

He considered mathematics to be of no great importance.

You will find mathematics a dry study at the beginning, but it is useful in the business of life. At the same time, unless you find an inclination for it, I do not insist upon you being so versant in it, as *Sir Isaac Newton* was. This is warm weather for fencing. You would find it an excellent plan to have a flannel jacket, and to take off your coat, vest and shirt, and put on the jacket only. Flannel lets the perspiration pass off, and by having a towel to rub yourself with after your lesson is over, you would come out quite comfortable, and without danger of getting cold. If you wish to save your eyes, never fence with learners *without a mask on*.

It is not surprising that, by 1818, by which time George Kinloch had made quite a reputation for himself in Radical circles as a Political Speaker, he approved his son's invitation to join the well-known Edinburgh Debating Society, 'The Spec.'

I highly approve of your *joining the Speculative Society*. It was in high repute when I lived in Edinburgh, and I have often regretted that I did not attend it. It is an excellent school for making a young man feel his own powers, and by the time you have shaken off the diffidence which always accompanies a first attempt to speak in public, I prophesy that you will make a respectable figure in it, which will be of use to you afterwards. As you have joined it, pray be punctual in your attendance, and if you will communicate the subject of your essay, and of your debate, I shall give you some hints which may be of use to you, though I would not by any means wish you to shine in borrowed feathers. Speaking of joining Societies, there are several I would wish you to avoid, which some of your companions will be anxious for you joining. In particular, the Free Masons. It is altogether an unmeaning farce, and always leads to drunkenness and dissipation. *Their secret is*, that they have no secret. For if they had, you may be very sure that some 'Brother' in a fit of madness or drunkenness, would have divulged it long ago. I forget if I ever recommended to you to keep a journal of your daily transactions. If you do so, it will give you the habit of recollecting what you have been about, and when you look back to it in after life, you will find it both interesting and amusing.

All the time that his sons had been studying in Edinburgh, he was becoming increasingly worried about his personal financial situation, and unlike most fathers, he explained this to his son in the following letter, so that his son would not consider him to be miserly—

With respect to books, those which you require for your classes, you will of course, get from Robertson, the bookseller, and your Uncle Robert, or Margaret will give you the money to pay for them. As to other books for amusement, or instruction, no sum that I could afford to give you would be sufficient. Owing to the 'change of times' and the reductions which I have been obliged to give my tenants, I am under the necessity of practising the *strictest economy*, and for these two years past, I have laid it down as a rule not to purchase a *single article* which I could do without; not even *books*, although I see many advertised, which I greatly wish to possess. The truth is, that owing to the purchasing of Carnoustie and Chapelhill, I owe about £10,000, the interest of which must be punctually paid, whether I receive my rents punctually or not, and the fall in the value of land has made them of much less value than they were some time ago, while at the same time, the increase in the value of money has proved very hard on those who had borrowed it when it was plentiful. I cannot now reckon on receiving more than about £1600 a year, from which deducting £750 for interest and publics there remains only £850 clear. (This will show you the effects of the *glorious Pitt system*, and how it has melted away the wealth of the country, like snow on a summer day.) I do not think you have any propensity to extravagance in money matters;

but I think it right to state to you how my matters stand.

There was an economy campaign in progress at home as well as in Edinburgh—

Here we are trying to live as economically as possible. I can no longer afford to keep my carriage, which I regret on account of your mother and sisters, but there is no help for it. I need not therefore point out to you and John the propriety of avoiding every *unnecessary* expense. This country is in a sad state. God knows when it will end. Many of the poor people are absolutely starving, not being able to get employment.

The improper use of pocket money was explained:

Ices and ginger beer are very good things and, when you are with other people who take them, it is very right that you should do the same. But, on other occasions, I know of no money worse bestowed *than upon the belly* nor do I know a more despicable set than your loungers in pastry cooks shops etc. of which, I am sure, you will never be one.

The clothing for a family of eight was a heavy item, and so economy here was also necessary—

I wish you and John to get great coats for going out with, in cold weather. I would prefer a drab colour, such as the old coat you have of mine; with a cotton velvet neck. It is a colour which wears well. It should be made *very wide*, but not *too long*, say two or three inches above your ankle, and with the pockets behind, like mine. The arms *can hardly be too wide*. If Robert or Margaret [his Uncle and Aunt] go with you, they will chuse a good cloth, the cheaper, the better, and not too thick, as it would be clumsy and heavy. Get your initials sown in the inside of the back, and I need not put you in mind of taking care of them, and of all your other clothes. You can return my old one with the chaise bag, any convenient opportunity.

George Kinloch had his own ideas about health and hygiene and, for most people, his advice was a good dose of 'Dr. Calomel', as he attributed the usual complaints to constipation.

I wish you would get a box of calomel pills, three grains in each, of which you might take one when you have occasion

49

for it. It is the best of all physic, and if taken in time often prevents serious diseases.

and, quoting from Hamlet—

'Give Physic to the Dogs.'

The other essential protection against chills in which he believed was the old-fashioned remedy of wearing flannel next the skin—

I must beg you will take care of yourself. If you have not got flannel *next your skin*, put it on immediately, and you will also be the better of a flannel waistcoat with sleeves above your shirt. Never go without worsted stockings, and I would have you avoid as much as possible going out after dinner. If, at any time you are under the necessity of doing so, either take a coach or a chaise. I shall not grudge the expense. If you walk, get a pair of stout *cloggs* to put over your shoes, as nothing can be worse for you than wet, or even *damp* feet. The best cure I know for a cold is to bathe your feet at bed-time, and to remain in bed most of the next day, taking a gentle dose of physic, and living upon *slops*. During the winter you should never go out without your great coat, however fine the weather, and at night, add a good thick handkerchief round your neck. If, with all these precautions, your cough does not quit you, I must prescribe for you a journey to Kinloch, which you know is a sovereign remedy for all complaints. When you do come, you will need to use every precaution to avoid cold. You will put on flannel drawers, and two pair of stockings; flannel above, as well as below your shirt; a neckcloth under your shirt neck, and a large cotton handkerchief above all, as silk has no heat. Also put my great coat above your own, and then you will have a chance to escape cold. I hope you will continue to take care of yourself, for your life, depends in a great degree upon it, at present. Avoid exposure to cold. Keep your bowels regular; and don't exert yourself beyond your strength. I shall expect you over as soon as you are able, but you must not expect that for some time yet.

Perhaps in the case of his son George there was unnecessary alarm, as this son was soon pretty fit, and lived to be 81, in spite of a full life and good measure of 'Wine, women and song'.

At this time, however, his health was thoroughly suspect and he created more anxiety to his grand-mother by proposing to walk home from Edinburgh through Fife at the end of the summer term. To this proposal his father was quick to support grand-mother.

It seems your grand-mother is grievously alarmed at the idea of you and John walking through Fife, and your Uncle Robert is little less so. You have grown a *tall gentleman*, but have forgot to take the breadth along with you; you are out of practice, and for these, and for twenty other weighty reasons, walking is out of the question. Now I certainly don't wish you to walk, *unless* you are perfectly able for it, I would propose that you should come to Mountwhanny the first day, which is just twenty-four miles, and you may rest a day there if you chuse. Then to Dundee, which is seven miles, where the Gig would meet you. There is no doubt you could not walk, *unless you are in practice*, and whether you are to walk through Fife, or not, you would be the better to take a walk of 3 or 4 miles out of town every day or every two days. There is some beautiful scenery round Edinburgh, all of which you should see. Rosline, Lasswade, Dalkeith, Corstorphine, Duddingston, etc. I suppose your Uncle has a book describing all the remarkable things in the neighbourhood, and if he has, you should read it. Give my love to John, who I suppose has lost the use of his right hand, as we never see a letter from him.

The following winter both sons were ill again, and their father went over to see them in Edinburgh. He wrote to his wife to say—

In your brother John's room (in which our John sleeps), the old-fashioned grate is meant for ornament, and not for use and, for want of five shillings bestowed in rumfording, the chimney smokes so as to prevent having a fire at night. Economy is a thing of which I highly approve, but there are some sorts of it which put me quite out of sorts. I think it not unlikely that I shall move them to lodgings where they can have more convenience. It may cause a little demur, but in a case of this kind, there is no room for false delicacy.

Finally it was decided that young George must come home so that he wrote again to his wife to say—

In taking over George, I think the best way will be in one of the Waterloos [the Coach to Perth], suppose I should take all the places. The quickness with which they travel is an object as they reach Perth in six hours. It leaves this at 9 and reaches Perth at 3; so I wish that Angus should be in Perth with the carriage on Friday, by 12, so as to be ready to start with us as soon as the Waterloo arrives. It goes to the Salutation [the Salutation Hotel]. I have, as usual, given offence to your mother by not sooner telling my intentions, and there is no want of evil forebodings accordingly. However, I hope, it is of no consequence. You may look for us about 6, and have a fire on in the nursery, and his bed etc. well aired and ready for him.

Perhaps George Kinloch 'spoon-fed' his sons too much, and did not give sufficient attention to his daughters. The daughters did not resent this and always longed for letters from their brothers, Margaret writing to her brother said:

I have long and eagerly looked for a letter from you, but I have hitherto been doomed to disappointment, though I do think you might have paid some one of the five 'purple-faced girlies' the compliment of writing to them. What was the reason you were so extremely foolish to give up learning German? I assure you I would not have given it up when you have such a good opportunity.

When the boys were out in France, as described later, she wrote to her brother George, saying—

Tell me what you think of the French ladies, as I hear very different accounts of them, and, as you will never do for a lady's correspondent unless you can write about dress, whatever strikes you as particular, mention it, besides that it will make you quite a ladies man. You complain that you have nothing to write about, but whether should you or I have most to say? I who have been constantly at home, and you who have been in a strange country. I quite forget if I told you Cecilia and I were at a Ball at Lintrose lately; it was a very pleasant one indeed. I believe you have seen Miss Hawkins, she was there drest the most eccentric figure you ever saw, her hair was curled and hanging down her back the length of her waist, and her petticoats up to her knees about. She caused a great deal of speculation, as William Hunter was there, and it is said he is going to be married to her. This day was a fortnight,[1] Cecilia, Ann and I went in to Dundee to go to the 'Valentine Ball' which took place the day after. We went with Charles Kinloch and Mrs. Horsley; there were about 70 people and every person said it was a very pleasant ball, so I suppose it must have been so. We had four Colonels and a General at it, and three gentlemen from Arthurstone, but *we girlies* are not fine enough for them to dance with. They are a set of conceited wretches.

One can imagine that the formidable eldest sister Cecilia might have been a 'wall-flower,' but not Margaret or Ann, who were both full of vivacity and spirits.

Primogeniture — everything done for the eldest son — was the order of the day. Although George Kinloch was not prepared to accept many of the customs of his generation, this does not seem to have been one of the conventions which he thought needed reforming, and so the daughters and the younger son John, although greatly loved, did not receive the V.I.P. treatment accorded to the eldest.

Although it was rough and ready justice as far as the younger son or sons was concerned, it gave the younger son the impetus to leave home and seek the possibility of a fortune overseas. At this time the most sought after occupation for younger sons was the East India Company, or on plantations in the West Indies. Another conventional occupation was to buy a commission in the Army or the Navy, and at the end of the Napoleonic wars there were a large number of retired Army officers living in France on half-pay, because the cost of living was smaller there than that at home.

George Kinloch wrote—

I am afraid Captain Ogilvy will find it a very difficult task to get rid of his sons. I suppose they will be for the Army or Navy — bad trades at all times, but damn'd bad just now, and I hope will long continue so.

Around Kinloch some of the younger sons, or sons without Estates had more original ideas; the son of Dr Boyter who was one of George Kinloch's most constant shooting companions, was appointed First Lieutenant of the 'Rising Star,' one of the ships being fitted out by Admiral Cochrane for his expedition to South America to support the war against Spain for the independence of Chile.

A letter described this ship—

This ship of 450 tons was of very new design, being polacre rigged, her main yard 60 feet long, and everything in proportion. She had a steam engine of 96 horses which was expected to 'astonish the Dons not a little,' but unfortunately later, 'the steam apparatus not being found to answer, it was given up.' However, Lieut. Boyter sailed off with Admiral Cochrane 'to sink the falling star of the "Man of Petticoats"[2] to the bottom of the Atlantic.'

Another unconventional friend of the family — Donald MacPherson, who became a missionary, sailed from Leith in 1818, 'with a wife which he has taken to himself,' the pier being covered with people to see them depart, and wish them Godspeed. They arrived at Cronstat in the Baltic after 25 days, and travelled to Petersburg where they were most kindly received by fellow missionaries. Petersburg is described as 'one of the finest cities in the world, having commodious streets and canals, and being worthy of it's founder Peter the Great.' They set off again, and, after a tedious voyage of 75 days, down the River Volga, arrived at Astrakan in Asiatic Turkey on the Caspian Sea to start their missionary work. The last that was heard of these MacPhersons in the Kinloch Papers was that they were studying the language, so that it would be some time before they were much use as missionaries.

The Kinloch younger son John was expected by the family to become a Writer to the Signet and join the legal practice of the Smyths in Edinburgh, but he had independent ideas of his own against this. At first John's idea of becoming a wine merchant in London was not taken seriously although they nick-named him 'The Wine Merchant.' However John was seriousa bout this and eventually joined a wine importing firm in London and worked there until his premature death in 1829.

[1] In correspondence the expression 'Wednesday was a fortnight' or 'Thursday was a week' was invariably used where we would write 'a fortnight ago last Wednesday' or 'a week ago last Thursday.'

[2] 'The embroiderer of petticoats' or 'The Man of Petticoats.'
See also page 91. This description of Ferdinand VII of Spain may be a literal translation from the Spanish 'Hombre Faldero' [from Falda-A skirt] or 'Womaniser'.

CHAPTER FIVE

His Travels in Scotland

ONE OF THE great changes in the way of life in the country in the last century has been in the means and ease of travel and transport. In 1800 it was usual for the ordinary man to be born, to live, and to die in his home town or district, so that for Strathmore people to go to Edinburgh or to Glasgow would be the adventure of a life-time. Women ventured away from home even less than men.

The cost of travel was prohibitive for the working man, and this is illustrated by the following detail of expenses incurred by George Kinloch on a journey from Dundee to Edinburgh and back in 1804, which included crossing the estuaries of the Tay and Forth rivers—

1804.	Paid Thos. Bell for a boat.	£—:	2:	6
16 July.	Osler 6d. Hire & tolls to			
	Coupar 14/4d. Driver 2/-	. . :	16:	10
	Osler 6d. Hire & tolls to			
	Ely 17/1d. Driver 2/5d.	1:	—:	—
20th.	Hire & tolls to Kinghorn	1:	1:	6
	Porter & toll 7d.			
	Boat & Porter 3/6d.		4:	1
	Total expense of journey	£3:	4:	11.
	Return.			
29th.	Coach to Leith.	£—:	5:	6
July	Boat 9/-. Toll 1/-. Porter 3d.		10:	3
	Chaise & tolls to Pitlessie 21/4d.			
	Driver 2/6d.	1:	3:	10

Osler 6d. Chaise & tolls to Sth.
Ferry 19/5d. Driver 2/7d.   1 : 2 : —
Beer 1/- Boat 2/6d.   —: 3 : 6

Expense of journey back.   £3 : 5 : 1.

The military roads which General Wade had started to build after the rebellion of 1715 with the purpose of opening up the Western Highlands for transport of troops and artillery had not been properly maintained and, in consequence, these useful new roads had fallen into such a state of disrepair that by 1800 the road to Inverness through the Grampians was practically impossible for heavy wheeled traffic. The picturesque Wade bridges remain as landmarks on roads which were never a very dependable means of communication. Coach transport and the Turnpike roads were improving, and Meigle, near where George Kinloch lived, was on the route of the regular service through Strathmore from Perth to Aberdeen, but this did not become 'The Mail' until Roger and Barclay took over the 'Defiance Coaches' in 1832. Even then, although the Coach passed the gates of Kinloch House, it was not practicable to stand at the gates and hope to board a passing coach. The Booking, or as it was then worded 'to take a place' had to be done in advance at the Change Houses where fresh horses were harnessed, and the nearest Change House to Kinloch was Coupar-Angus, six miles west in one direction and Castleton six miles east in the other.

There was no coach service from Meigle into Dundee, so that the ordinary man had either to walk or to travel on the clumsy 'carrier's cart' drawn by a team of cart horses which took passengers besides the produce of the farms and the local linen industries. Letters were delivered by Post Runners which was a very expensive service.

The drive of Drumkilbo House may have been the scene of the first bicycle ever to be ridden in Scotland, as George Kinloch recorded in a letter of 17th June 1819 — 'The Drummie has been practising upon a velocipede lately but not with great success.' History records that the first two-wheeled device in the nature of a bicycle called 'The Dandy Horse' was introduced into England by Baron von Drais in 1818 and as

David Nairne's velocipede was probably brought back from Paris after his trip abroad with George Kinloch in the summer of 1818, it may well have been the first bicycle in Scotland. The rider sat on a beam connecting the two wheels and propelled himself by kicking the ground alternately on either side.

George Kinloch never spoke of riding a horse, and his normal means of transport on business occasions was the open gig. It may have been more expensive to keep a riding horse than a horse which could be driven. Except on business journeys, he would walk, and it was nothing for him to walk to Carnoustie eleven miles away as the crow flies to visit his property there, and home again the same day. The daughters made use of an old grey mare for their calls at Balhary or Arthurstone, but this was probably a work-horse which could be saddled for riding as required.

George Kinloch enjoyed any excuse to travel. Being a well-educated man, and in consequence of his experience of estate management and farming he was sometimes invited to make expeditions in an advisory capacity.

The following letters about his travels in Scotland have little significance on his life, but they illustrate his character in many ways. Like 'The Elephant's Child,' he suffered from insatiable curiosity and never missed an opportunity of going to see anything unsusual, interesting, new, or historically important.

Not only did he record all that he saw wherever he went, but he encouraged his sons to do the same, and to make a detailed account of their experiences.

I would advise you to keep a daily journal, not only of all occurrences, but of whatever strikes you at the time, as being anywise remarkable. You will find it highly amusing to refer to afterwards.

This advice was not taken by his sons, but fortunately both sons and wife filed away most of George Kinloch's letters, so that extracts of the occurrences which he found anywise remarkable may be found 'highly amusing' to the traveller of to-day.

FIRST.　*From Meigle to Perth and Edinburgh — on foot.*
　　(Letter to his wife from Edinburgh — 19th March, 1807).

I dined in Perth and went to Kinross, where I arrived a little after seven, and altho' the wind was bitterly cold, yet, as it was in our backs, we felt little of it. Next morning, I breakfasted at Dunfermline, which is a neat little well built town, with the sad remains of what has been a magnificent Abbey. After inspecting the ruins, I walked on to Torryburn, and examined Mr. Wedderburn's sea coast, but I do not think there is upon it, any station fit for a net. It was a remarkably fine winter day. I left Torryburn about three when it began to look very stormy, and got to the North Ferry about half past four, when it blew hard from the South West, with snow. However, we got over without tacking, and I was here by about seven, the ground and streets powdered with snow and very cold. I have felt no bad effects whatever from my journey. This day has been as cold as any we have had. One might either skate or slide along Queen's St. but walking was out of the question. T. Read's horse crossed in the boat with me, which looks like a good omen. I conversed the groom, who says he is a wicked devil in the stable, tho' peaceable to ride. I shall see how he goes at the sale. God bless you and all the bairns; give my love to them, and tell them if they behave well I shall be back very soon. Write me again on Saturday.

Those who, before the Forth Road Bridge was built, have waited in a queue at North Queensferry for the motor car ferry will remember their annoyance at prospect of being late for an important engagement in Edinburgh and will appreciate that it must have been even more frustrating in the days of ferries depending on sails with the uncertainties of wind and tide.

SECOND. *From Meigle to Dundee, Newport and Edinburgh on foot.*

(Letter to his wife from Hart Street, Edinburgh — 23rd January, 1815).

After I left you yesterday morning, we were detained a short time in getting a boat, so that it was half past eight when we landed at Newport, thus adding a mile to our first stage. We got on pretty well till near Mountwhanny, when we were obliged to slacken our pace, owing to the depth of snow, and the road not being tracked. Poor Rintoul [the

Editor of the Dundee newspaper] was sadly distressed. After going twelve miles, we indulged him with a five minutes rest in a toll-house, and after we had gone about four miles more he fairly gave up, and asked us to go on and send a chaise for him. We accordingly left him, and made the best of our way to the New Inn, which we reached a little after one, having gone the eighteen miles in five hours, altho' the snow for the last four miles was five inches deep. We dispatched a chaise for our broken-down companion, and immediately commenced an attack on a round of beef, until the tea and eggs could be got ready. After making a visible impression on the beef, we dispatched four eggs and a plate of toasted bread, and then ordered the astonished waiter to bring as many more, which immediately followed their companions, with a due proportion of tea, and bread and butter. By the time we had accomplished this arduous feast, and got our shoes and stockings dried, and ourselves made quite comfortable, the way-worn traveller arrived in his chaise, and continued also to eat some breakfast. We paid for all, five shillings, by which, I am sure the man was a loser. Yeaman and I were as fresh as when we started but as 'The Incendiary' [Rintoul] protested he would give up the ghost if we walked, we chaised it to Kinghorn, where, as the boat was not to stir till ten, we indulged ourselves in tippling gin toddy 'pour passer le temps.' We embarked at ten, and after making a reasonable quantity of noise, the crew thought proper to get under way in about half an hour more; we had a passage of an hour and twenty minutes, and as by this time it was nearly midnight, we took up our abode at the 'Brittannia', where we got very comfortable beds, and we walked up this morning in time for breakfast. I found all here in their usual. Yeaman called for me when we went and roused up Maule,[1] and went with him to see the preparations for the dinner. Hallyburton called while we were with Maule, and we had a short talk about the Harbour Bill, which both of them see in it's proper light. I bought a fiddle for Courtney and then came home for the day.

THIRD. *By coach from Perth to Glasgow, via Crieff, Stirling and Cumbernauld.*

(Letter to his wife, written from King's Arms Inn, Trongate, Glasgow, 21st Sept. 1814.)

I arrived here safe and sound, at eight last night. The day was as fine as possible, so that I kept upon *deck* till we got to Cumbernauld, when a *Glasgow* shower forced me to take shelter in the *hold*, where, by means of a fat Quaker, who abounded in flesh, whatever he might do in the spirit, I had the pleasure of being squeezed for the remainder of the journey; six of us being packed into as much room as might have held four with difficulty, and each person having about as much locomotive power as a herring in the middle of a barrel.

My miseries did not end here, for on arriving every place was full, and I had to hunt about for lodgings, and if I had not been well acquainted with Glasgow, I might have lain in the street. I at last got a tolerable room with a good bed in the King's Arms Tavern, which will serve me while I stay here.

I breakfasted this morning with Tailyour, and found him fancying himself worse than when I left him, tho' the Doctor tells me he has, on the whole, been better, till within these last two days. He fancies himself so weak as to be hardly able to walk, and that he has a terrible pain in his back. I have not yet heard anything about his plans, but shall see to get them settled to-day, as I have no great pleasures in remaining here. I had the pleasure of John Adamson's [a Minister] company from Coupar to Perth and of course, received from him a great deal of information on the subject of morality and gratitude. Dr. Gillies, who cut out the lump on Elizabeth Graham's cheek, was the only other passenger from Perth, till we picked up Obadiah and three others at Cumbernauld. I introduced myself to him, as a friend of Gourdie's, and we had some conversation, tho' as he was in the hold, and I generally aloft, not so much as we would otherwise have had, for after Obadiah joined us, we had enough ado to breathe; conversation was out of the question. About Perth and till near Crieff, the harvest was well advanced, and more in than with us, except certain good farmers. From Crieff to this, except about Stirling, it will take a month, at least, to clear the fields. I think, upon the whole, the crop is better than it some time ago had the appearance of, but I do not think it will lower the prices.

The purpose of this visit to Glasgow was to escort home Mr Tailyour — a neighbour who lived near Carnoustie, and who seems to have been a hypochondriac.

FOURTH. *The same journey continued from Glasgow to Edinburgh by coach.*

I wrote to you from Glasgow on Wednesday. I now address you from Robert's desk in Auld Reekie, where we arrived at four this afternoon, having left Glasgow a little after seven. I would your mother and the rest all well, and I arrived just in time to partake of their dinner.

Mr. Tailyour was as ill as he has been at any time, all yesterday, occasioned by the idea of returning home. In the evening, I told him my opinion in plain terms; that it was impossible he could be in so much pain as he pretended, and that he had hitherto been too much indulged in his caprices, and that there was a necessity for now resisting them. In short, I said a great deal to him, and I expect he will be the better for it. Mrs. T. was anxious to come by Edinburgh to arrange about her sister's staying with her, but he was extremely adverse to it. However, as her request was so reasonable, and it being the shortest road, I judged it a proper opportunity to show my authority, and accordingly here we are, and he has borne the journey quite well, and expressed very little uneasiness, and I have left him for the night, in the 'Black Bull,' quiet and composed.

The road from Glasgow to this passes thro' a very bleak country till within about fifteen miles of this. Beyond that, they were just beginning their harvest, and I suppose it will be far in November before it is finished. Near this, the corn is about all in. But the supper bell is ringing, and the oysters are impatient, so God bless you all my dearest Helen.

FIFTH. *Coaching by night in bad weather from Dundee to Aberdeen.*

(Letter to his wife from Aberdeen — Friday, 25th March 1808).

If the weather last night was as bad with you as we had it, I am sure you would be pitying me, but I cannot say I felt any inconvenience from it, as we kept ourselves snug with both windows up, and dozed as well as we could.

It was the most tempestuous night I ever saw, but the roads were good and the drivers anxious to get on, so that we lost no time. We arrived here a little after six, and went to bed till half past ten, but tho' I slept a little, I could never get my feet warm, which I found was the case with my fellow travellers also. We left Dundee at a quarter past seven with the coach full, and Mr. Grubb took an outside berth at Balgillo, as far as Arbroath, where we supped. We dropped another of our passengers soon after, which gave us some more room. I cannot say I saw anything the whole way, till we came to Stonehaven, when the day began to dawn, and we got a little use of our eyes. From the time we could see distinctly (about six miles from here), I never saw a more bleak miserable country, bogs and heather, and not a hedge or a tree to be seen, and this continues till within a mile of the town. I have not yet been out, so cannot say anything of this city. It still snows as if it had never snowed here, and no appearance of mending. We remain here all this night, and if the weather does not alter, I shall return from whence I came, for I will not encounter this sort of weather in an open carriage, upon any account. Love to all the bairns.

He did not care for Aberdeenshire in this March weather, and returned 'from whence he came.'

SIXTH. *By coach from KinlochHouse to Aberdeen, Fort George, & Cromarty.*

(Letter to his son George — 22nd December, 1817).

I left home on Tuesday morning, the 9th. and got to Aberdeen at nine at night. I left Aberdeen in the mail at six next morning, and journeyed on to Campbellton near Fort George, where I arrived at four on Thursday morning, and found Mr. Storrier and Jamie Grubb waiting for me, more asleep than awake.

After breakfast we walked to the Fort, about a mile and a half, and walked round the ramparts. It is surrounded on three sides by the sea, and defended by a high wall with bastions. On the south side towards the land, it is one of the completest fortifications in the world, having a wall about 24 feet high with a broad fossee, which can be filled with water, besides being completely commanded by ten six pounders. Beyond this, there is advanced work of uncommon strength with another fossee to the southward of it, and beyond that another advanced work, with stockades in front of it, and I don't know what all. In short, instead of being adapted only to keep off a few undisciplined Highlanders, it might, with a competent garrison, have bid defiance to Buonaparte's Army of Russia. The body of the place is a parallelogram, formed by the ramparts, the inner wall of which may be about fourteen feet high. In this hollow which they surround, are placed the houses, which are two stories high, regular and neat, and I suppose might contain between two and three thousand men; but when I saw them, there was only one company of the 88th. consisting of *75 men*. So you may believe it appeared to be the headquarters of Dullness. It is altogether a beautiful specimen of the modern art of fortification, and one can only regret that so much money should have been thrown away, on so useless a fabric.

After surveying the Fort, we crossed the Ferry, which is about a mile broad, and walked to Fortrose a mile further. Then to Rosemarkie and across a bleak heath to Ardoch where Mr. Grubb stays, on the bay of Cromarty; the entrance to the Bay of Cromarty is between two very high rocks, called 'the Souters,' and it is about a mile broad. Within, the bay expands to from four to five broad by about six, and might contain, I believe, all the ships in the world, as snug as if they were in a mill pond. The bay is skirted with cultivated lands, but the heath predominates in the background, and they seem to be but indifferent farmers. The carts of the poorer sort might contain as much as two large wheel-barrows, and the horses are in proportion, and wholly unused to shoes. The roads are pretty good, for when once made, as there are no heavy carriages on them, they last a long time. Gaelic is the language, tho' most people understand English.

I stayed at Ardoch all Friday, and having succeeded in getting a trustee appointed to Mr. Grubb's satisfaction, Storrier and I walked to Inverness on the Saturday, about sixteen miles, for post chaises or gigs are unknown there. It was a remarkably fine day, altho' hard frost, and we got to Kessock Ferry about half past nine, and to Inverness a little after two.

Storrier returned to Ardoch on Sunday forenoon, and I went to look at the entrance to that useless and expensive work, the Caledonian Canal. It begins about a mile north from Inverness, and taking a south-west direction, sweeps round a hill and then turns north-west till it enters Loch Ness, about six miles up. There are two superb locks near the entrance, and I believe other four take it up to the Loch. It is to be twenty feet deep, and will admit a thirty-six gun frigate. Loch Ness never freezes, neither does the river Ness, which is still more remarkable. I cannot account for it any other way than by supposing that the Loch is chiefly supplied by springs within it. Having satisfied my curiosity, I embarked in the Mail at three p.m. and got to Aberdeen next day at two p.m. having had the benefit of the dreadful storm which raged all that night, and in which several vessels were lost. However, I felt nothing of it, thanks to the boat cloak and other precautions. I left Aberdeen on Tuesday morning at six, and arrived here at six p.m. and found all well.

The Caledonian Canal, built by Telford, and begun in 1803, was not opened for through traffic until 1823, so that, in 1817 it may have been open only as far as Loch Ness.

These letters show that coach travellers had to be tough at the beginning of the 19th century and emphasise that coastal transport by sea for both people and goods was usually preferable.

The speed and reliability of the coaches on the main routes gradually improved and an advertisement by the Mail Coach Office in Edinburgh dated May 1825 described the service to London as follows—

The direct Edinburgh and London Mail will, on and after the 6th. current, leave the Black Bull Hotel, every morning at a quarter before eight o'clock; and, passing through Haddington, Dunbar, Berwick, Belford, Alnwick, Morpeth, Newcastle, Durham, Darlington, Northallerton, Borough Bridge, Wetherby, Ferry Bridge, Doncaster, Newark, Grantham, Stamford, and Huntingdon, will arrive at the Bull and Mouth Inn, London, the second morning at six o'clock.

The whole distance will be performed within forty-six hours, including all stoppages. The most ample time has been afforded for the several refreshments, so as to enable travellers to go the entire journey with the utmost facility and comfort; and the greatest care has also been taken that the refreshments provided shall be of such a description as to meet the wishes of the most superior class of passengers.

This being the first attempt which has been made for any public carriage to travel regularly so great a distance in so short a time, the proprietors think it necessary to give the public every reasonable assurance, not only of the comfort, but of the safety of this conveyance. A mail-coach carries few outsides, and can in consequence go a fast pace with the greater security. An ample number of horses has been allotted for this establishment; the stages will be very short, to prevent any distress or difficulty; and the coachmen have been selected for their ability and good character.

An article in the *Scotsman* of the same date advocating horse-drawn rail roads said—

What a vast improvement would it be if travelling were rendered general and passengers carried at the rate of ten or twelve miles an hour on all our roads.

We have no doubt that the opening and shutting of Parliament, a Westminster dinner, a remarkable trial, a new opera, would call up some scores of persons from the Scottish Metropolis to London.

The public was ready to travel, but the means was still confined to the 'most superior class of passengers,' and George Kinloch must have been considered to be in this class of passengers for which the coach proprietors were catering.

1 William Maule (1771–1852) who later became Lord Panmure of Brechin was a wealthy landowner. He was Member of Parliament for the County of Forfar from 1805 until 1831, but seldom spoke in the House.

CHAPTER SIX

Involvement in Public Affairs

THE EARLY YEARS OF George Kinloch's married life corresponded in time with the Napoleonic war years. Scotland was far away from the battlefields of Europe but, when the South Coast of England was being threatened by the French invasion army in camp around Boulogne, authority had been given to Lords Lieutenant of Counties to recruit a Volunteer Force. These Volunteers, a territorial army, had the dual role of defending the country from invasion and suppressing riots and tumults at home.

In his capacity as Depute Lord Lieutenant of Perthshire, Mr Mungo Murray of Lintrose House, Coupar-Angus, wrote to George Kinloch, in a very unsteady and almost illegible hand, inviting him to command the Coupar-Angus Company of the Volunteers. The letter dated 16th March 1797 read—

My Dear Sir,
　　　　　Last night at a very full meeting of the Volunteers of the Parish of Coupar, they made a choice of you to be their Captain and Messrs. Charles Hay, David Clarke and Robert Blair Younger, of Cronan for Subalterns.
　　　　　There are two Sargents come out to Coupar from the Regiment to assist in orderling them.
　　　　　If you are pleased to accept of the Command of the Coupar Company, I shall do myself the pleasure of meeting you to-morrow by 11 o'clock forenoon, to introduce you to the Volunteers.

I have the pleasure to be
Dear Sir,
Your most humble servant
Mungo Murray.

George Kinloch was then an active young man of 22 and many of his friends such as James Rattray of Craighall, Alexander Whitson of Parkhill and Alan Macpherson of Newton Blairgowrie had already been enlisted. The Volunteers wore a smart uniform including a redcoat with blue facings and gold lace for the officers with white breeches or pantaloons; it may have appealed to him as an amusing new experience or a good club and he became enrolled as Captain of the Coupar-Angus Company.

The only known active service operation of the Coupar-Angus Company, besides a lot of orderling, inspections and reviews was, in September 1797, when Mungo Murray called out the Company to defend his own house at Lintrose against what he described as a 'Mob from Meigle.' The 'Mob from Meigle' consisted of furious but probably peaceable folk from Meigle who had gone to Lintrose to protest against the enforcement of the Militia Acts. As a result of these Acts, Meigle husbands and sons were being pressed into the Militia by ballot and many people thought or suspected that the 'Pressed Men' were going to be shipped off to the West Indies where disease took toll of so many British soldiers. This tumult was easily suppressed, nine of the rioters were taken and escorted to Perth where they would doubtlessly be severely punished.

Before long the Perthshire Yeomanry and Volunteers became a much larger organisation and by 1808, George Kinloch's name did not appear any longer on the Roll of Officers. George Kinloch, who considered that the cost of maintaining a large standing army in time of peace was a waste of public money must have felt that to continue in the Volunteers was contrary to the principles which he advocated and so he resigned his Commission.

Another responsible appointment which he undertook was that of Justice of the Peace for the County of Perth.[1] This was an honour and a public duty which was more to his taste. His letters describe how he used to attend the Justice Court in

Coupar-Angus with his shooting dog, Vixen, sitting beside him and where the dog behaved with more dignity and decorum than she did on the Tullyfergus braes.

He received a lengthy document of commission which made it clear that the King 'has assigned to you to keep all Ordinances and Statutes for the good of our Peace within the County of Perth and to chastise and punish all persons that offend.'[2] This appointment was no sinecure, as at that time the Justices were expected not only to judge the cases brought before them in Court but also to 'take steps to get any person guilty of a breach of the peace brought to trial.'

It was only a question of degree of seriousness of the crime whether a Justice dealt with a case himself or remitted it to the Sheriff of the County for trial with a Jury as 'they seem fitted to judge all petty crimes and petty acts of theft or pickery but cases which are truly infamous should be tried by a Court which proceeds with a Jury.' This was the official direction to Justices. The document of Commission ended by requiring the Justice to declare on oath that he would 'do equal rights to the poor and the rich after your cunning, wit and power.' It was therefore highly important that a Justice should have some legal knowledge besides his native 'cunning, wit and power' and with this George Kinloch was better equipped than most of the country Lairds who undertook this responsibility.

These two appointments of Justice of the Peace and Captain in the Volunteers were positions which were in keeping with his position in Society as a Laird. It might have been thought that, with this work, and with his farm and country pursuits, his family and his music, there would have been enough to keep him busy but, in 1815, his interest in public affairs began and led to continuous involvement with the public affairs of Dundee.

The first step towards this involvement came as a result of his good offices in getting work started on the new harbour. Without the harbour, Dundee would never have developed as an important nineteenth century industrial city, so that his career and the growth of the City of Dundee are linked together. He had been born in Dundee, and one can imagine that, as a small boy, it may have been one of his favourite walks to go down to the harbour and watch the sailing boats coming to anchor outside the breakwaters, furling their sails and kedging their way into the pier. At that time the harbour consisted only of a small tidal basin, protected from the wind and breaking seas by a breakwater of rubble and a wharf where all merchandise and passengers were landed, rather resembling one of the small fishing harbours which remain along the Fife and Angus coasts, but not an impressive harbour for a town with a considerable and expanding import and export trade of flax and linen. The small boy, by the time he was grown up, had seen much of the world and, from his knowledge of other towns and ports would realise the importance of a good harbour and that much progress was needed at Dundee.

The management of his property at Carnoustie involved frequent visits there and back and his usual custom was to spend a night 'en route' with his friends the Blairs in Dundee. These visits to Dundee brought him in contact with three prominent business men of that town; first Captain Blair, his host, who was a merchant in the linen trade and eventually became the stamp-master with responsibility of stamping all the linen goods which were manufactured in the town; secondly Mr Robert S. Rintoul, the editor of the 'Dundee, Perth and Cupar Advertiser' an antecedent of the present 'Dundee Courier' which was then the only local press with any general circulation and which held strong Radical Political views, and thirdly Mr James Saunders a Solicitor with the same political opinions.

In 1814 there was much criticism of the Town Council by the Trade Guilds to which publicity was given by the newspaper. At that time, as was the case in all Scottish Burghs, the Town Council was a 'closed-shop'. The Council members appointed themselves and co-opted their friends to fill vacancies so that Provost Riddoch and Provost Guild had taken it in turns to hold office for the past twenty years. They were able to levy rates and spend the income of the town however they liked without fear of losing office.

The matter, about which the Trade Guilds were complaining, was that improvements were greatly needed at the harbour, that the Town Council was doing nothing about it, and that the Harbour Dues had been squandered on other town expenditure.

There seemed to be a good case for taking legal power by a

Bill through Parliament to remove the responsibility for the harbour from the Town Council and to form an autonomous body with sole responsibility for the harbour who would see that all the revenue was spent on it.What was needed was some responsible people to put the case to the authorities and to pilot a Bill through Parliament so that an independent Board could be appointed. This was a battle against the vested interests of the Town Council, a cause which George Kinloch was delighted to get his teeth into, and in which he was very soon to become the moving spirit.

As described in the previous chapter, the purpose of an expedition to Edinburgh on a snowy day in January 1815 by George Kinloch and the unfortunate Robert Rintoul who got stuck in a snowdrift, was to prepare the ground with Mr Maule, then Member of Parliament for the County of Forfar, and Mr Gordon Hallyburton of Pitcur, a close friend of George Kinloch, so that a Bill to promote a new Harbour Board could be drafted and have an easy passage through Parliament. According to the record in a letter to his wife he persuaded these two important people to 'see the Harbour Bill in its proper light'.

Although the details of the Bill and the plan of campaign were probably worked out by the lawyer Saunders, with Rintoul and David Blair, in the book-shop of George Miln where they used to meet, George Kinloch was able to pull some useful strings behind the stage. Whether it had any effect or not in getting the Hallyburtons to see the Bill in its proper light, he addressed and dedicated a book of 'Quadrilles' which he had composed himself to the Hon. Mrs Gordon Hallyburton of Pitcur, and at any rate it was an original way of saying 'thank you' to her husband for his help in sponsoring the Harbour Bill. If the dancing of quadrilles ever comes back into favour, this composition may become better known and be called 'The Dundee Harbour Quadrille.'

The Bill was duly drafted and, when all was ready, he was asked to go up to Westminster, representing the Dundee Guildry with a Mr Chalmers representing the Town Council. Although the main purpose of his expedition was to sponsor the Bill, he knew quite well that he would meet a lot of interesting

71

people in London and find out what everyone was thinking and saying. Perhaps he thought that he had been getting into a groove with too much domestic life, and that it was time that he had a holiday. In any case he undertook to go to London at his own expense but, as usual, was faithful with his letters home to his wife, to whom it was unnecessary to be discreet in describing all that he saw and his opinions about everyone that he met.

The following letters written from the Cannon Coffee House, Cockspur Street, London, described his views of the sights of London in the spring and early summer of 1815—

19/4/15.

My Dear Helen,

I wrote to you from York on Saturday night, and from this on Monday morning. I have very little to inform you of; but I shall give you a bulletin of my motions in this city of noise and bustle. I called on Mr. Campbell, our Solicitor on Monday, but missed him. I then wandered about, taking latitudes and longtitudes, till dinner-time, after which I adjourned to Drury Lane to see Kean in Richard the 3rd. Being farther off than I could have wished, I could not mark the changes of his countenance accurately, but his acting pleased me very much. The accounts you have seen of it in the 'Champion' give a just idea of his performance. He has broke through the fetters of the Kemble school, and acts from an intuitive knowledge of his part. He is wholly absorbed in the scene, and you see Richard, but not the actor. His battle scene with Richmond is very grand, he is struck down, apparently severely wounded, but he rises again, and fights in desperation all round the stage. Even after his sword is struck out of his hand, he continues his impotent attempts till his strength wholly fails him, when he dies hard, as the fox-hunters term it. I staid the after-piece, called the 9th. statue, as stupid a performance as I ever witnessed. Yesterday, in going to Mr. Campbell's I met Charles Kinloch and took a short walk with him. He lives just opposite. I found Mr. Campbell who went with me to Mr. Chalmers, the town of Dundee's agent. We had a discussion about the Bill, and all, as yet, appears fair. I afterwards went and called on the Wedderburns and Gra-

72

hams. I went to Covent Garden in the evening, to see Miss O'Neill in 'The Gamester.' She acts on the same principle as Kean, is wholly absorbed in her part, and judges for herself. It was not so well calculated to display her powers, as some of the deeper tragedies, but she did it most correctly and was very much applauded. I, this forenoon, went to Mr. Campbell's who took me to the House of Lords to hear an appeal discussed. The 'house' consisted of the Chancellor, a poor, crabbit looking wretch; Lord Redesdale, do. and two other Peers, and a fat Bishop. It did not at all tend to exalt my idea of the dignity of our hereditary judges. Mr. Campbell left me, and was to return to show me the way to the House of Commons, as I wished to hear the debates to-night, but after hearing four lawyers argue the point, my patience was completely exhausted, and I left them to settle the matter at their leisure. I then went to enquire for Capt. Ogilvy in Wimpole St., but having lost my latitude, I stumbled into Hyde Park, from whence I piloted myself by the help of my map which I never go without. I took my dinner, my pint of porter, (not Scotch measure) and my pint of negus, and then began this epistle to one, who, however far from me, is never far from my thoughts, and to whom, and to hers, I wish all happiness, while I subscribe myself her own,

Geo. Kinloch.

He wrote again on 3rd May 1815—

My Dear Helen,

I last night had the pleasure to receive your letter of the 24th. April, with the others you sent; none of which happened to be of any consequence. Since my arrival here, the weather has been almost uniformly cold and rainy, till Monday last, when it became very warm; as the first fruits of which, I had a violent contest with a party of bugs, which made such incessant attacks on my rear and flanks, that I was obliged to quit the field of battle in despair. However, as daylight was coming in, I reconnoitered the enemy, and having seized sundry of them, I precipitated them into the Jordan, and last night they left me unmolested. This is the first time in my life I was ever annoyed by them. Yesterday, we had a great deal of thunder, and about 6 o'clock, a very heavy rain, I went in the morning to Robt. Graham's and he accompanied me to the London and to the West India Docks, which are most stupendous undertakings. I dined on Monday at John Wedderburn's who lives in great stile. Capt. Ogilvy and his family are here, but I have not yet seen them. The Capt. has been very unwell. I met Tom Irving in the Park, and have been twice at his house of an evening. He, his son, and his sister-in-law board in a house, and have a parlour to themselves. His son is about 14, a clever, ugly, good-natured boy, and a little deformed in consequence of a fall his nurse gave him. He is a good musician, and plays very well on the Piano Forte. There is a young lady in the same house who likewise plays well, and I accompany her on the violin. I intend going there tonight to meet Sir George Clark, who plays the Violincello and is a keen musician. I have been in perfect health since I left you, till Sunday last, when I had an attack of bile, which has not yet left me. I mean tonight to apply to Dr. Calomel, who will rid me of it. Mr. Small arrived on the 26th. ulto. and like Guynd and Barclay, he and I met on an amicable footing. He lodges here and we have a good deal together, and our business goes on smoothly. The report on our Bill is to be given into the House of Commons on Friday, and I suppose a fortnight after that will finish it. I could be very well pleased to turn my face northwards, but cannot say how soon it will be in my power. Even supposing our business was finished, I should most likely stay some time to look about me, as I don't intend soon to repeat my visit to this city. I am often with you, in imagination, and I hope it will not be long 'ere I be so in reality. I dine here for from 3/- to 4/6d., exclusive of what I drink, which never exceeds half a pint of sherry, or a glass of negus. It is provoking that they neglected to forward my letter from York, as I believe I mentioned some things in it, which I have now forgot.

Wishing all that is good to you and yours, with you, I remain always most affectionately and sincerely your,

Geo. Kinloch.

On 10th May, he wrote—

My Dearest Helen,

I was very happy to receive your letter of the 3rd. which arrived here on Monday, no letters being delivered on the Sunday. I am glad to learn that you are all well, and the weather was pretty good. As far as I can judge, it will be the beginning of the week after next before I can turn my face northward. Although there is no want of amusement in this place, I would be as well pleased to be home.

The prices of Spermacite candles are 3/- for a lb. Women's silk stockings 8/6. Do. with cotton feet 6/- Women's finest cotton stockings 2/6, silk gloves 2/-. Silk plaids 5/-. Write to me what of them I should buy. I have bought a watch for Margaret, and a pocket compass for each of the boys, but you need not mention them. I dined on Sunday at Mr. Drummond's our M.P. I dined yesterday at Mr. Turnbull's, and today I go to Mr. John Wedderburns at 6 o'clock, and we shall get dinner about seven. I dine with Mr. Gerry on Sunday, Mr. Rintoul having given me a letter to him. I mean to ask him to get me a sight of the machinery etc. of the theatre. I went yesterday to Hammersmith about 4 miles out of town to see Mr. James Smith, who asked me to come and stay some days with him.

The hedges here are fully out, and in blossom, and so is the horse chestnut. Cherries on a wall, the size of large peas, but the late frosts have nippit the fruit sadly.

Always most affectionately,

Yours, Geo. Kinloch.

Kind love to all the young folks.

He left London on Friday 2nd June and wrote from the house of his mother-in-law at 1 Hart Street, Edinburgh, on Tuesday 6th June—

My Dearest Helen,

I wrote to you on Thursday last that I was to leave London the following day, and I accordingly set out at 6 in the morning. On taking my seat in the coach, I found Dr. Turnbull was one of the party. We had only one more inside, as far as York, where we arrived at 2 p.m. on Saturday. We left it at 9 next morning, and reached Newcastle at 10 at night. The Doctor being tired, I left him

75

there to rest a day, and I came forward to this place last night at a quarter before eleven. I came straight down here and found them all well, and just done supper. As I have nothing very particular to do here, and as I am beginning to weary to see you, I mean to set off for Dundee tomorrow morning. I must stay there all Thursday to give an account of my embassy, and hope to embrace you on Friday, and to find you all well. You may tell John Miller to send in a single cart for my baggage on Friday morning, to Captain Blair's and with kind love to all the young folks,

I remain, Most sincerely and affectionately,

Your George.

The Bill received final approval on 4th July 1815, so that the Guildry of Dundee were well pleased with 'his Embassy.'

The immediate result of the mission, as affecting George Kinloch was that he was appointed to the new Harbour Board, as one of the four landowner representatives and he began to come into Dundee regularly for Harbour Board meetings. Thomas Telford, who was at the height of his success as a Civil Engineer, was entrusted with the design of the new works and all was ready by the 9th October of the same year, for the foundation stone to be laid. This day was a 'Red-letter day' in George Kinloch's career and was also a milestone in the prosperity of the City of Dundee.

The 'Dundee Advertiser' described the events as follows—

At an early hour on Monday last, the population of Dundee, with many visitors from the surrounding country, were in motion, either to join or to witness the grand procession to the Harbour, for the purpose of laying the Foundation Stone of the extensive new works. Every street through which it passed was thronged, every window and every spot from which a view might be obtained was crowded, every deck and mast and shroud of the ships in port was manned, every flag, and streamer was given to the winds. We have never heard of such a day of rejoicing in Dundee.

The cause of this is easily explained.

After a long struggle the people have succeeded in obtaining an Act of Parliament on the very principles for which they have contended, for the improvement of the

Harbour. All the money levied upon it is to be expended upon it and the management is placed on a broad and liberal basis, the Commissioners being annually elected from the various public bodies, of whom the Town Council party is a minority.

About eleven o'clock a long line of quarriers, carters, and carts with stones from the Commissioner's quarry at Lochee, decorated with flags, and accompanied by two pipers, entered the town, and proceeded through the High Street and Castle Street towards the Shore, and between twelve and one, upon a given signal, the whole moved forward to the enclosed ground, where the stone was to be laid. The Procession included:

Band of the Seventy-Ninth Regiment of Foot.

The Fraternity of Masters and Seamen,

preceded by four boys in naval dress, supporting a large and beautiful model of a ship.

Three Town Sergeants.

The Provost supported by the Sheriff of the County.

The Magistrates and Council.

The Superintending Engineer, with a plan of the Harbour. The Clerk to the Commissioners with the Act of Parliament. The Commissioners for erecting the Harbour, accompanied by Naval and Military Officers, County Gentlemen, and others not connected with any of the Public Bodies.

The Nine Trades in the order of their Precedence. The Guildry Incorporation, preceded by a new banner of blue silk, with characteristic symbols & embellishments. Mr. Jobson, as the Lord Dean of Guild walked at the head of the Incorporation and the whole members were dressed in black. The Honourable William Maule, Provincial Grand Master supported by the Grand Wardens.

Arrived at the enclosed ground, the front of the procession halted, and properly arranged, the Right Worshipful and Reverend H. Horsley as Grand Chaplain, invoked the blessing of Heaven. Corn, wine, and oil, were then poured over the stone; a glass bottle containing coins of the present reign, an Almanack, various newspapers, a copy of the Harbour Act, and a copy of the printed papers in controversy was deposited in the cavity, which was then covered by an ornamental plate, bearing a Latin inscription. The weather was favourable and the day passed without an accident, save that a woman and a child were considerably stunned and covered with mud by falling from some eminence into the west harbour.

The afternoon and the evening were spent in universal and increased festivity. Mr. Maule dined with a numerous party of his Masonic Brethren, and entertained them with a liberality which bordered on extravagance. The Magistrates and Commissioners gave an excellent dinner in Merchant's to the Military Officers and the County Gentlemen. A dinner, no less excellent in its kind, was set out in the Poultry market by Ferguson, at the desire of the Harbour Commissioners. Other Societies, amounting in all to nearly eight hundred persons, dined together and spent the evening in good humour and gaiety. But the most interesting scene of all, from the numbers, the composition and the public spirit of the actors, was exhibited in the large Hall belonging to the Nine Trades — better known to strangers by the name of the Exchange Coffee Room. About two hundred and twenty members of the Trades and Guildry, with a few Gentlemen invited by the Convenor and the Lord Dean, sat down to dinner, and the number was swelled in the course of the evening by deputations from other meetings.

About 7 o'clock Mr. Kinloch of Kinloch, accompanied by Captain Blair and Mr. Saunders, from the table of the Commissioners, entered the hall by invitation, when the whole company stood up to receive him, the music playing 'A man's a man for a' that.' Mr. Kinloch being seated on the Dean of Guild's right hand, the Lord Dean presented to him, in name of the independent inhabitants of Dundee, a rich silver vase (value £110) which was purchased by voluntary subscription, in testimony of their respect for his character as an excellent and accomplished country gentleman, and of their gratitude for his zealous services to the community in the matter of the harbour bill. Mr. Jobson concluded his speech by proposing the health of Mr. Kinloch.

When the long and loud applause had subsided, Mr.

Kinloch, with an emotion which almost deprived him of utterance, declared that his services had been far over-valued, but that he should always be a warm and ready friend to the interests of Dundee. He returned thanks for his friend Colonel Hallyburton, who was abroad, but who would no doubt have been delighted to be present at such a scene as Dundee this day presented.

Mr. Kinloch then gave the toast of 'The Liberty and Independence of the Press, to which the inhabitants of this town have owed so much during the late discussions and may the Light which has burst upon us continue to expand until Corruption shall not have a hole wherein to hide it's head.' He said 'You have all, of late, had an arduous struggle which is not yet over but in which, if you continue firm and united, and, if you give a long pull and a strong pull, and pull all together, there can be no doubt of your ultimate success. There is another Corporation, of which we are all members and on the rights of which sad encroachments have been made by Princes, Papes and Priests, I mean the "Sovereign Rights of the People," and which I beg leave to propose as a Toast.'

The Meeting was dissolved about half past nine o'clock, having been conducted, according to the newspaper report, with a spirit and propriety never excelled in such a large assembly. George Kinloch went back to spend the night with Captain Blair and, when he woke up next morning, he must have realised that he had become committed. He had shown his hand in public. Whether it was on the spur of the moment in the excitement of finding himself suddenly become a popular figure, or whether he had intentionally taken the opportunity of this big occasion to give publicity to his advanced opinions, is not clear, but he had said it. His words would be printed in the papers and he would have to stand by what he had said as champion of 'The Sovereign Rights of the People.'

He had greatly enjoyed the evening, and he had achieved a personal success; he had been accepted by the people of Dundee who could do so little for themselves to express their feelings on local or national affairs, being without a vote or representation of any kind. He saw the potential development of Dundee as a great

City which would come with its Harbour, in the same way that the City of Glasgow was developing by dredging the River Clyde and making it navigable for ocean-going boats.

He felt sure that what the people of Dundee most greatly needed was encouragement and not repression and that, if they were given responsibility and opportunity they would go ahead and develop their industries. He had no reason to think that, by extending the vote to the people, it would lead to a revolution to overthrow authority or to take land away from the land-owners. He knew that many of his fellow-landowners did not think this way, that many, such as Mr Mungo Murray would have classed the people with whom he was mixing in the same category as 'The Meigle Mob' who had threatened his house, that they did not understand the people whom they regarded as 'The lower orders' and were frightened of them.

He went home to Kinloch House taking with him the silver cup which he had been given and one can imagine him reading the inscription which the Guildry had engraved on it 'in testimony of their respect for his character as an accomplished country gentleman, and of their gratitude for his zealous services to the community in the matter of the Harbour Bill.' He must have pondered a good deal about this and realised that this was the parting of the ways. If he was going to be the champion of the people, then he would most certainly lose a great number of his land-owning friends. They might no longer invite him to come and shoot the muirfowl in the Angus glens or the roe deer in their woodlands. If he pledged himself to the people, there would be a great coldness towards him from many of his good friends.

From this time onwards, George Kinloch felt himself committed and, having said that he would always be a ready friend to the interests of Dundee, there could be no turning back. He had the same cause at heart as the Dundee newspaper which gave expression to Radical opinions whenever occasion offered and he was to remain true to this commitment through all the difficulties and dangers of later life.

[1] Treatise on the Office of Justice of the Peace in Scotland by Gilbert Hutchison, Advocate, 1815. Vol. 1. Chap. 1.
[2] Military History of Perthshire by the Marchioness of Tullibardine.

CHAPTER SEVEN

His Political Philosophy and Involvement

ALTHOUGH, as described in the previous chapter, George Kinloch did not come into the public eye before the year 1815 as a champion of the cause of the people, his anti-establishment views were not of sudden growth.

He had been too young in 1793 to be involved with the agitation for Parliamentary Reform which culminated with the arrest and trial of Thomas Muir of Hunters Hill, the young Scottish Advocate, who was found guilty of Sedition and was sentenced to fourteen years transportation, but he must have been well aware of this sensational trial as his native town of Dundee was very much concerned. At this same time, Thomas Palmer, a Dundee man, was given a similar sentence for having printed the text of an address on the subject of Reform by a Methodist Preacher in the Overgate of Dundee. Muir and Palmer set off together in chains in a Revenue Cutter first to work from the 'hulks' on the Thames and then on to Botany Bay. Another Dundonian, George Mealmaker, was sentenced to fourteen years transportation on a similar charge five years later. The authorities may have hoped that these severe sentences would put a stop to insubordinate talk about Rights of Man and Reform but memory of the martyrs of that time was kept alive by George Kinloch's friend Mr Robert Rintoul,[1] the free-thinking Editor of Dundee's newspaper. Continuous devotion to the cause of Reform in this part of Scotland is shown by the fact that, when Reform eventually came, the new shopping streets of Dundee, Arbroath, Kirriemuir and Blairgowrie were all named 'Reform Street.'

As early as 1812, during the later stages of the Peninsular War, George Kinloch wrote a letter under the pseudonym of 'A friend to liberty all over the World' in which he questioned the purpose of the War in Spain. This letter was published in the 'Aberdeen Chronicle' and the following extract shows that he was not prepared to go along with conventional public opinion. He said—

In the present momentous crisis of affairs in Spain, and when every post may bring intelligence of a battle which may finally decide the fate of that harassed country, I beg leave to offer my sentiments on so interesting a subject. I shall begin by observing that Lord Wellington has done as much as it was possible for a commander to do, with the force supplied him. That he has done more with such a force than any one could have expected, is clearly evident to all. But it is equally evident that those for whom he is ostensibly fighting, and for whom we are expending so much blood and treasure, are not cordial in the cause. After every victory, people exclaim 'Now, if the Spaniards would only exert themselves! If they would, now, take advantage of this glorious opportunity; but the Spaniards do not exert themselves; they do not take advantage of the glorious opportunity; they allow us to run fighting all over their country, without joining us, or assisting us in any one respect. What can be the reason of this?' After being repeatedly told by the newspapers that 'the universal Spanish nation is with us,' that 'to a man they hate and detest the French, while they caress and adore the British,' it must sadly puzzle the readers of these excellent prints to account for the circumstances of the Spaniards allowing us to reap all the honour of fighting their battles, without reserving for themselves the smallest share of it! But, to those who take the trouble to think for themselves, the reason is plain!

The Spaniards have been long an enslaved and most oppressed people. The country was enjoyed by haughty nobles and lazy priests, who looked upon the people, as formed for their pleasure. When the late King and his dutiful son abandoned their country, the people feeling themselves freed from the oppressions of their old Government, rose, as one man, to shut out those who had so long ground them to the earth. At this time, had the British Government come forward to assist in restoring the people to their natural rights, the people, seeing they were to be benefitted, would have united heart and hand, to repel the unprincipled invader of their country. Long before this time, not a Frenchman would have been seen in Spain; for where is there an instance of 12,000,000 of people being conquered, when the people had an interest in resisting the invader? So long as the people thought they were fighting for freedom, they fought nobly; and tho' often defeated, they were never overcome. But from the moment that George Canning gave us a toast 'Ferdinand the Seventh and the universal Spanish Nation,' the 'universal Spanish nation' sunk down into a profound apathy, reckless of what might happen. And who was this King whom we were to thrust upon them? A weak young man, known to the world only by an unprincipled attempt to dethrone his father. The truth is, that had they been allowed to erect a free Government, and thereby to get rid of the monstrous abuses of the old one, the example might have been contagious; it might have spread into countries where our ministers would have been by no means pleased to see it. The fact is, that instead of fighting in the cause of the Spanish people, we have been fighting for a worthless King, an insolent nobility, and a useless clergy. We have been fighting to prevent the Spanish people from being restored to those rights, to which, God has given all men an equal claim, and which it has been the uniform endeavour of almost all modern Governments to prevent them from enjoying. Seeing this, can any one be surprised at the sullen apathy of the Spaniards?

Battles, storms and sieges may follow one another in rapid succession; blood may continue to flow, and treasure to be squandered; but we shall not be one jot nearer our object, until we leave the Spaniards at liberty to chuse a

Government for themselves, with Ferdinand, with Joseph, or without a King at all. Had we, at the beginning of the contest come manfully forward and said 'Spaniards, we Britons, enjoying ourselves the blessings of freedom, rejoice to see that you likewise are determined to be free. Go on in the glorious work; frame a Government adapted to your habits.' If such language had been held, how different would have been the scene. Every Spaniard, animated by the glorious prospect of liberty, would have been a soldier. The intrusive Joseph, with all his followers would long ago have been driven out of the country. The British would everywhere have been hailed as real deliverers.'

In September 1814, when Napoleon Buonaparte was thought to be safely stowed away on the Island of Elba, George Kinloch wrote to William Cobbett on the subject of the continuation of the American War. William Cobbett, who later became an intimate friend of George Kinloch was then the author of 'The Political Register' and had only recently completed a two year prison sentence for having written a severe article against military flogging. An extract from this letter which was written in a humorous vein is as follows:

Since the close of the grand drama entitled 'A War against Buonaparte,' we have had a little more leisure to attend to the lesser drama entitled 'The American War.' While the former was going on, the latter was deemed too distant and too insignificant for 'the most thinking nation in the world' to think anything at all about it. Now, however, the case is different. As we have got Boney, like Prometheus, fairly chained to his rock, with, I suppose, the accompaniment of his vulture too, we have leisure to look about us, and to consider this nice little bit of a war, in all its bearings. John Bull has bawled himself hoarse, huzzaing for the peace, and after all the noise and fuss is over, wondering how the deuce this peace feels so very unlike what he expected. This may be peace, but also, it feels somehow or other, devilish like war.' 'The Times' talks of 'crushing the Americans at once,' just as a giant would crush a blind puppy! But, easier said than done! We have been repeatedly told of the unprovoked aggression on the part of the Americans! All they now ask is that we shall not stop their ships, and take what of their crews we think proper, without proving them to be British subjects. This is on their part, the sole cause of the war.

Suppose that an American frigate is stationed off Milfordhaven, and that she brings to a British merchantman, and sends a midshipman aboard to examine her. The 'mid' sees a man on board who he thinks is an American; 'No, by Jasus' says Paddy, 'there you are wrong now, for I was born at Ballynabog, and my father and mother can both testify it, only they are dead and gone.' 'Damn the fellow,' says the 'mid,' 'he's speaking like an Irishman to make believe; but I know he's an American, I've seen him at New York, so come along you dog.' Now can anything be more proper than this? The man may be an American, and who can be so good a judge in these matters as a Midshipman? And if the man after all, should really be an Irishman, he will be no worse of cruising about for half a dozen years, in a trim frigate, and will have the advantage of seeing the world. These are arguments which I have repeatedly heard used by those who should know best, and it is certainly very perverse in the Americans not to be convinced by them. What can we do then? We must use iron arguments with them, and thus convince them whether they will, or not.

You, Mr. Cobbet have been among the Yankees! Pray write a friendly letter to Jonathan[2] advising him to give up the point. Advise him, as a good woman in this country once advised her husband, who had been condemned by one of our petty tribunals to be hanged, but who had barricaded himself into the prison so that they could not get at him — 'Oh Johnny said she 'come out an' be hanged an' dinna' anger the Laird!'

As soon as the Napoleonic Wars ended, there was a revival of interest in the demand for Parliamentary Reform. This movement had been rigorously opposed after the French Revolution by the vast majority of the English and Scottish landowners who feared that any liberalisation might lead to a revolution in this country and seizure of their estates. George Kinloch, however, was one of the few landed people in Scotland who considered that such fears were groundless and the toast which he frequently proposed at political dinners — 'May the Reform for which we ask, come before the Revolution which we fear' expressed his thinking on this issue. It is this issue, of the need for Parliamentary Reform on which George Kinloch's political importance depends so that the situation of the franchise before the Reform Bill needs some little examination.

A report of a meeting of Radical Reformers held in Birmingham on 13th December 1815,[3] illustrates very clearly to what extent the nomination of Members of Parliament had fallen into the hands of a few people. The Report showed that, as a result of the Rotten and Pocket Borough anomalies and the common practice of buying and selling votes, one hundred and fifty-four individuals could and did return a majority in the House of Commons. It was also claimed that it was impossible to produce a list of sixty-six members of the House, no one of whom owed his seat to borough patronage or aristocratic combination.

In Scotland the system was almost equally unrepresentative of the people. Under the Treaty of Union it was appointed that 'Forty-five shall be the number of Representatives of Scotland in the House of Commons,' and of these, thirty were to be elected by the Counties and fifteen by the Boroughs. The County system was much the same as in England, where families and their friends dominated the polls. In Angus, the Ramsay and Strathmore families had a gentleman's agreement to take it in turns who would nominate the Member, and in Perthshire, the Murray family had a virtual control of the seat. There was always a certain market value attached to sale of property which included a vote. Another feature of the Scottish system was designed to exclude those with unacceptable religious or political beliefs, such as Roman Catholics and Jacobites. Freeholders, before voting, had to declare on oath that they did not believe in the infallibility of the Pope or doctrine of transubstantiation, so that this effectually excluded the Roman Catholics. Members of the Scottish Episcopal Church, which had always been suspected of Jacobite leanings, had to declare that they had not attended an Episcopal Church where the Pastor had not prayed for the Royal Family.

In the Scottish Burghs where the Councillors were self-elected, there was no direct vote by the townspeople, and with fifteen seats distributed between sixty-five Boroughs, it meant that a large town like Glasgow had to share its one Member with Dumbarton, Renfrew, and Rutherglen.

It seems obvious today that George Kinloch was justified in saying — 'The House of Commons, as at present constituted, does not represent the people of these Kingdoms. This is unfortunately as notorious as the sun at noon-day.' Quite correct, but nevertheless dangerous to say so because most of those who exercised power and influence by reason of their voting rights were jealous of that power and intended to retain it as long as possible. The trump card which they were able to play was to allege that speeches or writing in favour of Reform was inciting the people to rebellion and so sedition against the realm.

Remembering the severe sentences of 1793, the small man had found it too dangerous to take a leading part in the new campaign for Reform and in London the agitation was being led by well educated men of reputation and standing. It was with these men that George Kinloch became closely connected and whose efforts he supported.

In 1812 some of these men with liberal ideas had formed themselves into a Society called 'The Hampden Club' in memory of John Hampden who was one of the opponents of Charles I.

The Chairman of 'The Hampden Club' was Sir Francis Burdett, an English country gentleman, who rode to foxhounds, who had been educated at Westminster school, and who was very much the English counterpart of George Kinloch. He had married a member of the Coutts family, the Bankers, and, being a man of wealth as well as of standing, was able to help to a great extent with the finance of spreading Radical ideas. He had been elected as Member of Parliament for the Borough of Westminster in 1807, which was the first success for the Parliamentary Reformers. Westminster was one of the few seats with a wide franchise and so the voters were too numerous for any prospective Parliamentary candidate to bribe. A distinguished Scottish member of 'The Hampden Club' committee was Lord Cochrane but his interest was short-lived, as he went off to command the Chilean Navy, or as George

Kinloch put it, 'he was on his way to sink the man of petticoats.'

The main driving influence of 'The Hampden Club' came from Major John Cartwright, who was known as 'The Father of Reform.' Major Cartwright was a good deal older man than George Kinloch; he had been originally a promising naval officer like Lord Cochrane, but resigned his commission at the outbreak of hostilities against the American Colonists as he could not reconcile himself to the purpose of this war.

In August of the year 1815 Major Cartwright came to Scotland and his tour is described in a printed circular letter addressed to possible new subscribers to the cause of Reform of which George Kinloch was one.

> It was not for Fifty Pounds, that, by an infirm old man with his servant, England was left far behind; that Scotland was traversed from sea to sea; that the traveller visited Greenock and the coast of Ayr; Renfrew and Paisley, Stirling and Alloa; Dunfermline, Newburgh, and Perth; Cupar in Angus, Forfar, and Brechine; Crail, St. Andrews, and Aberdeen; that he went twice to Stonehaven, Inverbervie and Montrose; twice to Dundee, Cupar in Fife, and Kirkcaldy, twice also to Lanark and Hamilton, thrice to Glasgow, and thrice to Edinburgh; returning into England by the road of Kelso.
>
> Nor did he travel in vain, if he have proved how the work we have undertaken may be accomplished.

The circular continued by emphasizing the value of petitions and ended by saying—

> Who were the parties so encouraged by Earl Grey, Sir Samuel Romilly, Mr. Wilberforce, and Mr. Whitbread to stand forth by petition that an immediate stop might be made to the nefarious traffic in human beings, by a complete abolition of the foreign slave trade? Can we follow a better example? It was their wish to save from slavery the black men of Benin, of Congo, of Guinea and Angola. It is ours, to redeem from slavery the white men of England, of Scotland, of Wales and Ireland. When seats in Parliament are bought and sold by the Ministers of our own nation,

all the People, all Law, all Liberty, all Property are bought and sold.

Major Cartwright included in his tour a visit to Kinloch House, but George Kinloch was away from home. Correspondence followed however and Major Cartwright wrote on 15th September from Edinburgh saying -

Sir,

It is not possible for me to express the satisfaction which your letter of the 12th afforded me. Your frank and unreserved sentiments have induced me to trouble you with a parcel containing a score of the Hampden Club's Circulars which, no doubt, you will be able to distribute in channels favourable to Reform, as occasion may carry you to Dundee, to Coupar-Angus, or to Perth. On my second visit to Dundee, the gentlemen undermentioned namely, Doctor Ramsay, James Duncan Jr., Esq., Messrs. James Ogilvy, and Saunders Writers, Mr. Jobson, Cashier of the Bank and Mr.Rintoul, printer, joined me in the evening when we supped together, and I had reason to conclude that Petitions from Dundee would be a certain consequence. It may interest you to know that Mr. Maule of Brechin Castle, Mr. Ferguson of Perth, Mr. Oswald of Auchincruive in Ayrshire, and Lord Cochrane are members of The Hampden Club. We have also two Burdetts, two Blounts, Bernard Howard, heir to the Dukedom of Norfolk, Faulkes, late Member of Yorkshire, Lord Byron, Earl of Oxford, Sir I. Throckmorton, Sir W. Pilkington, Sir J.D. Broughton Esq. At our next meeting we ballot for I. Johnson Esq., author of the letters signed Timothy Trueman in the Statesman and others.

This letter went on to say that he would be staying with the Duke of Roxburgh near Kelso, on his way back to England, and ended—

Should you on consideration incline to enrol yourself with such a band, I should be most happy to propose you.

George Kinloch told in one of his letters how he appreciated the honour, but that he had to refuse as he could not undertake the financial responsibilities of Membership of 'The Hampden Club' which involved so much travelling.

Major Cartwright kept on writing, encouraging him about the importance of Lectures and Petitions, but in January 1816, George Kinloch replied that he was not so optimistic and wrote —

I have been sounding all round here to see how the land lay with respect to petitioning for Reform, but I am sorry to say with little success hitherto. The people are astounded by their misfortunes, and they are not yet sufficiently recovered from their confusion to understand the cause of what they suffer. As we all read in this country, I expect a great deal from the Press and fortunately the Editor of the Dundee Newspaper is a most decided Reformer. We have in contemplation to publish some short Tracts adapted to the lower orders, tracing the evil from it's source and pointing the remedy. This will, no doubt, take some time but, by making the people understand what they want, they will then speak in a voice of thunder that will dust all the powder out of the Speaker's Wig and make even the Mace shake under the table. After the mouldering fortifications of the rotten Burgh system shall have been assailed by this advance attack of Sharpshooters from the Press, then will be the time to follow up the assault by a concentrated broadside in the shape of a lecture; and if, by that time, no one better qualified shall be found to volunteer on the forlorn hope, I trust that I shall muster courage sufficient to mount the Breach.

Although George Kinloch could not afford to become a member of 'The Hampden Club', he was greatly influenced by Major Cartwright's example and leadership, and in his speech in Dundee four years later held up Major Cartwright's book and said — 'This little book, my friends, has never been answered for the best of all reasons because it is, in fact, unanswerable'.

In the spring of 1816, George Kinloch's enthusiasm switched from Reform of the Franchise to Reform of Taxation which involved much correspondence in the Dundee newspaper. On 14th March of this year he made a valiant attempt to defeat the resolutions of the noblemen and freeholders, who came together for a County meeting under the Chairmanship of the Duke of Atholl, in Perth.

It must have involved no small moral courage on the part of an impecunious laird, who could not even afford a 'Chaise' for his family, to oppose the resolutions sponsored by the Lord Lieutenant of the County and supported by most of the wealthy lairds of Perthshire including the Atholl and Murray families. The resolutions on this occasion were long-winded congratulations to the Government on the successful outcome of the War, and to approve that the same rate of taxation which had been necessary to carry on the War was still necessary, because no substitute could be found. The motion was moved by Sir Patrick Murray of Ochtertyre, Bart., and seconded by Sir Alexander Muir Mackenzie of Delvine, Bart.

Mr. Kinloch then rose and said—

I am obliged to differ from the respectable mover and seconder of the Resolution. I admire the conduct of the Army, and none could be more sensible of it's merits but, as it was useful only in War, why load the country with it in time of Peace? Much has been said about the necessity to preserve the Liberty of Europe as well as our own Liberty. But from one end of the Continent to the other, where are we to look for liberty? Is it in the well-filled dungeons of the paternal and legitimate Louis, whom we have restored at such an expense of blood and treasure? Is it to be found in Spain, under our beloved Embroiderer of Petticoats? Is it to be found at Naples under Ferdinand the Fowler whom we have restored? Is it to be found at Rome, at Milan, at Venice, or in Austria? Is it to be found in Prussia, or in Poland, or in Russia? As to Income Tax. It was unnecessary and to continue it now would be to violate what was universally regarded as a positive pledge to the nation. I recommend retrenchment, cut off sinecures and diminish the salaries of Government Officers.

This forthright speech did little good and the voting for Sir Patrick Murray's Resolutions was 41, and for Mr. Kinloch's 9.

Although the voting had gone so hopelessly against him, George Kinloch received congratulatory letters from two important Perthshire noblemen who were outside the Murray

Atholl circle, and who had been absent from the Meeting.

Lord Breadalbane wrote from London on 24th March 1816 -

My Dear Sir,

I accidentally noticed the Resolutions from the County of Perth which were voted by a majority on the 14th. and which were so much the subject of well deserved ridicule a a few nights ago in the House of Commons. I confess I blushed when I read them to be connected with a County which could in these times send such stuff to Parliament, but I was a little consoled when I found that they had not passed unanimously, and that there was still some spirit and patriotism as well as good sense in the County and when I read your excellent amendment, which I cannot sufficiently commend, it afforded a cordial against the nausea and stuff of the previous resolutions.

The time is now arrived at for the nation to speak out plain truth in intelligible language divested of every species of sycophantish flattery to those in power. The voice of the nation for economy and retrenchment must be heard.

I do not dispair through the exertions and perseverance of such patriotic individuals as yourself, it will reach it sooner or later. Tho' your Minority was small, yet I honour and respect it. You would oblige me if, at your leisure, you could furnish me with the names of those who divided with you.

Believe me, My Dear Sir,

Very truly yours,

Breadalbane.

Lord Kinnaird also wrote saying -

I cannot deny myself of sending you my best thanks for the stand you made at the County Meeting on the subject of the Property Tax, and of expressing my entire concurrence in the manly and constitutional resolution which you proposed for adoption. Perseverance in such principles may at some period be of effective service to us all and ensure the gratitude of every well-wisher to the Country.

I have honour to be, My Dear Sir,

Ever faithfully yours,

Kinnaird.

Besides his political connections with 'The Hampden Club', a regular outlet for George Kinloch's political views was provided by the annual dinners held to celebrate the birthday of Charles James Fox. Fox dinners were being held at this time all over the country by people with liberal ideas but many of them were informal affairs, involving a lot of hot air and good fellowship. Under the influence of a good deal of 'punch' those taking part were persuaded to adopt resolutions and give their names to petitions which, in their more sober moments they would not have approved. Family letters showed that George Kinloch's children were only interested if their father came home with some good stories and gossip about who had overdone 'the punch'.

In January 1817, however, at the 'Fox Dinner' in Morrens Hotel in Dundee, thirty-two gentlemen sat down to dinner, with George Kinloch in the Chair, and instead of the usual convivial party, this meeting had serious resolutions before them which prolonged it to a late hour. The principal matter under discussion was whether the Magistrates of Dundee should be approached to allow a public meeting to be held so that resolutions could be adopted petitioning for Parliamentary Reform. In the end it was remitted to the Chairman and to Mr. Mudie of the Dundee Academy to see whether a meeting would be approved, and to make arrangements. An advertisement appeared in the newspaper saying that on 21st February a meeting was to be held in the Magdalen Yard Pleasure Ground, and that although no approval had been given by the magistrates, George Kinloch would be present. When the meeting assembled George Kinloch was called on to speak to a crowd estimated at over 6,000 people. It passed off without any trouble, and included the adoption of a long list of the conventional resolutions and petitions which were common to all Radical Meetings. According to the Press report, it was a very stormy day, and so it is probable that the Speaker found it difficult to make himself heard against a strong wind blowing in from the Firth of Tay.

This public meeting did not arouse very much interest or opposition in the correspondence columns of the newspapers, but led to a certain amount of recrimination about 'the two and thirty friends of liberty' who had dined together to celebrate

Fox's birthday but who had not put in an appearance at the public meeting. George Kinloch felt that he had been let down by his friends and blamed 'the middle-class respectables' for failing to support him.

He therefore refrained from public utterances for the rest of this year and throughout most of 1818, although his political opinions remained quite unchanged. This is made clear in an unusual way through incognito writings of which he was undoubtedly the author .

On July 4th, 1817 the first of his monthly reports on the agriculture of Strathmore appeared in the 'Dundee Advertiser'. These reports are not shown under his signature but his style is easily recognisable and many of the farming facts are repeated in letters written to his sons which is proof of the authenticity of the writer. Extracts are given here to show only how he felt about the poverty of the labouring man.

In July after saying that the prospect of an early harvest may be realised, that potatoes, very long of making any progress have come forward rapidly, that the turnip season has been to a wish, that pasture grass affords a good bite and other matters, he concluded —

> If the old ladies and young gentlemen who now hold the helm of state would cease to libel and gag the people merely to conceal their own incapacity, and relieve us of some of the most oppressive taxes, there is every probability that British happiness would have a real and operative existence.

and in August he wrote —

> Labourers are plentier than labour. Good workmen only a shilling a day without victuals; women only sixpence. The incubus of taxation, like the nightmare in dreams, presses us down; and while it continues to its present extent, there is little prospect of relief to the country.

In September —

> Wages still only one shilling for men and sixpence for women, without victuals; which is far too little, being hardly sufficient to afford the coarsest food, without leaving anything for clothes or other necessaries.

In October —

> The common oats are very backward but, luckily for this

district, very few of them are now sown. Indeed the introducer of the potato-oat is much more worthy of a monument from his country than the whole set of those who are falsely called great because they have been knocked on the head. Without these, we should probably have done well enough; but without the potato-oat, one half of the people of Scotland would have died of starvation. Upon the whole our opinion at present is that the wheat is about two thirds of an average crop, the barley nearly average and the oats considerably above average; so that it is to be hoped, the distressing scenes of misery and starvation which were everywhere to be met with last season, will no longer exist; and the industrious labourer will no longer be found on the poor's list for want of employment.

In November —

Rumours begin to circulate of the renewal of the income tax, which, if Parliament can be got base enough to enact it, will prove a death-blow to the last hopes of the country.

In December —

No demand for labourers; and many of them are likely to be very ill off. Poor-rates everywhere increasing.

In January 1818 —

There is no prospect of meal being cheap this winter, which, with the lowness of wages and the want of employment, will bear very hard on the poor people. We hear of trade and manufactures reviving in other places; but we are sorry to say, that as yet there is no symptom of either in this quarter.

In February 1818 —

Labourers 10d. to a shilling a day.

In April 1818 —

Strangers jocularly tell us that our year consists of nine months of winter and three months of cold weather; and really we begin to think they are not far wrong. The month which has ended has been anything but a spring month. One or two fields of oats have been sown and several parcels of Heligoland beans; the farmers not being deterred from trying them again by the total loss of them last year.

In May 1818 —

Cattle, both fat and lean, still in demand; and at prices we have not for some time been used to. At last term, farm servants obtained from 15s. to 30s. more for the half year. Labourers also advanced about a sixth or from 1s. to 14d. per day. Nobody should grudge the rise for they were far too low.

Against the background of the farming scene George Kinloch's sympathy for the working man stood out in contrast to his scorn of the indifference shown by the Government. He believed that the best way of curing economic distress was to give employment and that handing out charity or reducing the price of bread was no solution to the problem. Writing a few years later he said – 'Lancashire seems to be in a dreadful state and still no prospect of amendment. Ministers propose to let out the bonded wheat but how, reducing the loaf a penny or so, it is to do any good to those who have no pennies, I cannot see. Employ the poor fellows and then they will be able to get loaves.

[1] Robert Stephen Rintoul (1787–1858) Advocate of Political Reform. Editor of the 'Dundee, Perth and Cupar Advertiser' until 1825. 1828/1856 Editor in London of 'The Spectator.'

[2] 'Jonathan' was a once popular nickname for the typical New Englander and later for the whole American people. The original Jonathan was Governor Jonathan Trumbull of Connecticut whom George Washington habitually consulted because of his solid common sense.

[3] Extract from the Independent Whig of 15/12/1815.

CHAPTER EIGHT

A Visit to France; Summer 1818

IN THE SPRING of 1818 George Kinloch wrote to his eldest son who was then a young man of eighteen as follows—

I have been of late thinking of taking you and John to France during the vacation, and to leave you boarded in a French family during the summer. It will be a little inconvenient for me [this inconvenience, for anyone who knew George, would be quite easily borne], but I suppose you would prefer me to any other *bear-leader*. You would learn the language, and you would be able to study 'The Great Book of the World', which is the most useful of all. Write what day you propose to come that I may send for you to Perth.

This was one of the happiest summers of George Kinloch's life, and, although the excuse for the expedition was his son's health, he was delighted at the prospect of studying 'The Great Book of the World' for himself, with the gay David Nairne of Drumkilbo as his companion.

The letters addressed to his wife read like a journal, and will therefore be transcribed in journal form.

The party set off in 'The Bridport Packet,' one of the Dundee, Perth & London Shipping Company's sailing 'smacks' on 6th June, 1818

Bridport Packet, Off Sunderland.
Wed. 10th. June 1818. ½ past 10 a.m.
Not having a great deal to do at present, I sit down to give you an account of our progress hitherto, without knowing

when I shall get this sent ashore. On Saturday, we dined and supped at Captain Blair's; but as we were ordered to be on board by half past three, we did not go to bed, but came on board about half past one. I lay down for a few hours, but the younkers (the boys) kept on deck. It was a most beautiful night as any I ever saw in Scotland, and we went down the Tay without a breath of wind, and the sea like a mirror. We left the harbour exactly at five, Rintoul [Editor of 'Dundee Advertiser'] stayed to see us off. By the time we got to the bar some of our fellow passengers began to look queer, and before we were over it, some were enjoying all the horrors of sea sickness. We had previously made a hearty breakfast which I suppose helped to keep us free of it. Before night George and John both paid their tribute to the oceanic Deities, but neither Nairne [David Nairne of Drumkilbo] nor I were under the necessity of doing so, though I felt a little uncomfortable all day. Next morning we were able to do justice to the breakfast, and our appetites have not fallen off since then; quite the contrary, for eating and drinking are almost our only employments.

On Sunday night we were off St. Abbs Head, and on Monday night, off the Staples, to the southward of Holy Island; last night we were off Shields, and this morning a few miles to the south of it; the wind having all along been almost directly against us. In other respects the weather has been as fine as possible, and as we have plenty, we do not vex ourselves with useless repinings at the want of wind.

Our fellow passengers are – No. 1 Thos. Lighton, late Surgeon of an India-man which was wrecked last March. No. 2 a lame man, whom we have set down as a dissenting clergyman. No. 3 a man who has been in various parts of Europe, but whom none of us can make out, a *second-hand* sort of shentleman. No. 4 Mr. Stevenson, brother of Grubb's friend. No. 5 a man whom nobody saw for two days, as he was sick to death, but he is now come alive again, but we don't know what he is. These are all our cabin passengers, except the Captain, Captain Wishart, who is an old man, a little particular, but very attentive to us, as well as to his duty. We have for steerage passengers an

98

artillery man and his wife, who proves to be a daughter of a man Valentine who was once miller at Blacklaw. She is a strapping wench, newly married, and if the soldier is not jealous, it is not her fault, for there is abundance of flirtation. Also a lass who is a servant to Dr. Ross, and who is going to London to see her brother. As there is one spare bed between the two cabins, she has got possession of it, and the soldier's rib gets a bed on the floor. We have had a great deal of jawing and laughing, and on the whole, pass our time comfortably enough; only the beds are confounded hard. We have suffered very little from their *privileged occupants*. We get four meals a day, and luncheon if we chuse it. We have small beer and porter, and one glass of rum, but we generally add to it quantity sufficient of whisky toddy. Though we are getting on so slowly, we passed one of the great Leith smacks, the Czar, and are leaving her behind us. Since this morning we see a great number of colliers, from Shields and Newcastle, and as we are never out of sight of land, we get a distant view of the coast, as we move along.

Sunday, 14th. June, 11 a.m. We are now at anchor in the Swynne, about ten miles to the southward of Norwich. A dead calm, the tide against us till 2 p.m. and very warm. To continue my log book. On Wednesday night we were off Whitley. On Thursday morning off Flamborough Head; at night, off the Spurn. Friday morning off the Humber, at night off Cromer, having coasted all along from St. Edmond's point, getting a distinct view of the coast of Norfolk, which presented a most beautiful landscape. Yesterday (Saturday) morning we found ourselves off Yarmouth, where we came to anchor, and sent ashore for some beer etc. George, John, Nairne and Stevenson went ashore, but had no time to make very profound observations. It looks well from the water but, I am told, does not improve upon a nearer inspection. The great number of windmills give it a very lively appearance as we sail along. Had I known of the boat going ashore, I would have closed this letter and sent it, as you are no doubt somewhat anxious to hear of us. We passed Lowestoft

99

and Southwold, both of which look beautiful. We are frequently so near the shore that we can see the people at work, and that the hay is mostly cut. At night we were off Aldborough, and this morning we passed Harwich. We came to anchor last night, when the Czar, whom we had not seen for two days brought up a breeze with her and passed us, and is now about a mile ahead of us. We had a great deal of thunder and lightning last night, with some rain, and it now looks like more. No. 2 proves to be a Mr. Adie, an agent or writer from St. Andrews. No. 3 a pleasant enough man, but we have not yet learnt his name. No. 5 a boot and shoe-maker from Perth,[1] taking a sail for his health. There is also in the steerage a barber's boy from Perth, who has made a wonderful reformation on the snouts of the crew. He has afforded some amusement by his simplicity. A breeze is just sprung up; so I must conclude for the present. We all continue in perfect health, and most noble sailors, as far as eating and drinking go.

28, Suffolk St. Cockspur St.

Monday 15th. June, 3 p.m.

The breeze proved so favourable that it carried us through the Swynne to the Nore about 6 p.m. and we got up to the wharf exactly at 11, having been impeded by about an hour by the boats at Gravesend taking out the salmon. The scenery on entering the Thames is very beautiful. First, Sheerness with a Guard ship, and a great many men-of-war, lying in ordinary; then Gravesend and Woolwich, and then Greenwich, with houses and villas interspersed and in-numerable vessels moving up and down. Just before reaching Greenwich the *humane* and *pious* Sidmouth [Lord Sidmouth —Home Secretary, of whom there is more later] has added much to the *picturesque beauty* of the scenery by an exhibition of ten men hanging in chains.[2] I think I could without much trouble, pick out other ten who deserve that *honour*, at least as well as the poor devils who are left to dangle there. By the time we got to Woolwich the day-light failed us, but we had the advantage of the moonlight. We slept on board, and also breakfasted there this morning, and No. 3, who proves to be a Mr. Nelson from Forgan-

100

denny in Perthshire, took the ladies in tow, while I remained with the baggage. However, it proved so long before they could get it out, that I tired, and left it to the ships steward, who arrived with it, all safe here. The town is all in a *bushel* of confusion with the elections. That for the city begins tomorrow, and for Westminster on Thursday. I find we can get to Boulogne by Hastings for 21/- outside (that is on top of the coach), and 25/- inside, or from here to Paris by Valenciennes, Cambrai, and Brussels for £5; 5/-, but I would prefer the first. We had four bottles of whisky left, which are all snug here, altho' the excise man breakfasted with us. I would fain be off from here by Monday 22nd. if possible. You have fine weather for your bathing [at Carnoustie], and I trust you will be much the better of it, and of the change of air.

14 Suffolk Street,
London, 19th June 1818.

I wrote to you on Monday last, which you would receive last night. After making enquiry, I am induced to think that Rouen in Normandy is a fit place for George and John, and it has the additional recommendation of being easy of access from here. We leave here on Sunday for Brighton, and from thence we sail for Dieppe, which is within 30 miles of Rouen. The coach leaves here, nine in the morning, and gets to Brighton about three in the afternoon, and if a packet sails that evening, we may reach Rouen the following evening. From Brighton to Dieppe is about 74 miles, but as we are *seasoned* sailors, we shan't mind that. The younkers have been at Vauxhall, Drury Lane and Covent Garden, and have wandered over most of the town. I have been mostly engaged with Dr. Gilchrist and Major Cartwright, (Radical affairs), at whose house George and I dined on Tuesday. I saw Sir Francis [Sir Francis Burdett] there before dinner, and had the honour of a shake of his hand. I called for Lord Cochrane,[3] but missed him. Lighton who came up with us is appointed his Surgeon, and expects to sail in eight days. We have just been applying for pass-ports, and are to get them tomorrow. I was on the Hustings yesterday, as one of Cartwright's friends. The noise and bustle baffle all description. The Reformers have lost themselves by splitting into parties, and it is thought that Romilly and Maxwell[4] will be elected, but it is too early to judge yet.

In the city it is expected to be Wood, Wilson, Waithman and Curtis. In the borough Calvert and Wilson.

I must conclude as I have only a few minutes. Kind love to you all.

Write to me immediately,

A Monsieur G. Kinloch. — Anglais,
chez Messieurs Jacques Laffitte et Co.
Banquiers
a Paris

Pay the postage.

Dieppe, June 24th. 1818

Here we are all safe and sound, within the territories of the Grande Monarque.[5] I wrote to you on the 19th. from London, which we left on Sunday at half past nine, and arrived at Brighton at five o'clock. Monday proved as stormy that we could not cross, so we were obliged to saunter up and down Brighton, in a nasty drizzling rain. Yesterday proved calmer, and altho' there was enough of wind it was pretty fair, and we arrived here at one this morning, having been fourteen hours on the passage. I find I have not time to say half what I wish, as we leave here for Rouen at two, and it is now past one, so I shall postpone the rest, till night.

Rouen, 25th. June 1818.

We took our places on the top of the coach at two o'clock, and arrived here a little after seven, having passed thro' a country, which, were it *free*, would be one of the finest in the world. The road broad, and excellent without tolls, bordered almost the whole way with apple trees, covered with fruit. Few or no fences, but remarkably fine crops of all kinds of grain, principally wheat, then rye, then barley, and oats, also pease, tare and red clover. The fallows remarkably clean, and some of them already dunged. Beautiful and fertile as the country is, it has two great wants, houses along the road-side and cattle pasturing, the want of which give it a dead like appearance, for which, the fine crops by no means compensate. We saw hardly any cattle, and those we did see, were milk cows; three or four flocks of sheep, herded by a shepherd and a dog who keeps them from the corns.

The coach we came on holds six inside, six in a covered place behind, four on the top in front, and two on the driver's seat besides the guard. There are five horses, three in front and two behind them. The driver rides on the near wheel horse, with reins to the two outer leaders, with which, and with a long whip, he manages very dexterously, with the assistance of occasionally, hooting, whistling, singing, and cursing. The traces are made of rope, the collars of a size out of which we would make four, and all the rest of the harness, excessively clumsy, and they never take time in cleaning it.

We passed safely through the ordeal, both of the Custom house and the police office. They were very civil, and merely put their hands to the bottom of the trunks without disturbing anything. At the police office, we had to show our pass-ports, and to get new ones, in which we are all drawn to the life. Here is my picture — forty-two years of age, height 5 ft. 10, cheveux gris, front découvert, sourcils gris, yeux bruns, nez gros and long, bouche moyenne, barbe noire, menton rond, visage ovale, teint coloré. Nairne's age de 21 ans, taille d'un metre 11 centimetres (5 ft. 9) cheveux bruns, front moyens, sourcils blonde; yeux bleus, nez bienfait, bouche petite; barbe brun, menton rond, visage ovale, teint clair coloré. George and John are equally minutely described. We were very glad to get ashore at Dieppe for the vessel we were in was small, only 55 tons and her tackling none of the best. The sea was mountains high, at least what appeared to us, such, and our lee side was gunwale-in most of the way. John was a little sick, but we others had the pleasure of laughing at the sick folks, including all the passengers except ourselves and other two. I find I get on with my French wonderfully well and my ears are getting accustomed to the sound of it. There is a great deal of shipping here at present. We walked through the town last night for a short time. The streets are very

103

narrow, and like all French towns, without foot pavements.

Paris, 2nd. July 1818.

I wrote to you from Rouen on the 25th. June. I went that day to a French master who receives boarders — a M. Delalande, and agreed with him for our sons at 125 francs per month for each, for bed, board and teaching, which is equal to £12 : 8 : 4d. per month for both. They have a large and a small bedroom, which communicate, and the use of a large room which is used as a school room and dining-room. The mistress is an English woman. They get either coffee or tea and eggs to breakfast, a plain dinner, chiefly in the English fashion, with cider instead of beer, and cheese and fruit for supper. As there were some spare beds, Nairne and I boarded with them while we remained. There is in the house a Mr. Balingall from Scotland, a young man, who lost a leg in Spain, [the Peninsular War], and two Frenchmen. The situation is retired and airy. The only objection to it, is it's dullness, with which George was much dissatisfied. John, poor man, is quite pleased and contented. I asked Mr. Delalande to introduce them to an English family or two, which would be some resource to them, till they acquire something of the language. But altho' they are, in other respects, quite well situated, yet, if George continues dissatisfied, I must endeavour to get a place more to his mind; for, in his delicate state, it would not do well to let him fret himself. We took the best seats in the cabriolet, which is where with us, is placed the coachmen's seat, and has a cover or apron like a Gig. We travelled ninety-six miles or thereby, for 14/8d, leaving Rouen at a quarter before five in the morning, and getting to Paris at a little after three, altho' the heat was intense. The Diligences are all driven in the way I mentioned in my last; the postillion riding the near wheel horse, and guiding the three leaders with the reins and whip. On level road we frequently went at the rate of twelve miles an hour, literally at the gallop.

Rouen is most beautifully situated in an ampitheatre, opening to the south, where runs the Seine, navigable thus far for vessels of between two hundred and three hundred tons. From thence goods are transported up the river in immense flat bottomed barges, carrying from three to four hundred tons. It is impossible to figure more beautiful scenery than that with which Rouen is surrounded; the hills rising about four hundred feet, and showing the finest landscapes in all sides, which vary with each change of position. Country houses, Manufactories, gardens, orchards, and corn fields all intermingled; the town with it's steeples, and fine rows of trees on the Boulevards; the river winding below and covered with ships of all nations, form all together a scene not easily to be equalled. The town on a nearer inspection, does not answer the idea one is led to expect from it's external appearance, for the streets are very narrow, and not over clean, and like most French towns without foot pavements. The principal street does not average more than twenty feet wide, and is crooked to the bargain. The best houses are shut off from the streets, and form small squares, the windows of which, of course, look into one another. The Quay on the river side is very broad, and the Boulevards which encircle the town form a delightful walk, having four rows of fine trees with a broad carriage road in the middle, and walks for foot passengers on each side. One of these is at present occupied with a fair, which lasts three weeks, and forms a very pleasant lounge for a stroll. The river is crossed on a bridge of boats, which rises and falls with the tide. The centre is paved for carriages, and there are wooden foot paths having seats in the recesses which of an evening are always filled.

The country between Paris and Rouen continues just the same as from Dieppe to Rouen. The road bordered with trees, chiefly apple trees. Fields covered with all kinds of grain, with a sufficiency of trees to make them appear well wooded, but still no pasturing, so that the traveller, after looking again and again, and seeing nothing but trees and wheat and oats and barley, and barley and oats and wheat and trees, is very apt to fall asleep, overpowered by the sameness and stillness of the scene. About thirty miles from Rouen the vines begin to make their appearance and, as they require almost constant attention, the labourers among them somewhat enliven the scene. Instead of apple trees, cherry trees red with fruit, and fine walnut trees with the fruit nearly full grown, border the road. Near Paris, these give way to fine elms, which continue to the town and all round it, on the Boulevards.

We have wandered over most of this quarter of Paris, including the Tuilleries, the Champs Elysees, along the Quays, and the bridges, and not forgetting the Palais Royal. We mean to go tonight to the Gardens of Tivoli, where there are fire-works, music, rope dancing etc., something I believe in the style of Vauxhall. We have subscribed to a reading-room where most of the London papers are received, together with the Edinburgh Courant, Dublin Post, etc. As we are thus far from home, it would be a pity not to see all we can. Altho' there are no want of ever varying amusements here, yet I assure you that, in the midst of them, I often think of thou who are dearest to me, and that this little ramble will only make me relish home more, if possible, than ever. The weather has been very hot. We have been sitting and sleeping with open windows. I hope you also have had good weather, and that everything is going on prosperously.

God bless you and those with you, and believe me, however far off, always,

Your most affectionate husband,

Geo. Kinloch.

P.S. Single letters pay here by the weight; so when you write use thin paper. Address to me:

À Monsieur, Monsieur Kinloch,

Chez Messrs. Jacques Lafitte et C.

Banquiers, Rue de Mont Blanc, Paris.

Pay the postage, otherwise it won't come.

Paris 5th. July, 1818.

Just as I was taking out my writing things to begin this letter, a rap at the door announced the arrival of your long expected letter of the 23rd, June, from which I rejoice to find you are all well, notwithstanding the stormy weather. We are here at Madame Tomasinis, an English woman, whose mother was from Scotland, and she, of course, is

partial to *sawney*.[6] We have each a tolerable bedroom, and
a parlour mostly to ourselves, breakfast and a plentiful
dinner, with half a bottle of wine for five francs per day,
equal to 4/2d. each; which you will allow is not *very
extravagant* for two Strathmore lairds. There were ten
dined yesterday, most of them English, which is not so
agreeable to me as if they had been French, to give me an
opportunity to rub up my French lingo. I bought a best
large silk umbrella for 21/8d, six pairs best silk stockings
at 8/4d. the pair, three pairs white at 10/-, six India silk
handkerchiefs at 5/10d. each, a sealskin cap with gold band
20/-. I have bought a watch for Eliza at 100 francs. She
must, of course, be satisfied with it, because it was bought
from the Horloger du Roi, who, although a very con-
scientious man, took 25 francs less than he asked. At the
silk mercer's I bought a silk scarf for a certain *friend* of mine
at 23/4d.

There are swarms of English here. David's Quaker hat
attracted so much notice, that I have been obliged to
Frenchify him with a Parisian hat, and as he has already
a Parisian coat, he is quite the tippy. He has bought some
pretty expensive things for his mother and sister, but you
will, of course, say nothing about them. We have subscribed
for a month at Galizanis reading-rooms, where most of the
London papers are received, also the Courant, and in it
today, I had the first notice of Gourdie's death [Kinloch
of Gourdie]. He was my oldest friend and his uniform
kindness to me, I shall never forget. When I took leave of
him lately, I was afraid it was for the last time. Peace be
with him. I have no doubt he is happy.

We went on the 2nd. to the Gardens of Tivoli, containing
mountains for hurtling down in cars; roundabouts; an
aerial fleet, consisting of four boats holding four each which
go round ascending and descending in a way I should not
think very agreeable; jugglers, music, rope dancing; and
very brilliant fire-works. The cars hold two, generally a
lady and a gentleman. They have small wheels, and go
thundering down an inclined place with immense velocity.
Those at Tivoli go straight forwards, but some of the others

were curved and at one of them an accident happened two nights ago, which has caused them to be prohibited. A Nobleman, his niece and a little boy, his nephew, set off in one of the cars; one of the wheels broke and threw them all out. The lady escaped, but the boy was run thro' by the broken rail, and the uncle killed on the spot also. The straight ones are still permitted, as in them there is little danger. We have also been at the Opera Francaise, which the Parisians look upon as the first place of amusement in the world. That night we were there, the music was execrable and the singers very indifferent indeed. The ballet in some degree made up for it. It was a serious pantomime and so well performed that it was difficult to avoid crying. The dancing also was good, and the scenery beautiful. But I am called to dinner.

Wednesday, the 8th. July.

We put off going to St. Germains on Monday, as we wished to see Talma act, but as there was such a crowd we did not attempt to go in. David has got a French master, and is to get a fencing master today, of which he will be the better. Indeed if he would take a few lessons at dancing, he would be no worse of it. He is quite well, and much pleased with his jaunt. He is to write to his mother today.

Gask[7] is here. We have exchanged calls without meeting. Our landlady having belonged to the Corps Diplomatique, the English Ambassador allows her letters to go in his bag, and we avail ourselves of that opportunity. In answer to this, tell me how everything is going on. The hay crop. How the turnips and potatoes are looking. Also the crops in each particular field. The water cutting etc., Kennedy's house, and everything else you can think of. Paris is much improved since I saw it last, thanks to 'him that's far awa'.[8] This quarter of it, (the west end) is really a fine town; the streets in general sufficiently wide, and the houses handsome, but no pavement for foot passengers. We are within five minutes walk of the Tuilleries, and two of the Boulevards, which lead all round Paris, and being shaded by trees form a very pleasant walk. Some of the public buildings are of prodigious extent, and very elegant. The Government is going slowly on with some of Napoleon's half finished edifices; but the soul that animated Paris, seems to have fled. They have made pitiful attempts to scratch out his emblems. Since the 25th. the weather here has been very hot during the day, and very pleasant at night. I sleep with one thin blanket and a part of my window open. We generally muster from eight to twelve at dinner, mostly English.

Apparently the boys were not very happy at Rouen, on account of 'the dullness of their situation' — in fact, they were bored. Captain Ogilvy one of the Airly family, who was an Angus friend had suggested St. Germains, just outside Paris as being more sociable and their father found accommodation for them there. He wrote to his son on 8th July—

My Dear George,

St. Germains is twelve miles from Paris, in a fine vine country, and a most beautiful situation. I could not hear of any boarding-house fit for you, but I was shown a very good room at a pastry cook's, with a closet off it, fully better than those you have. Captain Ogilvy said he would be most happy to pay you every attention, and to introduce you to the few English who are there. Now, if you like this better than where you are, you may come as soon as your month is out, or a few days before it.

If you resolve on coming, you will need to tell Mr. Delalande immediately, and perhaps he may claim something additional from you, *in place of warning?* You must go to the Mayor to get pass-ports for Paris, and *after* obtaining them, and fixing your day, take places in the cabriolet of the Diligence which leaves the Hotel Natel at a quarter before five in the morning. You will have to pay twenty francs, for which you get a receipt, you afterwards pay the conductor, ten more at Magny where you breakfast; also four or five sous for himself, and your extra baggage besides, which will probably amount to six or seven or more. On your way, there is a very steep hill which you will be asked to walk up, and at the top of it there is a hut where you will be offered breakfast; but you will find it better to wait till you get to Magny about ten o'clock.

If you chuse you can buy a sweet biscuit or two at the hut, or some cherries. David was so much stared at, he was obliged to doff the Quaker hat, and is now a smart Parisian. We have almost walked our feet off, rambling thro' the town in this hot weather.

He wrote again on 13th July, to fix the details—

As I suppose you don't care how soon you leave Rouen you may take your places for Monday next, the 20th., or any of the two following days you please. You shall have the remainder of the week here in Paris, to see the lions [himself and David Nairne]. I shall take lodgings for you, for the 16th. As to Mr. Delalande's demand of a guinea each, it is what he has no manner of right to; but as I should be sorry you left him on unfriendly terms, say I have desired you to give him twenty-five francs in full for both. If he asks payment for candles, a pound costs eighteen sous, and I suppose you have not burnt that quantity. You will give each of the women three francs, in full, and you will also pay for your shoes cleaning. Get your pass-ports *before you take any* other steps. I desired you to take your places at the Hotel Natel, because the cabriolet has a cover, in case of rain. Tie your umbrellas and sticks all together. Then, the night before you are to set off, pay Mr. Delalande. Be perfectly civil to him, but *firmly* resist every demand you think improper. Before paying his account, take it to your own room and examine it minutely, and satisfy yourself that is is all right. I may observe to you, that you should be perfectly civil, yet that much less delicacy is necessary on these occasions with a Frenchman, than with ourselves; and that what to a Briton would be an affront, a Frenchman receives it merely with a shrug of the shoulders. I again repeat it, be civil, but firm.

He wrote to his wife about the new arrangement for the boys—

I heard from George on the 12th. and as I foresaw, they are both very happy at the idea of removing to St. Germains. The landlord is an apothecary, and his wife is a respectable like woman, and they both promised to show them the same attention as they would to their own children. As to their eating, there is a 'traiteur' directly opposite who agreed to give them what they may want, either in his house or in their rooms. During the day, the entrance to their rooms is thro' the shop, where the mistress always sits, and which serves her for a parlour. It is a large room, and as the large doors and windows are always open, the smell is not near so powerful as that of Dr. Ogilvy's fragrant bower in Dundee. Upon the whole, I think they will find themselves comfortable. They are within ten minutes walk of the forest, which is of great extent and affords shady walks at all hours. We went to Versailles and St. Cloud, at which latter place the Court now is. We went on Sunday, as that is the day on which the water works play. While waiting for them, we got a full view of the Duchesse d'Angouleme, who returned our bow with royal condescension. We also saw our *fat* friend Louis taking an airing before dinner, but it was only at a distance; as one of the servants directed us to a wrong place to see him alight, a very common thing here, for, if you ask a Frenchman the way to any place, it is two to one but he tells you to go to the right when he means you to go to the left. This stupidity of theirs has sometimes cost us more shoe leather than we approved of.

On the 14th. we went to the Catacombs, where the bones from all the old burying grounds within Paris have been piled up, and where millions of skulls grin at you in the pleasantest manner possible. The Catacombs were the quarries from which a great part of Paris was built, and they are about sixty feet below ground. About twenty people went down at the same time with us, and among them two pretty English girls, whose plumpness and rosy cheeks formed a strange contrast with the furniture of the place. Each of us carried a taper, which served to show the horrors of the place, but to us they had no terrors, for none of the party seemed to think that the grim king had any business with them, and mirth and laughter echoed along the dark and winding passages.

We afterwards went to the Pantheon, formerly the Church of St. Genvieve, the Patroness of Paris, now intended as the burying place of great men. They have been busy effacing the inscriptions in front of it, but I was surprised to see the following ones untouched — 'The Rights of Man,' 'Law is the declared Will of the whole Nation,' etc. etc. We yesterday went to the 'Jardin des Plantes,' which by no means merits the encomiums which have been lavished upon it. Indeed, I suspect it has fallen off very much since Nappy's departure. We have also seen the Museum of Pictures, which is the largest in the world. It is, I believe, upwards of fifteen hundred feet long, and filled with pictures, which from their number, confuse and embarrass the spectator. We have now seen nearly all we wish to see, and if I had the young men fairly settled, I care not how soon I bend my course northwards, for tho' time glides on here almost imperceptibly, yet I shall be very well pleased when I again see the green fields and heath clad hills of Caledonia.

The way we spend our time is this. Breakfast at nine. If we have no sights to see, we remain in till two or three o'clock, then go to the reading-room, or take a walk on the Boulevards, dine at five, sometimes go to the theatre at seven o'clock; other times, stroll on the Boulevards for an hour or so, which are crowded from eight till twelve. Then adjourn to the Café d'Apollon in the Palais Royale, where for twenty sous, we get an ice, and as much music as we chuse to take, as there is a band of thirteen or fourteen people who play the whole evening. When tired of it, we saunter about in the Jardins a little, and then steer homewards, where we chat a while and take a glass of brandy and water, and then to bed.

There is a Captain Doig here of the 21st. and a Lieut. Cameron of the 79th. both Scots. The latter is a good natured, young fellow, and he and Nairne generally ramble about together, while Doig and I bring up the rear. The other day while I was at St. Germains, all the three got themselves properly 'toxicated,' and staggered home about nine o'clock, as drunk as Lords. They dined at a Restaurateur's on the Boulevards, and drank four bottles of Claret, four of Champagne, and one of common wine, and the bottles here are full quarts. This was pretty well in this hot weather.

PLATE 1
Kinloch House, Meigle, built 1797. From an old pencil and water colour drawing on an early version of 'scraper-board'

I am well pleased with the account you give of my farm operations, and the appearance of the crop, and also with the sale of my barley. I should think the crop would be at least a month earlier than last year. As there is a Fête at Tivoli tonight, with a nocturnal ascent of a balloon, I mean to take the young men to see it, as it is not far from here. Nairne takes an hour at French from seven to eight, and then we both take a lesson at fencing. He is quite well, and in great spirits, buying rather too many clothes, and eating too many ices, but as he is not to be long here, it is as well to let him take his swing.

Paris, 30th. July 1818.
I wrote to you on the 21st. the day after the young men arrived from Rouen. I mean to go out and dine with them before we set off for the Land o' Cakes, to which both Nairne and I are beginning to look anxiously. I took the young men to Tivoli the day after they arrived. It was a 'grand fête', the gardens all illuminated, a nocturnal ascent of a balloon, with Madame Blanchard who went up in fine style, letting off fire-works when she was about two hundred yards up; music, jugglers, an aerial fleet, ups and downs, roundabouts, and the Lord knows what. John and I went down the mountains of which Miss Biddy Gudge gives such an ecstatic description, but neither Nairne nor George would venture. You set off, two in one car, like fire and fury, pass beneath an arch, and then ascend a gentle acclivity which checks your velocity before you get to the end. The whole length is about two hundred yards, I think. When you are descending, you go at the rate of about forty miles an hour. The sensation is pleasant, and has the effect of a dram in exhilarating the spirits, but without the intoxication, and I really believe it is good for the health. It is the fashion for a lady and a gentleman to go together, and the Cavalier, of course, puts his arm round the lady's waist, which no doubt, makes the journey more pleasant. The cars are returned empty, by machinery, and if inclined for another trip, you walk up the slope till you arrive at the summit, when off you go again, and so on. At the Beaujou

(where the accident happened), you was dragged up in the car, so that invalids or gouty people could enjoy it also. In crowding to see the balloon, some obliging person was kind enough to relieve me of my pocket-book, which altho' of no value to them, was annoying enough to me, as I had my journal in it, and some memorandums, etc. also my passport and my letter of credit, but I have got both of them provided for. In London, I used to carry my banknotes in it, but here they are not blessed with these beautiful specimens of our paper manufacturing, so that the thief got little for his pains.

Before leaving for home Father wrote some last minute advice to his son;—

8th. August, 1818

My Dear George,

I hope you have found yourselves pretty comfortable since I left you. I told them you would settle the bill once a week, and I think a franc a week will be enough for the garcons. Do not indulge in lying abed. It is very weakening, therefore make it a rule to rise every morning at eight o'clock, or before it. If you can take your fencing lesson at that hour, so much the better. Shift immediately after it; wash yourself, and then to breakfast. I leave the choice of your studies to yourself, only I am anxious that you should be a good French scholar, when you have so good an opportunity. It is not the hour your master is to be with you that will teach it to you; you must study hard by yourself, and above all, write it; first turning English into French, and then the French back again into English. This you will find most useful. As to the pronunciation, you must get it by conversing with Mr. Asseree, his wife, or any other French person you meet with. At first, you will feel awkward and difficult, but never mind, blunder on, thro' thick and thin. They will always put you right, and you must not mind being laughed at occasionally. You are well aware that if a person were never to speak a language till they could speak it correctly, they would never speak it at all. To revert to your health, nothing is more weakening than women, and therefore avoid them as much as you can.

This is all that occurs to me at present, and I beg you will let John also read this letter, as it may be useful to him as well as you. God bless you both, and believe me to remain,

Your affectionate father, Geo. Kinloch.

On his return to London he described the journey home from France in a letter dated 18th August, 1818.

Here we are, so far on our way to the Land of Cakes. I would have bought some stockings, which I knew would be useful, but we heard so much of the difficulty of getting them ashore, that I was afraid to venture them. When I came to land, I found we might have brought three or four dozen pairs easily, as they never looked at us going ashore. But the knowledge came too late. We left Paris at six on Sunday morning, David having sat up eating melon and brandyfying the night before, so that he was quite *ree* when we set out. Dined at Clermont, where the landlady was the prettiest woman I have seen in France, supped at Amiens; got to Abbeville about three next morning, breakfasted at Montreuil, and arrived at Boulogne at three p.m. on Monday We went up to the heights where the *Army of England* was encamped, and we went to the top of the scaffolding put up to erect an immense pillar as a trophy to the French arms. There is about one fourth of it erected, and the marble for the rest is all hewn, ready to put up. I don't know the height of it, but there are four hundred and eighty-six steps to the top of the scaffolding. They told us it was to be finished next year, and made a light-house of, and certainly it will be the most magnificent one in the world, and worthy of it's founder. We left it at half past three p.m. on Tuesday, and landed at Dover at eight, the sea breaking over us all the way. Nairne staid on deck, and got wet to the skin, while I stretched myself on a parcel of trunks in the after cabin, which was so full of luggage that none of the sick folks could come in, so I escaped both the ducking and spewing, of which there was a vast. The motion was infernal, and I was all but sick myself, and not at all sorry when I heard Dover announced. We went to the Custom House next morning, and passed muster without difficulty, tho' Nairne had some contraband goods. He got all his things safe also, tho' he was in a terrible funk about his boxes and decent prints. They were by no means so strict as they had been represented to us. We left Dover outside at ten, and arrived at Charing Cross at half past nine, having dined at Rochester, which adjoins to Chatham. We breakfasted at our old quarters there, and lodge directly opposite. As to our motions, I think we shall not exceed a week here, and that we shall stage it down, stopping every night. We shall, of course, stop a day in Edinburgh, and then for home, which I can assure you I long very much to see, as well as some people who are there. I have been quite well since I left you, and I have certainly been much gratified with my journey. You will also find David no worse of it, tho' I could not prevail upon him to take a dancing master, of whom he certainly would have been the better. He has been very extravagant in throwing away his money, but I trust he will learn better to look after it. He has been particularly extravagant in clothes, and in the wine he drank and gave away to our fellow-lodgers. He has a good heart, but the head, as yet, is light. Upon the whole he has had a happy time of it. I must conclude.

Yours affectionately,

George Kinloch.

George Kinloch returned home in very good spirits, and was 'much gratified' by the whole expedition.

---

1 A boot and shoe-maker from Perth — was one of the well-known Norwell family of Perth.

2 This crude punishment of hanging in chains just above tide level on the river bank where all boats passing up and down the river could see them was considered to be a useful warning to sailors and pirates of what would happen to them if they misbehaved. One of Hogarth's pictures illustrates this punishment.

3 Admiral Lord Cochrane was at this time preparing his expedition to take command of the Chilean Navy in their war of liberation from Spain.

4 In the Westminster Election of June 1818, the two Reform candidates, Sir Samuel Romilly and Sir Francis Burdett were successful over the Ministerial candidate Sir Murray Maxwell. The election took fifteen days to complete and the state of the poll was published at the end of each day.

5 This 'Grande Monarque' was Louis XVIII.

6 By 'Sawney' is meant 'Sandy' e.g. a Scot.

7 Gask is Laurence Oliphant, 8th Laird of Gask.

8 'Him that's far awa' ' is Napoleon by this time in exile on St. Helena.

116

CHAPTER NINE

The Way of Life of a Strathmore Laird
(1818-1819)

G EORGE KINLOCH's activities between August 1818 and August
1819 which covered the period immediately before his arrest
are described in letters to his wife and family. From these
one can judge with hindsight whether he could possibly have
constituted any threat to the establishment.

He did not attempt to disguise the fact that he was a critic
of the existing state of Government and wanted to see radical
changes, but there is no evidence that he was the leader of any
subversive organisation, and it is clear that he was only expressing his own personal views and opinions for what they were
worth. A man with a sense of humour such as that of George
Kinloch would be unlikely to disturb the peace of the country.

These months, between his return from France and his
speech in Dundee in November 1819, were on the whole quiet
ones. He never went further away from home than Perth or
Dundee and, except for occasional outbursts of anger about the
state of the country, one sees him living quietly and taking a
responsible interest in local affairs.

His doings are described in journal form taken from his own
writings in letters addressed either to his wife or to his sons in
France.

AUGUST 1818.

The return from France, as described in the previous
Chapter, coincided with a large political dinner in London,

organised by 'The Hampden Club,' at which the Hon. Douglas Kinnaird M.P., son of Lord Kinnaird presided. The Chairman spoke about the progress of Reform in Scotland and coupled his speech with the health of Mr Kinloch of Kinloch whom he described as the distinguished supporter of Reform in Scotland. George Kinloch wrote to his wife:

At the dinner, I had the honour of being on the Chairman's left hand, Sir Francis being on his right hand, and you will easily imagine that it was an honour I could have dispensed with when I tell you that, on my health being drunk, along with the Reformers of Scotland, I had to get up upon the table and to address upwards of 300 strangers and that too, after Sir Francis and Mr. Kinnaird had spoken. I would rather have been in your arms, I assure you. However, I took care not to weary them with my *oratory* and I acquitted myself tolerably well for a beginner. It felt somewhat like taking the cold bath in a winter's morning; and I was damn'd glad when it was over. Wooler[1] spoke and his speech was like music. He spoke with great rapidity, with a happy choice of words, and a great deal of humour, and he never misplaced or repeated a word. The great folks, of which I was one, left them about half past nine. In going out, several people whom I did not know, shook me by the hand and, among the rest, Thos. Hardy[2] who was tried for High Treason in 1794, along with Horne Tooke etc. so that some of my neighbours will think me quite contaminated.

There followed invitations to dinners here and there around London and George Kinloch thought nothing of tramping out to dine at Woodford in Essex, a distance of better than ten miles where Mr Webster of the London Docks had asked him to dine. 'He has a very good house with large gardens with hot-houses etc. and everything in excellent stile. He was very kind and gave us everything of the best.'

He embarked on the 20th August on board the Dundee Perth and London Smack, 'the Good Ship, The Defiance, Capt. Mill, to reach Dundee in five or six days time.' He had bought seed wheat in London and a second-hand grand piano for Mrs Nairne, 'but you had better not mention it to them,' and so a cart would be needed at the harbour for their baggage. He was anxious to get home as soon as possible to help with 'the hairst.'

In September he wrote to his sons who were still in France—

SEPTEMBER:

The harvest is nearly all housed everywhere in this neighbourhood. Mine was all in on Tuesday last. A good crop on the whole, tho' not so bulky as last year. The prices are high and I expect to make a good rent of it.

I have been out three times at the partridges and averaged four brace and a half each day. They are plentier than for some years past, and the hares are said to be very plenty also; but there is so much foggage in the fields, it is not easy finding them. Yesterday Kildrumbo, Blair and I went to Tully where we saw several Roe of which Nairne and I killed one each. We saw only three black cock but we had not much time to look for them. Old Sambo still makes a shift to shuffle over a good deal of ground and Kirsty, if she does little good, does as little harm as she is very obedient. It seems Kirsty produced a son and heir during my absence which Angus has brought up. Nairne's three hounds were with us yesterday and got a tasting of the blood. They are pretty and offer well.

Here they have had a great quantity of small fruits and very fine. Some apricots and figs. A good crop of plums particularly greengages and a great quantity of apples on the walls and loads of both pears and apples on the standards. They have been exporting potatoes already from the Tay for London, and they talk even of exporting turnips.

His daughter Margaret added to this letter to her brother—

How do you do with the French language? Papa is giving us lessons and I intend to make great progress so that I expect to be able to converse with you by the time you return. I suppose that you will have heard of Betsy Stormont's marriage. She is married to a brother of James Maxwell in Dundee with a large fortune.

OCTOBER 1818.

At the beginning of October, George Kinloch was elected to a Joint Committee representing the Counties of Forfar and Fife to take advice about the ferry service across the Tay. The important question was whether they should introduce a steam ferry and a report from Liverpool, on the steam ferry 'Aetna' which was working across the Mersey was in its favour. 'Horses, cattle and carriages are disposed of on one side and passengers on the other, the wheel is in the centre and the power is a twelve horses one which carries the boat seven knots an hour.' It was necessary to collect £20,000 by local subscription in order to get a Government Grant of £5000, but the money was well subscribed and George Kinloch gave £100 although he had very little spare cash. He had to sell the small farm of Chapelhill at this time to his brother-in-law John Smyth to relieve himself of debt and produce some ready money. On the 9th of October, he wrote to his son —'We have had no frost yet. The Ash trees are just beginning to lose their leaves and the other trees to assume their variegated autumn coats. The pastures are quite green and the turnips stronger than I can ever remember them.'

At the end of this month there was a party at Kinloch to celebrate his eldest son's birthday, although neither son was present.

> We had a grand turnout on your birthday. Miss Austin and Captain Burns, she brought with her; young Hay and two Miss Hays. Margaret and Sarah Smyth, David and Margaret Gray; David Nairne, two Boyters; Mr. and Mrs. Wedderburn, L. Brown etc. We had a ball in the house and another in the barn to which we occasionally adjourned. The house party left off about three but the barn folks kept it up till five and Davy Reid was telling next morning that he got some kisses as sweet as *succré*. We had young Kenny and Willy Cruikshanks as fiddlers.

Some unknown local lady under the pseudonym of 'Lady Stripside' also gave a party from which—

> the vulgar were excluded. I did not go, but Dr. Gray and two of our girls went, so you see we have been tolerably merry.

George Kinloch kept himself well posted in world affairs, and commented to his son —

> I am glad to see that the allied troops are to be withdrawn from France and still more so to find that a great reduction in our red coated slaves is to take place. The hum of politics

has for the present almost ceased in anxious expectation of what the new Parliament will do.

This letter ended with a rather unkind reference to the approaching death of Queen Charlotte, wife of George III —

Poor old Snuffynose has been dying by inches. She is a tough old b. . . , but she must kick in a few days in spite of her heart if she has one. It is not possible that any human can regret her and there will be no tears shed except à force d'onions.

According to Horace Walpole who described her features 'her nostrils spread too wide,' so perhaps the nickname 'Snuffynose' although unkind, was fitting.

There was more notice in his letters of social activities than to any interest in politics —

NOVEMBER 1818.

There was a 'house-heating' party at Mr. Jobson's at Rosemount which went off in fine style. The lobby, staircase and drawing-room decorated in a very tasteful manner with flowers and evergreens and coloured lamps. There were about 120 people present and the dancing was kept up till half past five on Saturday morning. One half of the company supped first and, about an hour afterwards, the other half so that there was no intermission in the dancing.

His friends from Carnoustie, the Tailyours, were staying at Rothesay, the capital of Bute, for the winter—

They give a very favourable account of Rothesay but not so however, of the cleanliness of their landlady and her maid, who seem to think dirt a very wholesome ingredient in people's food; as a specimen of which, the second day after their arrival there, Mrs. Tailyour caught the maid drying their tea-cups with the bairn's dirty 'hippens' [nappies]. After making this discovery, she was glad to take the whole culinary department into her own hands. A steam boat goes from Glasgow three times a week, accomplishing the distance which is forty miles in about six hours or less.

It was an open winter and—

The grass is still green and the cattle out in many places. The hollyhocks and late flowers are still flowering and the

121

whins are very generally in blossom, also the broom in some places.

DECEMBER 1818.

In consequence of two women having died from the effects of the bite of a mad dog in Dundee, dogs are prohibited from going at large and I do not like to take out the hounds. I had taken them out at Johnshill on the 7th. where we saw two roe but they escaped owing to the insubordination of the troops who did not place themselves as ordered. The whole days sport was two hares.

George Kinloch was planning to build a windmill at Bank head Farm and, as he could not do so much shooting as usual, this occupation took up some of his surplus energy during the winter months.

JANUARY 1819.

At the beginning of this month, the family went to stay at Gourdie some few miles away, with their cousins, the Gourdie Kinlochs. There was shooting at Forneth and the Blair woods with the Goodchild family, also at Stormont Loch where 'we had no sport, not having fallen in with the deer.' This party ended up at Kinloch where they were joined by others, and on the 25th they went together by coach to attend the 'Fox' dinner in Coupar Angus. It was a more riotous affair than usual, and he wrote—

We stirred about the punch till about two o'clock in the morning when we parted and Dr. Boyter, in the going home, repeatedly declared that he was as drunk as ever he had been in his life. To show his steadiness, he insisted on walking along a seam of the carpet but, making a lee lurch, he pitched headlong into the book-case bed, to our no small amusement. The Toasts, being chiefly of my giving, were, as you may believe, prodigiously loyal. I think it will be followed with good effects.

Mr Rintoul of the newspaper who attended the dinner, printed most of the 'Toasts' in the weekly issue of the Advertiser and, far from being prodigiously loyal, can have done George Kinloch's reputation no good at all. These Toasts included the following—

The Rights of the People; May the People soon obtain them.

The House of Hanover; and whenever they forget the principles which seated their family on the Throne, may they be packed off as the Stuarts were.

Trial by Jury; not by Judges.

As the last House of Commons was one of the basest that ever disgraced the benches of St. Stephens, may the new one avoid their faults.

The complete abolition of the Slave Trade and Slaves throughout the World.

Catholic Emancipation, and may no man be disqualified from serving his country because he chooses to worship God as his fathers did.

FEBRUARY 1819.

There was more Roe deer shooting with the Goodchilds of Forneth which lies west of Blairgowrie on the road to Dunkeld, and close to the Atholl country.

We went to a place called Kincaidstone four miles on the road to Dunkeld. It had been hard frost in the morning, but the sun was very powerful as we climbed up the hills. Kincaidstone marches with the 'Guck's' property [The Duke of Atholl] so we trespassed a little on his Grace, and had very pretty sport. We soon found the roe and saw them running below and could trace all their windings. David Kinloch shot one and I another and, if we had had leave from the Duke, we might have killed four or five, but we did not like to venture too far upon his premises. I never saw a prettier scene.

George Kinloch on the other hand took quite a different line about trespassing when it concerned his own land, and so when it concerned his neighbours he wrote—

Young Hay is playing the devil as a poacher, killing everything. He had the impudence to come with another person and shoot all over Balmyle and Chapelhill, although I had given him leave on Blacklaw only.

MARCH 1819.

In March one of his wife's sisters, Sarah Smyth, then forty-two years old was married—

Your Aunt Sarah is to be married next week to Dr. Whitson of Parkhill. It has long been in agitation but all the preliminaries could not be settled sooner. [Being a Smyth wedding, there would be the most elaborate marriage settlement]. The Doctor is a quiet, sensible man with a snug little property and an excellent house upon it; so I hope she will be comfortable and happy, though neither of them are chickens.

In this month there was unusual entertainment for the neighbourhood — a visit from two packs of foxhounds;

We have had the foxhunters in our neighbourhood these ten days past; the Kintore hounds at Coupar and the Fife hounds at Forfar. The latter, on the 10th. killed three foxes hereabouts for which I owe them thanks. The Kintore Hounds tried Johnshill and Tullyfergus on the 20th. under the direction of Dr. Boyter, who was mounted on a steed of Mr. Wedderburn and by knowing the country and taking short cuts, contrived to be in at the death of the only fox they killed at the gates of Bamff. They ran other three but lost them.

The Doctor dined here yesterday but said that he had been a leetle unaisy in his nether parts in consequence of his long ride. He went to see them throw off behind Islabank yesterday and had the pleasure to see one of the fat Proctors thrown off into a whin bush where he lay jammed on his back and helpless as a turtle, and all the field laughing at him, till some of the pedestrians hauled him out of his nest, weel jobbit and bleeding in various places.

APRIL 1819.

In April the 'Dundee Advertiser' exposed a letter from the Rev. James Thomson, a Minister of one of the Dundee Churches written to Lord Sidmouth, the Home Secretary, which may have had considerable importance for George Kinloch. This Minister was suspected, rightly or wrongly, of being an 'Informer' to the Home Secretary against the supposed subversive elements in Dundee. The letter read—

My Lord, I need not inform your Lordship of the political state of this town and neighbourhood, as your Lordship is no doubt well acquainted with it. A few spirits have always existed here since 1792, fond of change and hostile to the happy constitution of our country and the spark of disaffection is kept alive by a weekly paper which owes its origin to democratic faction.

Two years ago, I made an attempt to get a newspaper conducted on Proper Principles in order to counteract a growing evil and to disseminate, among an often misled population, loyalty to the Best of Princes and respect for constitutional authority.

The only obstacle to our success is the want of funds for which about £500 will be necessary. For myself I ask and expect nothing. The whole profits shall go to the Printer and he knows nothing of anyone interesting himself in the matter except myself, as we are afraid of injuring the cause by giving publicity to our object. Your Lordship is perfectly aware that this matter requires Prudence and therefore must not transpire.

      (Signed) James Thomson
        One of the Ministers of Dundee.

The Editor[3] of the 'Advertiser' made sure that the matter did 'transpire' by giving the letter full publicity and said that he was preserving the letter as one of 'our rarer curiosities.' The reference to the Prince Regent as the 'Best of Princes' would have tickled George Kinloch's sense of humour, knowing as he did of the Prince's love affairs, first with Mary Robinson, the beautiful Drury Lane actress, then his secret marriage to Mrs Fitzherbert, and his love-less marriage to Caroline of Brunswick, besides the continual scandal of gambling debts and doubtful connection with horse racing. Nevertheless, Lord Sidmouth may have taken the letter seriously.

At the end of the month, George Kinloch spent three days in Perth attending the Circuit Court and a further day for the County Meeting. He made no comments on the severe sentences but wrote 'six or eight people were condemned to be transported, three banished from Scotland for life and one poor boy to be hanged for house-breaking'. The young boy, James Fraser, who had been charged with stealing food and servant's clothing from Miss Stewart of Cluny, and who might to-day have been put on probation, was condemned 'to suffer death at the common place for hanging, (which was at the foot of the High Street) in Perth on the 11th. of June 1819.' Notwithstanding such horrors, the seating of the gallery of the Court Room was filled to suffocation all three days. There were a number of ladies present, who were equally interested in the grim details and although these were noticed to leave the gallery when the case of Effy Mill who was charged with concealing pregnancy and abandoning her child, was heard, they only left the gallery to get a better view of her from another part of the Court.

This was less than one hundred and fifty years ago, and shows how ideas about crime and punishment have changed. Whatever one may think of the crude justice, the presiding Judge did not waste time over it and, having dealt with many criminal charges in three days, he attended the Court before breakfast on the fourth day to deal with the Appeals from the Lower Courts.

MAY 1819.

On 3rd May the annual competition of flowers, fruits, vegetables and wines took place in Grant's Strathmore Arms in Coupar-Angus. This Horticultural Show was attended by all the big houses of Strathmore. Mrs Kinloch may have been a little disappointed that she was beaten in the Flower Show by the newcomers at Arthurstone, but she held her own in the Currant Wine Section and also for apples, being last year's crop, in best state of preservation.

Spring came early, and a letter to the boys said —

We had pease in blossom on the first inst., an immense show of apricots, few plums, but a great deal of blossom on the apples, pears and cherries. No sale for grain of any kind. Lean cattle extravagantly high; fat moderate. Manufactures lower than ever known; a stout weaver not able to earn more than 5/- to 6/- a week, working fourteen hours a day.

On Political affairs all that was mentioned was that 'The Catholic question has again been lost in the Den of Thieves by a majority of two.' This Bill aimed at giving greater liberty of worship to Roman Catholics, was not to succeed for another ten years.

George Kinloch included in this month's letter full instructions to his sons about their return journey from France, and in this there was nothing left to chance—

As the time is now approaching when you will be turning

126

your face towards old Caledonia I shall recapitulate what I said as to your progress northward. You stay a week in Paris, or at most two weeks to see everything which you have not yet seen there, taking care not to get into any mischief. Indeed, if you make good use of your time, a week or ten days will be quite enough.

You then leave for Boulogne, taking the route either of Clermont or Beauvais, and stopping, if you chuse, a day at Amiens and another at Abbeville to examine these towns. When you get to Boulogne, your stay there will be regulated by the sailing of the packet for Dover; at which you may go to the French hotel or the King's Head. You must put your night things in your pocket, as your trunks will be all taken to the Custom House. I would advise you to remain a day at Dover to see the castle, etc. and to prevent disappointment in getting your things passed at the Custom House; at which you must attend in person. After the ceremony is over, you may secure places in, or on one of the coaches, taking care to make a bargain for your luggage at the same time.

I would not advise you to bring any smuggled goods, but if you do, put on *two* shirts, wrapping the smuggle round your body, between the shirts. At Dover they never search the person of any decent looking people; in which respect I suppose both you and John will pass muster. You must keep the smuggle about you, till you get to London, as they sometimes search the trunks at Canterbury. If your trunks will not hold all your luggage, buy a 'sac de nuit,' of which you will get the largest size lined with leather, at the Halle aux Pilliers. Each of you buy a neat plain travelling cap.

When you get to London, you will stay all night at the hotel where the coach stops, and next day I would advise you to try La Sabloniere Hotel in Leicester Square; which being a French house, you need not drink anything after your dinner, a great nuisance in other coffee houses. I suppose ten days or thereby will satisfy you of London. When you arrive in Dundee, you can leave your heavy baggage in the ship, and hire a gig to come out here, when you will find sundry persons most happy to see you. Now,

127

though I have sketched the outline for you, I leave it to your discretion, to vary the plan a little.

I shall now proceed to give you, at one view, a note of the things you are to buy and bring with you. 1st. A watch for Margaret as formerly described, with a good key, the neatest plain gold chain 3 ft. long; 2nd. Another gold chain, same length and price for Eliza, and four gold set seals, amethyst, cornelian, or rock crystal uncut. 3rd. a neat plain gold repeater for myself, with white dial plate, and engrained back, having the maker's name, and warranted both as to gold and workmanship. I would have you try L'Episse; this is all the jewellery. 4th. We shall now adjourn to the shop of Monsieur Nicholas on the Boulevard and the corner of the Rue Richelieu where, with the help of Madame Tomasini, or Miss Pruny you will buy 3 pieces of cambric (Batiste) for handkerchiefs. You will get each piece cut into nine, making 27 in all, hemmed and marked with a 'K' in red letters, and you and John can then wear them for cravats, neckerchiefs, and pack them up in different places unwashed. 5th. Six pairs plain white silk stockings, small men's sizes. Seven pairs white stockings full women's size. 6th. Twelve pairs black stockings full women's size. All to be marked with a 'K', steeped in clean water, so as to be thoroughly wet, dried, and then each pair drawn within one another, as if going to be washed, and packed in different places of your trunks. If you haven't time to dirty them, soak them in clean water, wring them, dry, and tumble them in, as dirty.

You will, of course, wear your own French watch. You can carry your old watches in your waistcoat pockets, and I would advise each of you to get a steel chain to wear round your neck, and your watch fastened to it, and when in London, to wear your old watches, for fear of pickpockets. This is all that occurs to me at present on the subject. Uncle John and Aunt Cecilia are living like two hermits at Balhary in the old comfortable mansion, the new one not being yet ready for them.

JUNE 1819.

There had been late frosts in Strathmore and on 29th. of

PLATE 3

View of Dundee Harbour before 1815 showing D.P.L. Smacks moored by the stern to the pier

By courtesy of The Librarian, 'Dundee Courier'

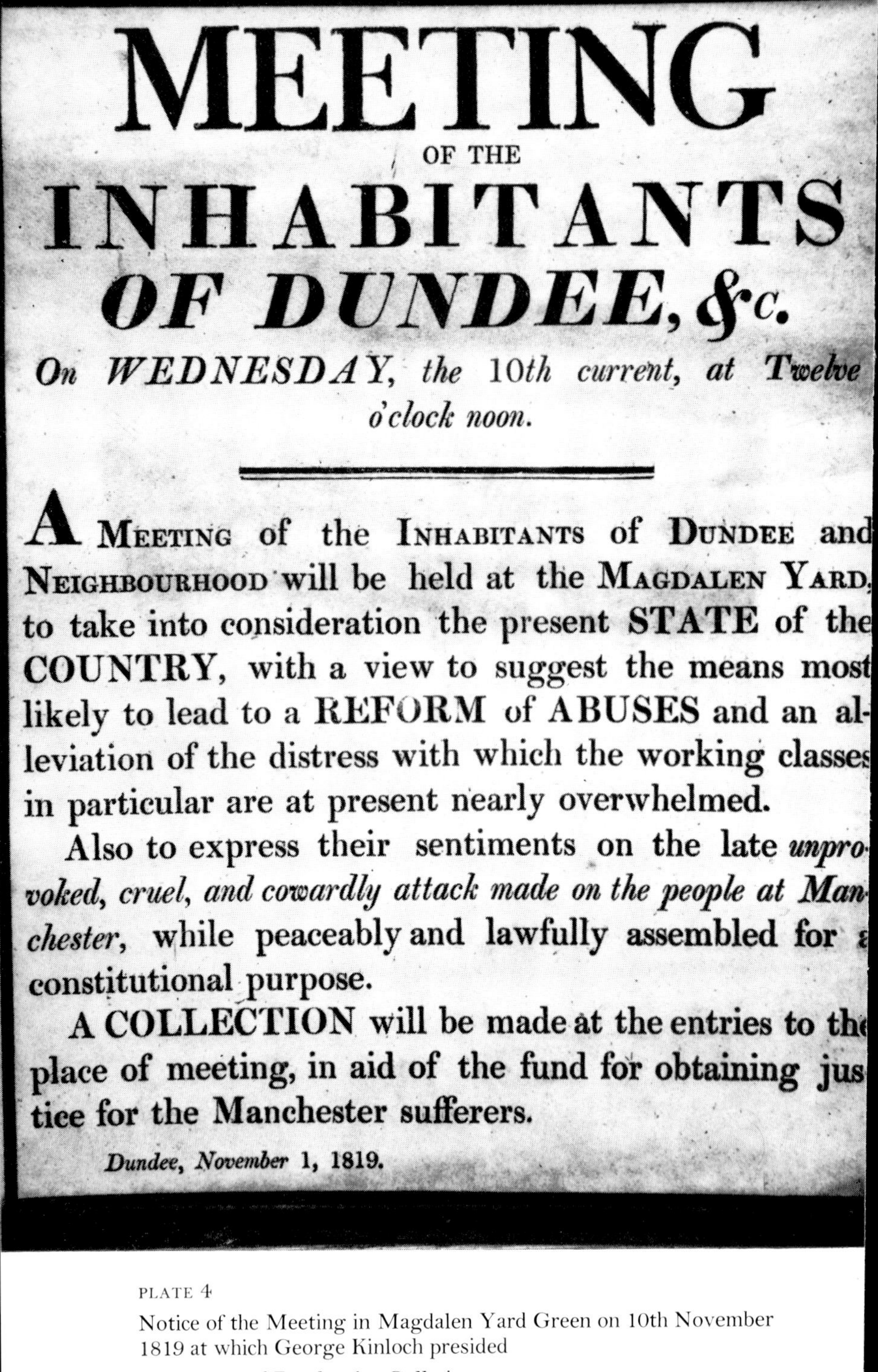

MEETING

OF THE

INHABITANTS
OF DUNDEE, &c.

On *WEDNESDAY*, the 10th current, at *Twelve*
o'clock noon.

A MEETING of the INHABITANTS of DUNDEE and
NEIGHBOURHOOD will be held at the MAGDALEN YARD,
to take into consideration the present STATE of the
COUNTRY, with a view to suggest the means most
likely to lead to a REFORM of ABUSES and an al-
leviation of the distress with which the working classes
in particular are at present nearly overwhelmed.

Also to express their sentiments on the late *unprovoked, cruel, and cowardly attack made on the people at Manchester,* while peaceably and lawfully assembled for a
constitutional purpose.

A COLLECTION will be made at the entries to the
place of meeting, in aid of the fund for obtaining justice for the Manchester sufferers.

Dundee, November 1, 1819.

PLATE 4
Notice of the Meeting in Magdalen Yard Green on 10th November
1819 at which George Kinloch presided
By courtesy of Dundee Art Galleries

May, there was snow on the Sidlaws as low as Auchtertyre Farm House.

I fear the frost and snow have done a deal of injury to the muirfowl. The hares are numerous and a good appearance of partridges. They have been cutting the oak wood at Ruthven lately and, when I saw it, they had 202 people employed. The price of bark has since then fallen very much so they have stopt for this season. Islabank gets £1260 for it, a very neat sum.

All the comments this month were of country affairs and there was no talk whatever of any involvement with the Radical leaders.

On 17th June 'We all go down to Carnoustie next week for to *see* bathing.' They had rented a house at Carnoustie for the summer as there was no house on the Carnoustie property and both he and his wife had been unwell.

I have been unwell for a month past with a weakness in my back but am almost well again. Your mother has also been ailing but I hope the bathing will restore her.

There was a large party of the family by the seaside as two of the Smyth cousins, Helen and Ann, came over in the Fife coach where they met two beaus to escort them in the persons of Sir James Ramsay and Mister George. 'They are all quite well and "doukin terribly."' He told his sons that they would 'know to find us at Carnoustie' on arrival in Dundee. Their return would be the next excitement and he was 'Expecting every day to hear from you.'

This was the pattern of his life for the twelve months up to August 1819, an active and full life based on his home and family, but always ready to accept responsibility in public affairs such as in the Committee to improve the Tay Ferry service or to speak at County meetings.

1 Thos. Jonathan Wooler (1786–1853), Journalist and Politician, Editor of 'The Statesman' and 'The Black Dwarf.' In 1819 took part in electing Sir Charles Wolseley 'Legislatorial Attorney for Birmingham,' an action which earned for him eighteen months imprisonment in Warwick Gaol.

2 Thomas Hardy (1752–1832) was born in Larbert and went to London where he set up in business as a shoemaker in Piccadilly. He was charged with High Treason in 1794 for issuing handbills of the London Corresponding Society on subject of Reform and spent six months in the Tower of London. He was acquitted after a Jury Trial.

3 In 1819 there were two Dundee newspapers, 'The Dundee, Perth and Cupar Advertiser' with Radical sympathies, owned and edited by Robert S. Rintoul with a large circulation and a Tory paper with a small circulation called 'The Dundee Courier' published by a Mr Colville who died in August of this year. Colville's paper went bankrupt so that the Rev. James Thomson's appeal to Lord Sidmouth for financial support must have been unsuccessful.

'The Courier' was revived in the interests of the Tory party in 1823 and was purchased by a woollen merchant and shipowner, Mr William Thomson in 1866. 'The Dundee Advertiser' came into the ownership of the Leng family until the two papers merged in 1926 to become the present 'Dundee Courier and Advertiser.'

CHAPTER TEN

The Dundee Meeting, Magdalen Yard Green, 10th Nov. 1819

ON THE 16th of August 1819 while George Kinloch was spending the time quietly with his family by the seaside at Carnoustie watching his children bathing, all 'doukin terribly,' one of the most discreditable incidents in England's social history took place in St. Peter's Square in Manchester. Here, when many thousands of working class people had assembled to hear a speech of protest from Henry Hunt about their misfortunes, the Magistrates of the City who had taken no action to prevent the meeting being held but had assembled a large military force to maintain order, decided, as soon as the speaker arrived on the scene that it was an unlawful assembly and ordered the troops to disperse the crowd. The Manchester Yeomanry charged in with sharpened sabres and so the massacre of Peterloo took place. This was the climax of many attempts of self-expression at public meetings throughout the country by poverty stricken people who wanted to make their voices heard but which led only to more repressive measures and a feeling of frustration by those with liberal ideas.

The effect which the affair had on George Kinloch was to convert him from being a theoretic, touch-line supporter of reform into a more seriously dedicated man, determined to devote his life to the cause of the people. It was not so much the conduct of the Yeomanry with their sharpened sabres which upset him, as the attitude of those in authority to the affair and this brought home to him that the system of Government and particularly of the Home Department under Lord Sidmouth was rotten.

Lord Sidmouth was to George Kinloch like a red rag to a bull. The Home Secretary depended for the loyalty of his representatives such as Lords Lieutenant, Magistrates and Justices of the Peace on the patronage system by rewarding those who supported him, and dismissing those who offended him. The patronage system and the system of accepting reports to the Home Department by paid informers were features of Government which George Kinloch particularly disliked. In accordance with the way patronage worked, one of the four Magistrates who had been responsible for the action of the military and who was an Anglican Clergyman was rewarded for his zeal by being promoted to the valuable living of Rochdale with a stipend of £1750 per annum and, on the other side of the picture, the Earl of Fitzwilliam, who was Lord Lieutenant of the West Riding of Yorkshire and who spoke out strongly against the massacre was dismissed from office. Criticism of authority could not be accepted and, to make this clear, Lord Sidmouth persuaded the Prince Regent to send a congratulatory letter to the Lord Lieutenant of Lancashire saying—

His Royal Highness requests you to express to the Magistrates of the County his satisfaction from the prompt, decisive, and efficient measures taken for the preservation of the public tranquility.

After this official blessing, there could be no official enquiry and the matter must be considered to be closed.

George Kinloch was not alone in being horrified by what had taken place and his friend Sir Francis Burdett said in a speech to his constitutents in Westminster [1]—

This then is the proof of our standing in need of Reform. What — Kill men, unarmed and unresisting and Gracious God women too, disfigured, maimed, cut down and trampled on by dragoons? Is this England? Is this a Christian land? Will the Gentlemen of England support or wink at such proceedings?

However 'wink at the proceedings' or 'couldn't care less' was exactly the attitude of most of the Gentlemen of England

and Scotland too. In Edinburgh, Sir Walter Scott, expressed the opinion of his fellow Tories by declaring 'The Yeomanry had behaved well, upsetting the most immense crowd that ever was seen and, despite the lies in the newspapers, acting without needless violence.'

In spite of the warning of Manchester that vigorous measures might be expected to suppress any unlawful assemblies, the demand for public meetings continued. These were attended by large crowds all over the country. In Scotland there were protest meetings in Paisley and Glasgow and, at the beginning of October, a group of weavers approached Provost Anderson of Dundee to call a meeting there. The Provost refused to do so, but replied to the organisers that there would be no objection from the Magistrates provided that it was properly sponsored.

The organising committee felt that they must have a man of standing to act as Chairman, and they immediately ran into difficulties over finding the right man, as Mr Maule, the M.P. for the County said that it would be presumptious for him to act as he was not an inhabitant of Dundee and every important person in Dundee who was approached made some sort of excuse. In fact no one, who had a position to maintain, wanted to have anything to do with popular meetings of this kind. Alexander Smart, one of the Committee, suggested that they might try Mr Kinloch of Kinloch who was known to be a Radical, and in consequence he went out to Meigle and called at Kinloch House with a letter asking him if he would agree to preside. George Kinloch was not at home but, when he returned, he found the letter waiting for him.

To accept such a responsibility at this time was a decision which could not be taken lightly. The political situation was much more explosive than two years earlier when he had addressed a similar meeting. Sir Walter Scott[2] writing about that meeting some years later, said—

It seems to have escaped Mr. Kinloch that the conduct of a man who places a lighted coal in the middle of combustibles and upon the floor, is a little different from that of one who places the same quantity of burning fuel in a fire grate.

George Kinloch knew full well that the organisers and

speakers at the Manchester Meeting had all been arrested and were still waiting for trial. It was an unenviable job but he felt himself to be in a strong position, being a man whom everyone in Dundee knew and trusted, and being a Justice of the Peace, a Harbour Commissioner, and a Landowner, it seemed hardly likely that the Magistrates would object to him. In any case he made up his mind that it was his duty to give a lead and he therefore accepted the invitation.

It was decided to hold the meeting on the afternoon of Wednesday 16th November and advertisement was made in the press and on public notice boards. One of the original advertisements which hangs in the Dundee Museum is illustrated in plate 4. This states that the business of the meeting is in general to consider the present state of the country, to suggest means to leviate the distress of the working classes and also to express sentiments about the cowardly attack made on the people of Manchester. The usual place for such meetings was Magdalen's Yard Green, an open grassy slope leading down to the River Tay from houses at the West end of the town. To-day, from the photograph on plate 5 it seems to be hallowed ground where no football, golf or even kite-flying is allowed but, in 1819 it was a convenient place for a public meeting, being only a short walk from the centre of the town and on sloping ground, where the speaker could at least be seen if he could not be heard.

George Kinloch was particularly anxious to see that everything was conducted peaceably and quietly and he therefore asked the editor of the 'Advertiser' to put a paragraph in the paper telling everyone how important this was and asking the groups and parties who planned to attend not to bring flags or banners. He knew that flags and banners had often led to trouble at other meetings, with clashing of rival factions who tried to capture and pull down one another's banners.

The Committee, not being well educated men, had asked George Kinloch to frame the resolutions which would be put to the meeting for adoption. He therefore prepared these at home and came into Dundee on the evening of the 9th to discuss them with the Committee and arrange the last minute details of the meeting. He agreed later that these resolutions, which were twenty-one in number, had been made 'as strong as possible provided that they could be reasonably considered legal.' Being over-sure of himself at this time, and thinking that he was in a privileged position, he over-stepped the bounds of discretion and resolutions such as No. 10 where he said — 'We are of opinion that, in preventing the voice of the people from reaching the Throne, the said Lord Sidmouth has been guilty of the highest species of treason, namely treason against the people and that dismissal from the Office which he so unworthily fills would be far too lenient a punishment for him,' was going a bit too far. It may have been the Resolutions which decided the Authorities to take action against him.

The Dundee Bailies, although they were alarmed and disliked the idea of the Meeting intensely, took a much more sane course of action than the Magistrates of Manchester had done. They recruited a number of Special Constables for the day but they themselves and their Constables remained in the Town Hall where they were well away from the Meeting on the Green. They rightly believed that Mr Kinloch would conduct the Meeting peacefully enough and that their best course was not to become involved. The Sheriff of Forfar — Sheriff L'Amy — took the same view. He decided to stay at Forfar and he asked the Military Commander to confine the troops to barracks as he was wise enough to realise that, if the Meeting was not threatened, it would pass off quietly.

On the morning of the Meeting, there was not much activity until about mid-day. Soon after this, several large bodies of workmen from the factories arrived and were described as 'in martial array,' linked arm in arm, marching to the sound of a scanty supply of music and unfurling a few flags.' These flags and banners, contrary to instructions, carried slogans such as 'We only want our rights in a peaceable and constitutional manner.' 'For the sufferers at Manchester.' 'The voice of the People is irresistible.' Other people, presumably trying to avoid the ban against flags and banners, carried emblems such as a pole from which dangled a broken tea-kettle and two broken tea-pots, and from another pole was hung a gill-stoup, fragments of wine glasses, tobacco pipes and snuff-boxes which were supposed to indicate luxuries which poor people could no longer enjoy. A party of sailors, about one hundred strong carried the figure of a ship's hulk, upside down, representing the ruined state of the shipping trade. Fortunately there was no anti-Radical element present, or at least they kept quiet, so that the banners and emblems did not have any bad effect, or incite any counter demonstration.

The Committee, with representatives from Arbroath, Cupar and other towns were dressed in 'decent mourning,' and they arrived about half past twelve and stood up on the Hustings. By this time about 10,000 people had collected on the Green. One of the Committee then introduced Mr Kinloch of Kinloch as being one of the ablest and most public-spirited of our country Gentlemen, and as soon as the applause subsided, George Kinloch began his speech by explaining how he came to be the Chairman and again emphasising the need for orderly behaviour.

You have this day placed me in a situation which, however honourable, I would not have accepted of, had I not been satisfied from long observation, of your orderly and peaceable behaviour and your respect for the laws of your country. Those laws have lately, in another part of the Kingdom, been violated, not by the people, not by those who are described as the 'lower orders', as if all men were not equal in the sight of God, but by those very individuals who have been appointed to enforce the laws and who consequently should have been the last to violate them.

Prominent among the lawless planners of the atrocious murders which have lately been committed stands the name of a Clergyman — it would be an abuse of terms to call him Reverend, who showed how little he chose to practise the maxim of his Divine Master and sorry I am to say, that in that part of the Kingdom, there are too many of his Profession, who, like him, prefer obeying the orders of an earthly master, to those of Him who has said that his Kingdom is not of this world. In Scotland, thank God, we have few instances of those busy meddling priests, who thrust themselves into every man's concerns, who dabble in the muddy pool of local politics, and who, to attain their dirty ends, don't mind using a sufficient quantity of calumny and misrepresentation.

Now, my friends, let us convince those who have for so long calumniated the working classes that you can behave more correctly than some of those who affect to look down upon you. I therefore trust that, when the business of the day is over, you will disperse peaceably and retire quietly to your homes. I am anxious to impress this most strongly upon you because nothing would delight your enemies so much as to say that you have been guilty of a riot. There may be amongst you wolves in Sheep's clothing. We know that Lord Sidmouth has at least one voluntary 'spy' in your good town, and there are probably more of these 'honourable' men. But heed them not. If any man attempts to lead you into acts of violence, you may set him down as your worst enemy and, as such, you will avoid him.

Having thus put you on your guard, I shall proceed to state the business for which we are now assembled, and also how I, who am not a resident in your town, come to take a prominent part in the proceedings of this day. You all know that your Magistreates were first applied to and that they refused to sanction this meeting by their presence. The Members for the Borough and for the County were next applied to, and that they likewise declined. Your Committee then turned their eyes towards me and, as I shall never shrink from occupying any post in which I think I can be of service to the cause of the people, I instantly wrote to them that I would attend in any capacity they thought fit.

Having been born in this town, and having daily communications with it, being one of your Harbour Commissioners and deeply interested in all your other improvements, I do not think that I can justly be accused of presumption in obeying your call. My motives may be misrepresented and, as has been the case before, I shall probably furnish a topic of abuse to the old women of both sexes. I shall probably be called an ambitious demagogue, and other hard names. Let it be so but, neither hard names nor hard usage shall ever make me shrink from doing my utmost to

137

rescue my country from the state of vassalage and ruin into which a contemptible Ministry are doing all they can to plunge it.

I have now to point out to you what appear to me to be the causes of that continued and complicated distress which threatens to overwhelm us. Few of you are old enough to remember the American War. That was a war waged against liberty but, God be praised, it was unsuccessful. The addition to the National Debt, by that War, was upwards of One hundred and ten Million Pounds. Well this was a trifle compared to the addition made to the Debt by Pitt's glorious wars, for the permanent addition to the debt was upwards of seven hundred millions. The sum which is taken from us to pay the interest on this infernal debt is upwards of Forty Millions annually. This is the cause of our distress. This is the mill-stone which weighs us to the ground.

Here he continued by calculating the National Debt per head of population which is unimportant to the tenor of the Speech.

Away then with all the nonsense of Edmund Burke, about taxes returning to us like the dews of Heaven. The dews of Heaven do indeed return to us to nourish our crops, and the sun shines forth to ripen them, but the taxes are like the pestiferous vapours from a marsh, sent to prevent us from enjoying the bountiful gifts of Providence.

Having thus endeavoured to show that our distress arises from excessive taxation, if I am right, it follows that distress cannot be got rid of until the amount of taxation be greatly reduced. How this is to be done, is a matter requiring serious considerations; one thing we are certain of that, as long as the House of Commons is constituted as at present, no effectual remedy will be either proposed or applied by them.

I shall not occupy your time by telling you what you already know, that the House of Commons does not represent the people of these Kingdoms. This is unfortunately as notorious as the sun at noon-day. Had the people really been represented in the House of Commons, would these foolish and unnecessary wars have been carried on? Would the wealth of this country have been squandered as it has been, in the support of chuckle-headed Legitimacy and for the restoration of that devil Ferdinand, the Pope, the Jesuits, and the Inquisition? No. If the people had really been represented, we would not have quarrelled with the French because they chose to shake off the fetters of priests and despots with which they had been bound for ages: No. If the people had been represented, free ourselves, we would have rejoiced to see the spirit of free-dom spreading far and wide, instead of wasting all our means in a vain attempt to arrest the progress of the human intellect, and to throw back the world into the feudal bondage and barbarism of the dark ages.

In short, the whole of our misfortune as a nation, the whole of our misery, the whole of our distress, can be clearly traced to the circumstances of the people being deprived of their share of the British Constitution, by not having a voice in the election of persons to represent them in the House of Commons. As to the extent of that Reform, there are various opinions. For my own part, after the most mature consideration, I am decidedly an advocate for a 'Radical Reform', on the base of first Annual Elections, secondly Universal Suffrage, and thirdly, Political Voting by Ballot.

First, as to annual Elections, a year is surely long enough period to put uncontrolled confidence in any man. If he has satisfied you in the discharge of his trust, you will re-elect him: If you have no longer confidence in him you will dismiss him.

Second, as to Universal Suffrage, seeing that all men are equal in the sight of their Creator, I cannot understand why one man should have a vote and another should not have one. Is not the life, the family, the property of the poor man as dear to him as the life, the family and the property of the rich man is to him? Do we not all contribute more or less, according to our means, to the needs of the State? Are we not all liable to be called upon at any moment to risk our lives for its defence? Why then should one man have a vote and another not, I confess I cannot comprehend.

Thirdly, as to election by ballot, I look upon it as absolutely necessary to neutralise the influence which would otherwise be exercised by unprincipled persons upon those whom they employ.

There are at present in this country three Political Parties — the Tories, the Whigs, and the People. As to there being a fourth party, desirous of a revolution, I know of none. If such a party does exist, their numbers must be very small indeed. We want no Revolution; on the contrary, we want a Reform to prevent a revolution. We want nothing but what is contained within the British Constitution, freed, indeed, from those abominable corruptions which have nearly converted it into a code of despotism and us into a set of slaves. As to the first of these parties, the Tories, they at least employ no disguise. They tell you they want no Reform, because the present is the best possible system — and so it is for them. As to the Whigs, they are for a Reform but then softly, it must be temperate, a moderate Reform. As none of them has ever given us the plan of their moderate Reform, it is impossible to judge of it, but this we can judge of that the moment you quit the straightforward path of universal suffrage, you plunge into an ocean of doubts and difficulties to which there is no end. I believe that of the two factions the Whigs are the most to be dreaded in so far as a pretended friend is worse than an avowed enemy.

But while they content themselves with railing at us, the venerable Cartwright, whom I am proud to call my friend, has, in this little book which I hold in my hand, shown that there is nothing either impracticable or absurd in what we ask. It is entitled 'A Bill of Rights and Liberties,' and shows not only practicability but the amazing facility with which the Elections for the whole Kingdom could be begun and finished in one or two days at most. This little book, my friends, has never been answered for the best of all reasons because it is, in fact, unanswerable; and withall so plain that he who runs may read.

We now come to a part of the proceedings on which I am almost afraid to trust myself to speak. I mean the late,

140

atrocious proceedings at Manchester. There, our defenceless countrymen, while peacefully and lawfully assembled, as we now are, were, without warning, attacked by a band of ruffians, sword in hand, their swords sharpened for the occasion, and hacked and hewn down without mercy. Neither age nor sex was spared. Nay, the most interesting of all Nature's works, woman with a child at her breast, was wounded and struck down by one of these brave yeomen. In reading of these atrocities, we cannot help exclaiming with the poet:

> *'Can such things be,*
> *And overcome us like a summer's cloud*
> *without our special wonder?'*

With a refinement in cruelty, worthy of the planners of this horrible massacre, every avenue by which the people attempted to escape was closed by a hedge of bayonets, pointed at them by beings, they could not be soldiers, who drove them back, to be cut and slashed at by the merciless yeomanry. Could these fellows be Britons? Impossible, for a Briton and a brave man have hitherto been synonymous terms, and none but the basest of cowards would attack an assembly of unarmed men, women, and children.

But, cruel and infamous as their conduct has been, it is nothing compared to the cool and deliberate villany of those who set them on. If these Reverend and worshipful monsters are not dragged from their hiding places, if they are not put upon their trials for the murder of their fellow citizens, then, there is neither law nor justice in England; and the time is near when we must either bow our necks to a military despotism, or be prepared to rise like men in defence of our liberties.

These gallant Manchester Yeomen have imbued their hands in the blood of their fellow citizens, and they may now exclaim like Lady MacBeth:—

> *'Out damned spot'*

or add in the words of her conscience stricken Lord

> *'Will great Neptune's Ocean wash this blood*
> *Clean from our hands? No, these our hands will*
> *rather*

> *The multitudinous seas incarnadine,*
> *Making the green one red.'*

Their offence is rank indeed

> *'It smells to Heaven,*
> *It hath the primal oldest curse upon it*
> *A brother's murder.'*

One more thing before I conclude. Allow me to point out to you that, although we were able to obtain our wished for Reform, it would not at once remove all our distresses. No, our wounds are too deep to be healed in so short a time, but the effects of it would begin to be felt immediately. Economy would pervade every department of the State, the Taxes would be diminished, the absurd restrictions with which Commerce is fettered would be done away with. Confidence between the People and their Rulers would be restored, Hope would spring triumphant on exalting wing, and Britain would once more smile, a land of liberty and peace.

The Speech was enthusiastically received and hailed with cheering throughout.

The prepared Resolutions were then read out, submitted and approved and at half past one a vote of thanks was accorded to Mr Kinloch. He then stepped forward again, acknowledged the thanks and promised that he would always be at his post when the country required a defender or the people a friend and finished by exclaiming — 'But where are all your City Respectables to-day? Why have they not come forward to assist you on this important occasion?' The Meeting ended with a final appeal to everyone to disperse quietly and orderly so that their enemies might have no cause to revile them and the large crowd immediately started to move away so that, within ten minutes, there was no vestige of the Meeting except the hustings and a few people wandering around discussing the Speech.

The collection which had been taken for the Manchester Sufferers and which consisted mainly of coppers which the poor people of Dundee could ill afford, produced £16 and George Kinloch generously added £10 himself.

In the evening he went to the Town Hall where the

Magistrates had been sitting all day in case of trouble, and spent rather a long time talking things over with them. A crowd had seen him go in and the rumour got about that he was being held in confinement so that shouting started outside and it was only when he showed himself at a window and explained to the people that he was under no constraint that they agreed to disperse. This was the only incident which could be described as giving any trouble. The newspaper report said that by midnight the town was hushed into a state of still and dark security which might have even beguiled to slumber the wakeful vigilance of my Lord Sidmouth. This, as will be seen, was wishful thinking on the part of the Editor.

George Kinloch returned to Meigle next day well pleased with the success of the meeting and his own performance. His daughter Margaret who wrote poetry and admired all her father's most eloquent phrases probably complimented him on his quotations from Shakespeare and liked his reference to taxes being 'like the pestiferous vapours from a marsh sent to prevent us from enjoying the bountiful gifts of Providence.' His own stock expression to the family in commenting on his own speeches was to say — 'I think it will have good effect,' but the 'effect' which this speech was to have was very different from what he expected and the consequences will be described in the following chapter.

[1] This quotation of a speech by Sir Francis Burdett is taken from the book 'Peterloo' by Douglas Read.

[2] Sir Walter Scott's Journal.

CHAPTER ELEVEN

'The Imaginary Revolution'

THE FIRST REACTION to the Speech was to produce a number of letters addressed to the Editor of the Dundee Newspaper. The text of the Speech had appeared word for word in the paper and the report described the meeting very fully. Most of the letters to the Editor did not comment on the main theme of the speech but picked out details such as some of George Kinloch's economic theories with which one correspondent disagreed and particularly how the break-down of the National Debt to head of population had been calculated. These letters appeared under pen-names such as 'A Friend of my Country,' 'Calculator,' and 'A Weaver,' but 'The Weaver' who went off at a tangent about protection for the Linen Trade, did not keep to the point.

George Kinloch replied patiently, politely and in great detail to all the letters, writing, as usual, under his own name and from his own home address, and there were some interesting points which he made in this correspondence in elaboration of what he had said in his speech.

First on the subject of Manchester he wrote — 'Our Friend is angry with me for saying that the swords of the Manchester Yeomanry were sharpened for the occasion. I assert it, on the evidence of the Coroner of Oldham, where the journeyman cutler who sharpened the swords proved that it was done only a short time before the fatal 16th. August. I quote from "The Statesman Newspaper" which, being a Radical one, dared to insert the whole evidence.' The 'Friend of his Country' had also disputed the implication by George Kinloch that it would please the Authorities if the Radicals became involved in disturbances which could be regarded as riots and he replied to this — 'This is entirely a matter of opinion but I still remain firmly convinced that nothing would give some of our humane rulers so much pleasure as a good thumping riot on the part of the Reformers.' Both of these replies indicate that he sincerely believed that the Manchester Massacre had been premeditated.

Secondly 'The Friend' had asked whether he really meant that all men should have a vote and to this he replied — 'I certainly do say this and I shall continue to say so until some argument is adduced to show why and where a line of distinction is to be drawn between those who are to have a vote and those who are not to have one. I am no advocate for the Quixotic doctrine of perfect equality — a thing which never has been and never can be. Industry and genius, wealth and rank will always have their influence while the human mind continues formed as at present.' This explanation is interesting in showing that he did not believe in the equality of man but only in equality of opportunity.

'The Friend' also criticised the vulgarity of George Kinloch's language, and to this he replied: 'I plead guilty. I have paid more attention to "language" than possibly our friend may be inclined to give me credit for. It may be bad taste in me but I seldom hesitate to use the expression which I think will best convey my meaning although it should not be the most polished which our language affords. But still, I must take the liberty to say that, either in writing or speaking, I shall continue to use such phrases as appear to me best calculated to convey my meaning without offence to whom they are addressed. Had our friend been present at the meeting, I rather think that he would have found that those very expressions which he censures told most. For instance, I called an English Judge "thick-skulled," because he had the folly to say that taxes were beneficial to those who paid them. As to "the old women of both sexes" were our friend an inhabitant of Dundee, he would have known to what I allude. As to "the humane Sidmouth" it is the designation by which he is generally known, whether justly or not, I do not pretend to say.'

Unknown to George Kinloch, however, while this newspaper correspondence was proceeding in a light hearted manner, machinery had been set in motion from some source or other, to see that he would not be in a position to give any further trouble to the authorities. Whether the Rev. James Thomson of Dundee was the evil genius operating against him or whether some other informer had brought the text of the speech to the notice of the authorities is not known, but, the wheels of the Law had been set in motion to bring a criminal charge against him. It seems probable that the initiative came from London by a directive to the Lord Advocate in Edinburgh to take the necessary action.[1]

The first news of what had been going on behind the scene came to him on the 22nd of November when a most unwelcome and unexpected visitor arrived at Kinloch House in the person of William Hutchison, the Procurator Fiscal for the County of Forfar. George Kinloch was most probably sitting in his business room at the back of the house, preparing further replies to newspaper correspondents or writing up his farm accounts after the Martinmas term, when this Mr Hutchison was announced. The Fiscal had brought with him an ominous and formidable document which was, in short, a Warrant for his arrest. The Warrant, addressed to Messengers at Arms and other Officers of the Law, instructed them to search for and apprehend the persons of George Kinloch Esquire, Robert Stephen Rintoul of Dundee the Printer, and James Saunders, Writer in Dundee, the publisher and vendor of the newspaper called the Dundee, Perth and Cupar Advertiser, all being charged as being guilty actors or actor, art and part of the crime of Sedition and to bring them before the Sheriff for examination. The Warrant was signed by Sheriff L'Amy of Forfar with the concurrence of Sheriff Husband of Perth and gave the Fiscal instructions to commit the said George Kinloch to the Tolbooth of Dundee until liberated in due course of law.

Mrs Kinloch must have been out of the house on some errand or other, perhaps visiting Arthurstone or Balhary, so that George Kinloch went away with the Procurator Fiscal without saying a word to anyone and left a message for his wife that he had gone to Dundee with Mr Hutchison. At this stage it looks

146

as if he had been more insulted than alarmed and his reaction was to try to make sure that neither the servants nor the neighbours got to know about this indignity. What he and the Procurator Fiscal, who had been his good friend up to this time, talked about in the carriage on the way to Dundee is not recorded but perhaps Mr Hutchison managed to convince him that it was a serious charge which could not be brushed off lightly.

On the following morning, after the first examination by the Sheriff, he wrote to Mrs Kinloch in the hope that it would set her mind at ease. Luckily she was used to his erratic behaviour and would not be so much alarmed as most wives.

> Dundee, 23rd. November,
> 1819.

My Dear Helen,

You would be surprised yesterday to find me flown and in company with the Procurator Fiscal too.

Sheriff L'Amy is upon his high horse and appearing to make things appear *very terrible*. I was examined first as to the Meeting, Resolutions etc. and dismissed at 4 o'clock, when I went and dined at Blairs. Hutchison tells me he does not think I shall get away tonight yet so I write this, lest you might conclude that I was *shopped*.

Sedition is the crime of which I am accused by the *Bigwigs*, so I suppose I shall be held to bail till their reverences take time to consider what they are to do with me and I have no doubt I shall be made to swell the *Doctor's Green Bag*. However, they may do their worst. I fear them not.

If a letter comes from John to me, you will, of course, open it.

> Always most sincerely yours,
> George Kinloch.

P.S. I wish Angus or John could bring in the Gig tomorrow morning to Donaldsons, the coachmaker, before I leave this.

'The Doctor's Green Bag' which he was made to swell was, in other words, Lord Sidmouth's Dispatch Case. Lord Sidmouth was nicknamed the Doctor and his green bag contained correspondence about all the 'disturbances' real and imaginary.

George Kinloch made the examination before Sheriff L'Amy

as easy as possible for all concerned. He denied nothing of the wording of his Speech and accepted the entire blame for this and responsibility for the Resolutions. He must have felt that, as a Justice of the Peace, he was the senior officer concerned and so must accept responsibility. In any case, he was in a much stronger position than was either Mr Rintoul or Mr Saunders, having many friends and county connections to support him. In fact he rather resented the fact that the charge included the names of Rintoul or Saunders who were responsible only for publishing reports of his Speech, as the subject and wording of his address was his own responsibility. He felt proud and confident of the truth of what he had said and did not want anything withdrawn from its wording. The only facts that he wished to make clear were that the meeting had been conducted in an orderly manner, that there was no disturbance of the peace of any kind, that no revolutionary society or political club was involved, that the organising committee was composed of a few simple people who had come to him to ask him to act as Preses and that therefore the initiation of the meeting had not come from him. The organising Committee in their evidence to the Sheriff did their best to support him in this and said that the idea of the Meeting had been theirs and that after failing to get the Provost and the Member of Parliament and Mr Guthrie Jr. and Mr Patullo of Langhaugh to preside they had approached Mr Kinloch as a last hope. They said that Mr Kinloch had been most meticulous in making sure that the Meeting was conducted in an orderly manner and had said that, if there was any trouble, he would not be inactive as a Justice of the Peace in suppressing it.

This examination before the Sheriff took two days to complete so that the warrant was extended for his apprehension but, as he went out to dine with Mr Blair and family at night, it does not seem likely that he was forced to endure the indignity of a night in the Tolbooth. In any case, Angus or John arrived with the gig on the 24th and, after bail had been arranged, he was allowed to return home to Meigle. Sheriff L'Amy told him that the matter was now out of his hands, that he had been instructed to investigate and return the papers to the Lord Advocate and that, therefore, the decision about whether any further action was to be taken would rest with Edinburgh.

George Kinloch began to see that the situation was distinctly critical. He lost no time in setting his affairs in order at home as far as possible; he collected money due to him at the Martinmas term day and paid it into his farm account at the Dundee New Bank, and some other private monies were paid into his private account with the Coupar-Angus Branch of the Perth bank.

Five days after his return from the Sheriff's examination, he wrote his last letter on the subject of his speech to the newspaper which was again a long reply to 'A Friend of my Country,' and this letter ended with the following significant paragraph—

But it would be a waste of words to attempt to argue with such an alarmist and I therefore take my leave of him and of your readers fervently hoping that the dark clouds which at present lour on our political horizon may be dispersed without a storm and be followed by the calm, bright sunshine of returning happiness and prosperity.

G. Kinloch. 29th. Novr. 1819.

'The Friend of my Country' had the last word in this correspondence with a letter on the 10th December and, in it, it is pleasant to see that he appreciated George Kinloch's sense of humour.

Sir,

Your reply to the remarks which I made on your speech does you credit, if not for the soundness of your political views, at least for the temper and good humour with which it is written. Your true friends will be pleased that I have given you an opportunity of showing that, although on the hustings you can speak like a Radical, at Kinloch you can write like a gentleman.

'A Friend of my Country'.

By this time the tide of events was running very strongly against him. During the fortnight between 24th November and 6th December when the Lord Advocate's decision on his case became known to him, a crisis had arisen in national affairs which made the meeting in Dundee appear to the authorities in London to be a matter of more than ordinary concern. The matter which gave reason for this alarm was the sudden

149

enthusiasm for public meetings, in the manufacturing districts of the country, which were being attended by large crowds. The people attending these meetings listened to speeches and then adopted resolutions on all kinds of subjects but the general purport was to express indignation over the Manchester Massacre and exasperation about the poverty of the poor. Although they were usually free from any rowdyism, the authorities became convinced that there must be some sinister purpose to explain the spontaneity of the meetings and that they must be stopped.

Typical of such meetings was one held at Kilmarnock on the 20th November which was attended by some twenty thousand people, at which one of the resolutions was — 'A vote of thanks to G. Kinloch Esq., of Kinloch for the admirable manner in which he conducted the Reform Meeting in Dundee and for being the First Gentleman that had espoused the cause of Radical Reform at this time in Scotland.' Such a vote of thanks from Kilmarnock might have justified suspicion that George Kinloch was an acknowledged leader of public opinion and was not therefore one that he would relish at that particular moment.

The Government had become so alarmed that Parliament was recalled on the 23rd of November and the Speech from the Throne delivered by the Prince Regent said—

My Lords and Gentlemen,

I regret to have been under the necessity of calling you together at this period of year, but the seditious practices so long prevalent in some parts of the manufacturing districts of the country have been continued with increased activity since you were last assembled in Parliament. They have led to proceedings incompatible with the public tranquility and with the peaceful habits of the industrious classes of the community so that a spirit is now manifested utterly hostile to the constitution of the Kingdom and aiming not only at the change of these Institutions which have hitherto constituted the pride and security of this country, but at the subversion of the rights of property and of all order in society. I feel it to be my indispensable duty to press on your immediate attention the consideration of such measures as may be requisite for the counteraction and

150

suppression of a system which, if not effectually checked, must bring confusion and ruin on the nation.

This Speech from the Throne had the familiar sound of alarm of Lord Sidmouth's Home Department but, as few Members of either Houses of Parliament lived in or cared to visit the manufacturing districts, they were easily convinced about the country being in a state bordering on revolution. Earl Grey was one of the few speakers in the House of Lords debate on the Speech from the Throne who spoke in favour of Reform and who said that he saw no signs of revolutionary danger but his speech was received in stony silence.

The Lord Advocate was asked to come to London and explain the situation in Scotland, and he spoke as follows in support of 'The Seditious Meetings Bill' on Thursday the 9th of December—

The Headquarters of the Reformers is the large city of Glasgow, which yields to none in the Island, except the Metropolis.

There is much distress among the Manufacturers, but the discontent is not confined to the distressed and those who are most distressed bear their suffering without a murmur. The reduction of the Army, the Scots part of which was chiefly raised in Glasgow, added to the distress. The progress of disaffection in Scotland has been most rapid. For six months after the last session the local authorities had no idea of it's existence, yet in six weeks more it has spread through Lanark, Renfrew, part of Ayrshire, Dumbartonshire, and Stirlingshire and reached the County of Fife and Forfar, where one of the meetings was headed by a gentleman of property, one of His Majesty's Justices of the Peace. (Hear, Hear).

Even the Highlanders are not exempt from infection and advantage has been taken of the discontent exerted by the changes effected by landholders in the disposition of their property to promote an un-natural union between the miserable Radical Reformers and the brave gallant, loyal Highlanders.

Another circumstance, which appears very alarming, is the great quiet and order which has for some time

151

pervaded public meetings of the Reformers in Scotland. At present, contrary to the nature of Scotsmen, 30,000 or 40,000 individuals will stand quietly for hours to hear the speeches of itinerant orators employed to corrupt them, and then disperse in the greatest order. This appears to me to denote some great but secret purpose on the part of the people. Indeed I am convinced that revolution and a division of property, whether belonging to friends or foes, is the object in view.

The Lord Advocate continued by saying that they had not stood with their arms folded but had armed and bade defiance to the monster by which the country was assailed. His final words were that he trusted that the discussions and the provisions of Parliament would open the eyes of the misled; and, he was persuaded, that as soon as they (the orators) manifested a sense of their error, they would experience the utmost indulgence and liberality.

This speech was received with loud cheering. Although George Kinloch was not actually mentioned by name, it described him clearly as the gentleman of property and Justice of the Peace in Forfar who was creating trouble and so was included under the heading of itinerant orators who were employed to corrupt the people. It was nevertheless distinctly prejudicial to the case of a man who had been indicted to appear in the Criminal Court in Edinburgh within a fortnight on the charge of Sedition. It may have been in order to avoid any loophole in the charge against him that the Lord Advocate made it clear that, if meetings were held in a quiet and orderly manner, this must be considered highly suspicious of some great but secret purpose, and, on the other hand, if they were riotous, the necessary action would be taken against riotous behaviour. It was 'Heads I win, tails you lose.'

The action taken to justify the Lord Advocate's assertion that they were not standing by 'with arms folded' was to enrol Volunteer Regiments to support the regular troops. The Royal Edinburgh volunteers took over guard duties in Edinburgh Castle so that the regular garrison could be spared and were used, according to a letter of thanks from Lord Sidmouth for 'repressing the Insurrectionary Spirit which betrayed itself in the Western part of the country.' The Midlothian Yeomanry and the Linlithgow Yeomanry were stationed in the vicinity of Glasgow and the East Lothian Yeomanry were used to defend Edinburgh.

According to Sir Walter Scott's letter to a nephew — 'the mob pelted the Yeomanry when they marched for the West and shewd a very wicked spirit. However nothing happened except that between Glasgow and Paisley a picket of hussars was so seriously pelted with stones that the corporal leapt his horse over a high wall, cut down one man and cut the hand off another who is since died. The corporal who belonged to the 10 Hussars has been tried and honourably acquitted. This is a lesson but the rascals will not stop till they get a worse.' Nothing happened!

Glasgow and Lanarkshire were considered to be the danger spots but Sir Archibald Hamilton who had followed the Lord Advocate in the Debate in Parliament and who came from Lanarkshire denied the extent of the disturbance. He said 'The cause of the discontent is distress and while that cause continues, the effect must also continue. If Ministers had any plan by which they could relieve the distress of the poor, they might bring it forward.' But Ministers had no such plan. The provisions on which the Lord Advocate trusted to restore order were not provisions for the poor, but the more repressive measures known as 'The Six Acts.'

An awe-inspiring picture of a country bordering on revolution was given by the reports of County Meetings held under the chairmanship of Lords Lieutenant at which fulsom Loyal Addresses were made to the Prince Regent and printed in the national newspapers.

These Loyal Addresses from the Noblemen and Gentry of every County singled out the Radical Reformers as the villains of the Peace. To quote from the freeholders of the County of Dumfries who said: 'We have viewed with feelings of horror and indignation the increasing activity with which the destruction of this country has lately been attempted by profligate and design-ing men who, versed in the arts of revolution, have concealed their infamous projects under the specious but shallow pretence of reform.' All county gentlemen seemed to be agreed about 'factious demagogues instilling false and pernicious doctrines,' but in many cases their findings were qualified by saying that 'nothing like this exists in this part of the country.'

The show of military force in the Western part of Scotland may have prevented mass meetings which could have led to trouble, but the Duke of Hamilton who lived in the industrial part of the country did not accept the panic rumours of approaching revolution. He made his position clear by publishing in the 'Edinburgh Courant' a copy of a letter which he had written with a donation to the Committee in charge of the Fund for the Sufferers in Manchester. In this letter he said that it appeared to him that the people of Manchester had been interrupted in a mode and with a precipitation and violence that awakened the most alarming reflections as he saw no reason why people should not meet together to consider their grievances.

The Duke of Hamilton was nearer to the way of thinking of George Kinloch who had said in his speech in Dundee—

As to there being a fourth party, desirous of revolution, I know of none. If such a party does exist, their numbers must be very small indeed. We want no revolution. On the contrary, we want Reform to prevent revolution.

Lord Sidmouth, on the other hand, did not want Reform and he was determined to use the accepted methods of repression and punishment to see that there was no revolution.

It was in this explosive situation, of the recall of Parliament, of the Lord Advocate's Speech to the effect that peaceful meetings were as dangerous as riotous meetings, of irregular military units being embodied and marched about Scotland to deal with illusory disturbances, and declarations by County Noblemen that the Radicals were leading the country into anarchy that George Kinloch had to prepare for his trial as described in the following chapter.

---

[1] The fact that George Kinloch's pardon required the consent of the Home Secretary and that The Lord Advocate could not grant it, indicates that the charge against him had been initiated from London.

CHAPTER TWELVE

Preparation for Trial

G EORGE KINLOCH, being a man who lived a well organised,
self-disciplined life was not one to panic in an emergency. In
fact, the emergency which had now, suddenly, sprung upon
him brought out the best qualities in his character and he
took charge of the situation in his usual practical, business-like
manner, without much help from friends or professional
advisers.

On Monday, the 6th of December, a copy of the Indictment,
at the instance of the Lord Advocate, Sir William Rae Baronet
of St. Catherine's was handed to him by a Messenger at Arms
from Perth who had come out to Kinloch House with two
witnesses to prove that the Notice had been duly served.

This Indictment summoned, warned and charged him to
compear before the Lord Justice General, Lord Justice Clerk,
and Lords Commissioners of Justiciary in a Court of Justiciary
to be holden by them within the Criminal Court House of
Edinburgh upon the 22nd day of December, in the hour of
cause, ten o'clock forenoon, there to underlye the law for the
crime of sedition charged against him. The whole Indictment
written out by hand covered forty-three pages and was signed
by Mr H. Home Drummond the Lord Advocate Depute.

It started by saying that 'Albeit by the laws of this and of
every other well governed realm sedition is a crime of an
heinous nature and severely punishable, yet true it is and of
verity that you, George Kinloch are guilty thereof, actor or art
and part in so far that, the Meeting being advertised, a great

155

multitude of persons, chiefly of the lower orders assembled at a place called Magdalen's Yard, Dundee and you George Kinloch did wickedly and feloneously deliver a speech containing a number of seditious and inflammatory remarks and assertions calculated to degrade and bring into contempt the Government of the realm and fill the realm with trouble and dissention.' It went on to say that there were many wicked and seditious expressions calculated to incite the people to resist lawful authority and propagate vain delusions among the lower orders as to the management of public affairs and the whole fabric of the British Constitution.

The Text included a word for word account of the Speech and Resolutions, a list of the witnesses who would appear for the Crown and the names of forty-five Jurymen from whom the Jury would be selected. The names of Rintoul and Saunders now appeared amongst the list of Crown Witnesses, as they were to be used to prove that George Kinloch had given the text of his Speech to the newspaper for publication. Otherwise the principal witnesses were Sheriff L'Amy and the Procurator Fiscal.

The Indictment ended by saying, 'All which or part thereof being found proven, you, the said George Kinloch, ought to be punished with the pains of law, to deter others from committing the like crimes in all time coming'.

There was no time to waste. Only a fortnight in which to instruct Counsel for his defence, collect witnesses and evidence, and also to arrange his affairs at home in case he should be imprisoned. Tuesday and Wednesday were spent at home instructing the farm people about the winter programme on the farm and he went in to Coupar Angus to withdraw his whole credit balance of £140 from the branch of the Perth Banking Company so that he would not be short of ready money. On Wednesday evening he had a heart to heart talk with his wife Helen and made it clear to her that, although he still felt confident of clearing himself, they must be prepared for all eventualities. He told her that, if he was parted from her for a time, he could not live without knowing all that was happening at Kinloch, every detail no matter how trivial, and begged her to start keeping a diary. Helen promised to do this and as a result 'Helen's Diary,' remarkable for its brevity of detail, which lasted from 9th December 1819 till her death on 28 February 1850 was opened with the first momentous entry.

Kinloch, Dec. 9. 1819.

Decr. 9 Mr. Kinloch & Margt. left us at ½ past 3 in the Morn. for Edr. Mr. Hay came.

From this first prosaic entry can be imagined the scene at the foot of the drive at half past three, in the darkness of a cold December morning, with the lanterns waving to stop the Aberdeen Mail Coach. Margaret, his adoring daughter, travelling with him to Edinburgh to look after his creature comforts and Mrs Kinloch making sure that her ample supply of provisions were properly stowed in the boot of the coach, and then farewell.

The Diary continued:

Dec. 10. Mrs. Blair came.
    11. C. & C. Smyth, Mrs. Murray, Mrs. Macnabb and David Nairne came. Jas. Yeaman came.
    12. A letter from Mr. Kinloch.
    13. A letter from Mr. Kinloch. Wrote Mr. Kinloch. J.Y. left us.

From these brief entries it can be seen that friends and relations gathered round to offer whatever help they could give.

On arrival in Edinburgh, on the afternoon of Thursday the 9th December, George Kinloch and his solicitor, Mr Patrick Pearson got to work preparing a note of relevant details which they thought would be useful information for the Advocates who were to conduct the Defence. They got in touch with a number of his influential friends and prepared a list of those who would agree to speak for the Defence.

These included the following names which seemed to give him a solid and formidable backing:

The Hon. Douglas Hallyburton of Pitcur, Coupar-Angus.
The Hon. Wm. Maule of Panmure, M.P. for County of Forfar.
David Ogilvie of Airly, claiming the title of Earl of Airly.
Gilbert Meason of Lindertis.
Charles Hay of Ballendoch, by Meigle.
The Rev. John Halkett, Manse of Coupar-Angus.

William Hutchison, Procurator Fiscal, Forfar.

David Blair Jr., Merchant, Dundee, and many others.

The line of argument which Mr Pearson suggested in his notes for Counsel was as follows:

The town of Dundee and the district around it is one of the most peaceable districts in the Country. No disturbance has happened, nor has there been made, even in this time of alarm, the faintest allegation as to training or military array there.

Mr. Kinloch in the first place says he is not a disorderly or seditious person. He humbly thinks he is in a condition to prove that, in private life he has lived for twenty-five years in a peaceable and exemplary manner, that during the said period he has acted the part of a local Magistrate to the entire approbation of those around him and acquitted himself well of the relative duties incumbent upon a properly disposed and well behaved Country Gentleman. He is a husband and father; a wife and seven children now grown up must be involved in his fate. His immediate neighbour Mr. Hay of Ballendoch will bear evidence that the Justice of Peace business for Coupar Angus and that district has been done for the period mentioned almost exclusively by him and Mr. Kinloch, and that they were for a number of years of it, brother Officers, — Mr. Kinloch, the Commanding Officer — in the Coupar Volunteers. His evidence on these points as well as to Mr. Kinloch's general conduct can be corroborated by that of the Hon. Mr. Maule of Panmure; and the Hon. Mr. Douglas Hallyburton of Pitcur, the latter also his immediate neighbours; if necessary, Robert Jobson Esquire, of Rosemount, and David Blair Esquire of Pitpointy, the present Dean of Guild of Dundee will speak to the same points.

These witnesses will also speak to the peaceable state of Dundee and the neighbourhood before, at, and subsequent to the time of the meeting in question.

Patrick Anderson Esquire, Provost of Dundee might be called as to the whole of these points also, and they will farther establish the important fact, that Dundee, with a population reckoned upwards of 30,000 has no police

Establishment, nothing more than five or six Town Officers, and although about the time of the meeting there were hundreds of unemployed, yet the people were as quiet the night of the meeting and have continued to be so, as if it had never taken place.

Mr. Kinloch distinctly disclaims the seditious or inflammatory purpose ascribed to him. The general tenor of his conversation, it can be proved, has not been seditious and the subject of an apprehended revolution of the Government was never mentioned by him but to be deprecated. He holds certain opinions as to the necessity and the extent of a reform of the House of Commons which, holding conscientiously, he is in the habit of avowing but nothing like disaffection to the whole frame of the existing Government can with truth be urged against him.

The Meeting, it can be made perfectly clear, did not originate from him. The first notice he received of the intention to hold the meeting was from the Dundee Newspaper and that the Advertisement of the meeting stated — 'We understand that Provost Anderson has declined to call the meeting but that no manner of obstruction will be thrown in the way of their orderly proceedings.' The circumstances that the Bench of Justices of Dundee agreed that the meeting should receive no interruption if orderly can be confirmed by Captain Blair, one of the Justices.

Finally it was noted for information of Defence Counsel that it looked as if information had been sent to 'The Official People' in London by the Rev. James Thomson, Minister in Dundee, an informer under the Spy-system, and that William Reid, one of the Crown Witnesses might also be an informer. The notes finished by suggesting that Counsel might emphasize the mis-rerepsentation of the Spy-like information upon the 'Official People' in London which 'may open the eyes of the Jury,' but it is left for Counsel to decide.

Having prepared these notes which seemed to George Kinloch and to Patrick Pearson to be a reasonable explanation of the meeting and a fair description of his character as a useful and reliable member of the community, he wrote as follows to

159

Mrs Kinloch, who would be pleased to hear that he had not lost his appetite with all the excitement and anxiety.

Edinburgh 10th. Dec. 1819.

My Dear Helen,

I received yours to-day and shall probably require Mr. Halket's attendance. I am obliged to Mr. Hay for his zeal at any rate. I can say nothing yet as to the business. Cranstoun and Jeffrey have been spoken to and have accepted the charge. Jeffrey cocquetted a good deal and, Pearson says, evidently felt nettled at the hit I gave the Whigs. They are to meet for a consultation tomorrow night or Sunday forenoon, when we shall see how the land lies. I would not be surprised if the thing were dropped, tho' I don't flatter myself with getting off so easily. Warrender, the Crown Agent, Pearson says, is very easy upon the subject and would have no objections to there being no more of it but, he says, the orders come from London. Maule arrived here with Radical Rinty [Rintoul] on Wednesday last. I am to see him tomorrow and expect to get him for one of my supporters.

George appears to be quite well and is surrounded by a long mantle of Stewart tartan.

Nothing can exceed Mr. Pearson's kindness, except his zeal in my defence. It seems entirely to absorb him.

If the lamb is as good as that which we were using and small, I think that you might send us a side of it, or a side of wedder mutton; game if you could get it from Nairne or Boyter; fowls or anything you judge best. If you can pay the carriage do it.

Always most sincerely yours,
G.K.

P.S. Streets covered with snow and damnation cold.

News of the forthcoming trial of a country gentleman from Perthshire was the principal topic of conversation in the Edinburgh drawing-rooms. Those who did not actually know George Kinloch himself were soon made aware that he was a connection of such and such a family — the Smyths, the Wedderburns, the Grays, the Ogilvies, the Grahams, the Oliphants, and others.

PLATE 5

Magdalen Yard Green, Dundee. One wonders whether the prohibitions are out of respect to the Reformer's memory

Photograph by Viking Studios, Dundee

FOOTBALL · GOLF
FLYING OF KITES
PROHIBITED
NO DOGS EXCEPT
ON LEASH
NO CYCLING

BY ORDER

PLATE 6

The entrance to Rue des Petits Peres, 2eme arrondissement, in Paris, looking from the Place des Petits Peres. From George Kinloch's description it would appear that his lodgings were in the building at the right of the photograph, although on which floor it is difficult to determine. The buildings in this particular district are virtually the same as they were in Kinloch' time.

The lower picture shows the view from his window looking left

Photographs by Reg Lancaster

On the 9th of December, Sir Walter Scott[1] wrote to a nephew in Canada —

Do you remember Kinloch of Kinloch who married a daughter of the very respectable Smyth of Balhary? He is under indictment to stand trial in a few days for his conduct at a meeting of Radicals at Dundee, when he used the most violent and inflammatory language which it seems he copied out in his own hand as well as the Resolutions which were adopted in consequence. For much less matter was Muir in 1794 'doomed the long isles of Sydney Cove to see.' The event of this trial will be very important.

Unfortunately the adjectives 'violent and inflammatory' were being commonly used to describe the strong and emotional speech which George Kinloch had delivered. In times of panic it is not uncommon for greatly exaggerated rumours to circulate but Sir Walter Scott was guilty of gross misrepresentation of the truth in writing on the 17th of December to Mr John B. S. Morrett and saying that George Kinloch in his speech 'had exhorted the people to right themselves by arms in case the Magistrates of Manchester, the Yeomanry etc. were not punished'. This was the exact reverse of the policy of peaceful demonstration for Reform to avoid revolution which George Kinloch had advocated.

Thomas Campbell,[2] the Scottish poet, who is best known for his poem 'Hohenlinden' was one of few who came near to supporting him and he wrote — 'On this subject, I cannot help saying that I feel a sort of Scottish pride in Kinloch of Kinloch. I don't like the cause but I admire the dauntless simplicity of his zeal and feel for his martyrdom'.

The Friends of Reform in Kilmarnock added a letter to their previous Vote of Thanks which wished him 'fortitude and comfort in the hour of trial from the knowledge that your conduct meets the approbation of the most discerning part of your fellow Countrymen, and although we cannot extricate you from the grasp and shackles of Tyranny, yet, if the fervent prayers of your Countrymen can console you, they are at your command, and that a jury of your Countrymen may break the Sword of Despotism that is suspended over your devoted head, is the sincere wish of the Radical Reformers of Kilmarnock'.

A letter received from some unknown friend in Edinburgh written in a scholarly hand under the pen-name of 'IGNOTUS' may have given George Kinloch the first indication of the way that the wind was blowing and may have prepared him for the first reports from Counsel who were, by this time, having daily consultations with Mr Pearson his Solicitor.

This 'Ignotus' letter read —

Edin. Decr. 13th. 1819.

Sir,

I know you not, but I have heard your character which in many points I highly esteem. My motive for writing to you is one of the purest friendship and if you shall despise the information which I am to communicate, you will at least think well of my intention. I was this morning at Breakfast with a gentleman of this City, and at table your approaching trial or reported trial was the subject of some conversation. I said that I had heard that Mr. K. intended to plead his own defences. I myself had previously approved highly of this intention, but the answer which my entertainer made to this bit of news completely altered my opinion. 'The more fool he' (said he), for if he pleads *ill* he must lose it and if *well* the Judges will most certainly condemn him. This was a firm loyalist too. They will say 'this is a most dangerous person and we will do our country a service and strike terror into the Radicals by showing them that no talent or ability will avail them if we make him an example of our severity.' Such a case happened in the latter part of last century. A man accused of Sedition pleaded his own defences to the astonishment and admiration of all who heard him, but the ability he displayed served only to add strength to their determination to condemn him considering him more dangerous than one of inferior abilities and therefore the more desirable a victim. The poor man was banished and ended his days in Botany Bay.

These hints are sent to you by a friend who considered it for your interest to know them, although he does not presume even to advise you what use to make of them.

Ignotus.

The two Advocates who undertook the Case for the Defence

162

were Mr Cranstoun and Mr Jeffrey.³ At the end of their consultations Mr Pearson wrote a letter to George Kinloch giving
a detailed summary of what transpired which describes the
extraordinary defeatest line which these two men adopted.
Their casual and off-hand manner may, or may not have been
typical of the Scottish Bar in the year 1819.

Mr Pearson's letter said —

It would be unworthy to mince matters and I will therefore
bring to your ear everything which has operated upon mine.

It explained that the papers had first been handed to Counsel
on Friday evening and that, at the first consultation on Saturday,
Mr Cranstoun appeared to have read the papers with interest,
but Mr Jeffrey confessed he had not done so and, in consequence,
the consultation was deferred until Sunday. Mr Cranstoun,
however, declared 'I am afraid that the Gentleman has destroyed
himself by these declarations and by giving up the Notes of his
Speech.'

On the Sunday, the two learned Gentlemen had been some
time together before Mr Pearson went in to see them and,
before long, they showed that they were at one as to the
hopelessness of the case. They discussed what had been said
about the Manchester business and construed that it was
tantamount to an invocation to Civil War. The Prince Regent
had approved the affair, there were no attempts to bring the
Yeomanry to Justice and consequently the remarks of the
accused were an invitation to Civil War. Mr Cranstoun paced
the room in great perturbation and remarks broke out involun-
tarily by bursts and starts. 'The case appeared to him worse by
studying it.' 'Worse than Muirs.' (meaning the Thomas Muir
Sedition case of 1794).

They both agreed that to escape conviction was out of the
question and Mr Jeffrey then made a speech upon the subject of
punishment which ranged from Imprisonment to Transportation
for Life. Mr Pearson's letter went on to explain that having
come to this conclusion, the two learned Counsel decided to
resort to 'back-stairs' information and 'string-pulling' to try to
find out what punishment had been decided upon by the Crown.
It had been hinted, but never expressed, that it might be best
for their client to get out of the country and avoid trial, although

both advocates became indignant about any discussion of such a matter which, they said, was entirely out of their province.

At the end of the Sunday meeting, Mr Cranstoun, still pacing about in much agitation had intimated that he could not undertake the case as he never practised in the Criminal Court.

Mr Pearson's letter finally described how, after the official consultation, Mr Jeffrey mentioned to him that Mr Home-Drummond, the Depute Lord Advocate had made some remarks on the subject of punishment. Mr Pearson thought that he might learn something more about this from Mr Cockburn,[4] another Advocate, who was married to a niece of Mr Home-Drummond, as it was said that 'There was daily communication between the families.' At this point he left Mr Jeffrey — 'We made our Bows and came off.'

After this consultation Mr Pearson may have conveyed some of what had transpired to his client because, on Sunday afternoon George Kinloch started writing a letter to his wife at mid-day and finished it at 2 o'clock, which showed a very different tone from the optimistic letter written on Friday.

It read—

Edinburgh, 12th. December, 1819.

My Dear Helen,

I wrote to you on Friday which I hope you received last night. The lawyers are now (12 o'clock) holding a consultation on the means and mode of defence. They are Cranstoun and Jeffrey, Mr Pearson and Robert.

I am sorry to say that from all I can learn a favourable result is hardly to be anticipated. Men's minds here are heated to a degree of which, in our part of the country, you can have no conception. Of course, I can hardly expect an impartial trial.

Circumstances too have occurred which make it still more unfavourable for me. There was yesterday a report that a general rising is intended to-morrow in Glasgow. In consequence, Hussars, Flying Artillery and a Regiment of Foot were sent off at a moment's warning. To-day, the Midlothian Yeomanry are also gone and the Castle duty is done by Volunteers. I don't believe the people are so mad as to throw themselves on certain destruction but in the meantime these alarms operate most unfavourably for me.

Whatever shall happen, I have the satisfaction of an approving conscience. My error, if it amounts to a crime, was unintentional. I shall feel no disgrace from anything they can do to me and I shall have the satisfaction of knowing that the persecution of which I am the object, will in the end, forward the glorious cause for which I contend.

I shall probably be imprisoned — Thank God, I can employ and amuse myself as well in jail as in a palace. They will probably inflict a heavy fine on me. Again I thank God that I shall still have enough left to make my family comfortable. — And above all, I thank God for having given me a wife and family of the comfort arising from which no earthly power can deprive me.

2 o'clock. Robert and Mr. Pearson are returned. My Counsel anticipate a conviction, just as I had guessed. However there are many alleviating features of which they are to avail themselves.

Jeffrey is to conduct my defence, assisted by Cockburn and advised by Cranstoun who does not practise in the Criminal Court.

I think that on the whole, you should remain at Kinloch. I remove tomorrow to George's lodgings, 11 Drummond Street where there is a spare room. You can send any provisions you think proper there.

With kindest love to you and the lassies,

I remain, always most affectionately yours,

G.K.

Still desperately cold and streets covered with snow.

Mr Pearson's summary of the consultations continued with the sequence of events as follows:

The suggestion that Mr Cockburn (later Lord Cockburn) might find out something about the scale of punishment led to his being approached and undertaking the case for the Defence in place of Mr Cranstoun.

Mr Cockburn was found disengaged on the Monday afternoon, the 13th, and at this meeting he quoted the opinion of his neighbour Lord Pitmilly, that 'Transportation was the appropriate punishment.'

On Tuesday Mr Pearson saw Mr Cockburn again whose opening remarks were — 'I never saw a more hopeless case.' Mr Jeffrey joined the consultation and the remarks recorded were — 'We were already prepared for Conviction and all our doubts were as to the quantum suff. of punishment.' Mr Cockburn had not liked the suggestion that he might be able to find out from the Home-Drummond family about the probable punishment and 'He got out of countenance, scribbled on the wall and made play to disguise his being caught.'

This day's consultation ended by discussing the distress which would affect the family of Mr Kinloch and their connections and Mr Cockburn said — 'A sentence of Transportation would come with a damnable thump upon them.' It seemed quite obvious that, once Mr Cockburn got over his indignation about being catched, he made it clear that he knew that Transportation was the sentence which had been agreed by the Lord Advocate's Department.

Mr Pearson's letter ended by saying—

In all periods of political effervescence, to retire seems to have been the favourite practice to the best informed of the time. Mr. Smyth and I will see you tomorrow and all we can do for the next twenty-four hours is to keep in view the way out.

Yours very truly,
Patrick Pearson.

In this letter describing the consultations, there was no reference to the Notes for Defence which the Solicitor and George Kinloch had prepared, neither was there any precognition of the witnesses who had been suggested, or of calling on the services of any of the many other distinguished people who were good friends of the accused.

The letter also made it clear that Counsel did not wish to meet the accused personally and in fact they seem to have thought that there was something very unsavoury about defending a man accused of sedition which might prejudice their own professional reputations.

Counsel came quickly to the decision that the accused was

guilty and being guilty that he deserved to be punished so that the only useful purpose which these three advocates served was in finding out and convincing their client that the verdict was a certainty and that the punishment had already been agreed.

Although Mr Pearson's description of the consultation was graphic enough, it was a pity that George Kinloch had not been admitted to meet Counsel, as he would have been sure to have made some amusing comments to his wife about the atmosphere of snuff and good claret in which one can suppose that the consultations were conducted.

Mr Cockburn, later Lord Cockburn, who was familiarly known as 'Cocky' when he came, in later life, to writing his book 'Sedition Trials in Scotland', included the case of George Kinloch. As he had been brought into the case late in the day for the main purpose of discovering, through family channels, what the verdict and punishment would be, he probably did not take time to read the speech or study the evidence at that time. However, when he came to writing his book thirty years later, if he had re-read the Speech, he might have given a fairer report on George Kinloch's eloquence.

In this book he wrote —

Although parts of this vulgar harangue might have been explained away or apologised for, we were clear that enough of sedition remained to make it certain that there would, and proper that there should be a conviction; and that a verdict of guilty would be followed by sentence of a long term of transportation. Kinloch undoubtedly did not hold himself to be guilty, and his ignorance made him rely far too much on the candour of a jury.'

A vulgar harangue seems an unkind description of the vigorous, emotional speech about which George Kinloch was justly proud and from which he never recanted a single word.

Wednesday, 15th December was one of the most critical days in George Kinloch's life. He had come to Edinburgh hoping that, with the help of his good friends and his reputation for quiet living, the charge against him might be dropped. He was prepared for a prison sentence or a considerable fine but, finding that the punishment was to be Botany Bay, this was too much for him. Besides the prospect of consorting with criminals

167

and the scum of the earth, he felt that there might be much popular feeling for him in Scotland that his martyrdom would lead to riots or revolution in which the people would be the sufferers. He wanted to avoid this above everything else. Until the last moment, it had not entered his head that he might be forced to leave the country but, after meeting Mr Pearson and his brother-in-law Robert Smyth on Wednesday morning, he realised that this was the only possible course of action for him to take.

Robert Smyth prepared a Trust Deed for him to sign handing over his property to Trustees and there were certain other arrangements to be made including a visit to a barber's shop for the purpose of preparing a disguise.

Once these matters had been dealt with, he retired to his son's lodgings at 11 Drummond Street and wrote a final letter to his wife. This letter, written in the hour of defeat, danger and disillusionment showed no sign of bitterness and even included a little joke about the prospect of a 'jaunt of pleasure.'

Edinburgh dated 15th December, 1819.

My Dearest Helen,

Your ample store of provisions arrived safe last night but I regret to say that it will not be in my power to partake of them.

The tide of the times sets so strongly towards despotism at present that I am advised to go out of the way for a short time to avoid the 'pelting of the pitiless storm.'

I mean to go to the West of England and from there to Havre and to remain in that neighbourhood till I see how the land lies. Don't be uneasy about me during this temporary separation, for, if I cannot return to you, you and the girls shall come to me. Robert and Mr Pearson are taking steps which will, they trust ultimately prevent any bad consequences from a pecuniary point of view and there are many contingencies which may enable me to return sooner than might otherwise be expected. If it was not for the uneasiness that you and the girls will feel till you hear of my arrival, I would consider it a jaunt of pleasure. Fortunately gifted with a pretty strong mind and deeply impressed with the conviction that everything which happens to us is for the best, I shall never repine. My cup of prosperity has hitherto overflowed and I hope that I have not been wholly unworthy of it. A dash of adversity may do me good. But what do I say of adversity? If you and the girls are not cast down, I feel nothing for myself. If our circumstances are to be reduced, you have many kind friends to assist you.

I know all of you too well to think that you will regret what is nowise conducive to real happiness. Hope therefore for the best. I have done nothing of which I am ashamed and better men than I have been persecuted for the same error. George will be with you in a day or two. Send down the handkerchief with the Carnoustie Papers to Jas Yeaman for him to collect the Martinmas Feus etc.

None must know this but you and the girls and John Smyth.

God bless you all.

Ever your most affectionate,

George.

[1] Letters of Sir Walter Scott edited by H. G. C. Grierson LL. D. page 49.

[2] Beattie's Life and Letters of Thomas Campbell.

[3] Mr Jeffrey — Francis Jeffrey (1773–1850), a Whig Advocate became Lord Advocate in 1830. He was editor of 'The Edinburgh Review.'

[4] 'Mr Cockburn' — Henry Thomas Cockburn (1779–1854) later Lord Cockburn or 'Cocky', the subject of Jack Ronder's successful play in the Edinburgh Festival of 1969. This play ridicules the needless panic in Edinburgh in December 1819 and the activities of the Volunteers and Yeomanry.

CHAPTER THIRTEEN

'The Hour of Cause'

Mrs Kinloch was not used to keeping secrets and, in spite of her husband's careful instructions that no one must know of his plans, she entered in her diary of 17th December — 'A letter from Mr. Kinloch telling me he was to leave the country.' George Kinloch may have feared such a possible security leak and so the route which he had spoken about in his letter to his wife 'to the west of England and then to Havre' was a false trail and he had no intention of going that way at all.

Otherwise the entries in 'Helen's Diary' between the 17th and the 22nd, are just of people coming and going, but they must have been days of great anxiety to all the family.

It is not possible to tell whether rumours had leaked out in Edinburgh that George Kinloch had disappeared but, on the morning of the 22nd, at the hour of cause, the High Court duly assembled and was presided over by the Lord Justice Clerk. The Lord Advocate and Crown Witnesses were ready to present their case and the forty-five Jurymen who had been cited to appear were in attendance. In view of the public interest in the trial, the Public Gallery was also crowded out with people who wanted to have a glimpse of George Kinloch about whom there had been so much gossip.

Mr Pearson and Mr Cranstoun, were sitting together in the Court and Mr Pearson made a number of notes and observations on his printed copy of the Indictment. His notes about the Jury were that — 'There are a few liberal men but the great

170

proportion of them are believers in the divine right of passive obedience,' and his notes continued — 'several of the Jury are known to have left the ranks of the Yeomanry this morning, with blood in their eye, and breathing vengeance against the damned Radical they were about to judge.' Mr Cranstoun's observations were more non-commital but commented on the Jury — 'There are enough to do the business.'

The Counsel for the Defence do not seem to have been asked to explain the absence of their client and the Minute of the Proceedings states bluntly 'the said George Kinloch being oft times called in Court and three times at the door of the Court House, by a Macer of Court, as use is, failed to appear.' This formality being over, His Majesty's Advocate, Mr H. Home-Drummond, rose and moved the Court to pronounce sentence of Fugitation against the said George Kinloch and craved that the Bond of Caution granted for his appearance might be forfeited.

The Lord Justice Clerk did not require much time for deliberation and pronounced his finding as follows — 'We decern and adjudge the said George Kinloch to be an Outlaw and Fugitive from His Majesty's laws and ordane him to be put to the horn and all his moveable goods and gear to be escheat and in brought to His Majesty's use for contempt and disobedience in not appearing this day and place in the hour caused, to have underlyn the law for the crime of Sedition in manner mentioned in the Indictment.' He also declared the Bail Bond to be forfeited and to be recovered by the proper Officer in Exchequer for His Majesty's use.

He then thanked the gentlemen summoned to act on the Jury for their attendance and, in the name of the Public Prosecutor, assured them that the law would be executed against the offender to the very letter and that, if he was found in any of His Majesty's Dominions, he would be brought to answer for the heavy charges preferred against him.

The Solicitor General also considered it necessary for him to make a public statement to the effect that —

The Lord Advocate would use every exertion to convince the public that the Law was inflexible in it's course, and would be administered with the same impartiality to this

171

individual as to the poorest of His Majesty's Subjects.

All that remained to complete the picturesque formalities of the case was for a Messenger at Arms to go out to the Market Cross and then on to the Pier and Shore at Leith, blow three blasts on his horn and denounce George Kinloch as an outlaw and fugitive from Justice.

There were, however, considerable repercussions. All sorts of rumours and suggestions, which had been going about in Edinburgh about the case, came to the ears of the Lord Advocate. Some were saying that the authorities had been aware of George Kinloch's plan to absent himself and had condoned this. Others of Radical opinion were saying that the Jurymen were framed and an article appeared in a Glasgow periodical on the 25th commenting on the case, which said that Juries were commonly packed by the Sheriffs of different counties. The Lord Advocate took quick action on this Radical article, addressed the Edinburgh Bar on the subject and charged the printer with contempt of Court. Gilbert McLeod who was the printer was sentenced to four months imprisonment, and after that three years surveillance for good behaviour, which in itself was a lenient sentence, but more of his misfortune will be told later.

At Kinloch unofficial messages had been coming in about the progress of the outlaw, but there was no definite news.

Mrs Kinloch's lawyer brothers had taken charge of the situation and given her plenty of work to do in this time of anxiety, making an inventory of all the contents of Kinloch, and Bankhead Farm House, for the purpose of the Deed of Trust.

The Diary of 27th read — 'Inventoried everything at Kinloch and Bankhead.' Her business-like brother John opened a Day-Book to record all transactions of the Trust and the first entries were 1/4½d. for postages, 2/9d. for this book, and then £166: 13: 4d. to pay for the Bail Bond. It was fortunate that Mrs Kinloch had the financial support of her brothers at this time but the Trust was to lead to very bad feeling between husband and brother before very long because, as often happens with family Trusts, George Kinloch could not get it into his head that the management of the Trust and so of his beloved farms was in the hands of his Trustees and out of his own control.

At last on the 1st of January, news came of safe arrival in France and the diary recorded 'I received a letter from Mr. Kinloch.' Now the tension was over. All the horrible nightmare of legal formalities, warrants for arrest, the long faces of the brothers telling her what disgrace her husband had brought on the family and on their respectable legal business, was over. George was well and safe and, God be praised, he had not lost his sense of humour nor his self-confidence, and this was all that mattered.

He wrote—

My Dearest Helen,

Here I am, seated in Mr. May's[1] parlour, in perfect health, and in as good spirits as can be expected, considering the distance at which I am from all I hold dear. I wrote a note from York, in a feigned name, to Robert, which I hope he received. Dr. Gilchrist was to write, under Kinnaird's frank, to Mrs. Nairne enclosing a letter to you, on Tuesday. I wrote to Captain Blair from Dover on Tuesday, also. From some, or all of these, I hope your anxiety, on my account would be relieved.

I left Edinburgh at five on Thursday morning with no one in the coach except one woman. I got to Newcastle about ten that night, and got a comfortable sleep. The weather was desperately cold. Left Newcastle at nine on Friday morning, dined at Northallerton, and got to York about half past nine. The fore part of the day the weather was exceptionally stormy. Wind, sleet, and snow. Left York about eleven at night, and jogged on to London without any accident. The weather quite mild. Met Mr. and Miss Ker from Durham in the coach, who knew the Oliphants, the Stewarts, Goodchilds etc. He asked me whether *Mr. Kinloch's* trial had come on, or not, to which, of course, I replied in the negative. All the way from York our party was very pleasant. Got to London at eight on Sunday morning. Took a coach and drove to Dr. Gilchrist's[2] who I found expecting me, as I had written to him from Edinburgh under the name of Oliphant. Wrote a note to Mr. Kinnaird, who

173

came to breakfast next morning. He got my pass-port,[3] letter of credit and everything arranged by three o'clock and I was off for Dover at seven that night. Got there to breakfast on Tuesday, placing my things at the Custom House, and went in board the packet about one. Took possession of a bed and never stirred till the boat from Calais was announced about half past seven — got into it, and after two or three thumps on the bar, which I did not by any means relish, landed in safety about eight. A Mr. Barber and I went to the White Hart, and got our supper. and tumbled into a most comfortable bed at nine.

Passed the Custom House, got my French pass-port, and at ten on Wednesday morning set off in the Swallow which was *to fly* to Paris in 30 hours; but alas, instead of getting in at six in the evening, it was three this morning before we arrived, most confoundedly jolted and sufficiently tired. The roads were bad and the weather rainy and stormy, though, on the whole, mild for the season. I came and breakfasted with Mr. May who had received me in the kindest manner. I have taken a bedroom in the hotel adjoining and am to mess with Mr. May until I see how the land lies.

On leaving Calais on Wednesday morning, I could not help thinking it fully as pleasant to be stepping into the Dilligence for Paris as into the *dock* before the *Big Wigs* with the prospect of a jaunt to Botany Bay. I wrote a letter to the Lord Advocate and left it with Dr. G. to be sent to him along with some documents in my vindication, as soon as he thought me safe. The Dr. was as kind as possible.

In all my journey, I did not meet with a single individual to whom I was known. I got a wig in Edinburgh, which I wore all the way, but which I have laid aside for the present. I brought £80 from Edinburgh with me, of which I still have eight Napoleons, besides circulars for the £60. Mr. Kinnaird also furnished me with a credit for £500. Not that I shall have any occasion for such a sum, but it looks respectable.

I would wish your brother to write a letter to Mr. Roberts [this was his Banker in Dundee], saying that he will be security for my drafts upon him, as I have no other

174

means at present of guaranteeing them. He will be no loser in the end.

Now having given you my history since I left you, you may believe that I shall be very anxious till I hear from you. Your brothers and George would explain to you the reasons which induced me to get out of the way, and that I had executed a trust deed, which we hope will protect my property. If within six months, there is no prospect of my being allowed to go home, I shall then look out for a place somewhere here about, where you and the girls can come to me, for I have been so long *accustomed* to you and them, that I don't at all relish the idea of being without you. Nay, should any circumstances occur to render it any wise improper for you and them to come here, I shall find means to go home in disguise, and keep snug among you, till I may again appear in my own character. Except so far as you and the young people are concerned, I feel no regret for what I have done. My conscience does not accuse me of having committed any crime, and therefore I feel no uneasiness. I hope you feel none either, except what the distance between us occasions.

There is no London post to-day or I would have sent this by it. I have not yet called for Madame Tomasini, but shall do so soon, as I shall probably board with her. Meantime direct to me, under cover to Dr. G. À Monsieur G. Smith, Petit Hotel, Montmorency, Rue St. Marc, No. 12, À Paris. Enclose the Dr.'s letter in a cover to the Hon. Douglas Kinnaird, M.P., 34, Pall Mall, London. As I can have little to say for some time, it will be as well not to write to you often, and I would not wish you to write oftener than once a fortnight or so, unless you have something of importance to communicate. I send this under cover to Dr. G. who will forward it under cover to some of your neighbours.

Make yourself as easy as you can, as I can assure you I am nowise to be pitied. Tell all inquiring friends that I am at St. Maloes in Brittany, under the name of Oliphant. I thought yours a better travelling name, only changing the 'y' for an 'i', and it already sounds quite familiar to me.

God bless you my dear Helen. Give my kindest love to our young folks and tell them to hope for better times. I shall write to David Nairne soon. I fear he and many of my friends got a deal of needless trouble on my account. Again God bless you all.

Ever most sincerely your affectionate George.

Rue St. Marc, No. 12. Paris.

Friday, 24th. Dec. 1819.

[1] Mr May, from whose parlour George Kinloch wrote on arrival in France, has not been identified. He appears to have been an official of the American Consulate who passed letters back to England through the Diplomatic Bag.

[2] Dr. John Borthwick Gilchrist who helped Kinloch to escape to France was at that time a Professor of Oriental Languages in London. He had been born in Edinburgh and educated at George Watson's College before going out East as surgeon in the East India Company service.

[3] *Passport Register.* Public Record office confirm entry in Passport Register under date 20th December 1819 of Passport No. 4313 for Mr Geo. Smith going to Paris and recommended by Morland & Co. The entry is completed by fee paid of £2 : 2 : 6d. Morland & Co. are listed as Bankers of 36, Pall Mall, London, of which firm Mr Kinnaird was a partner.

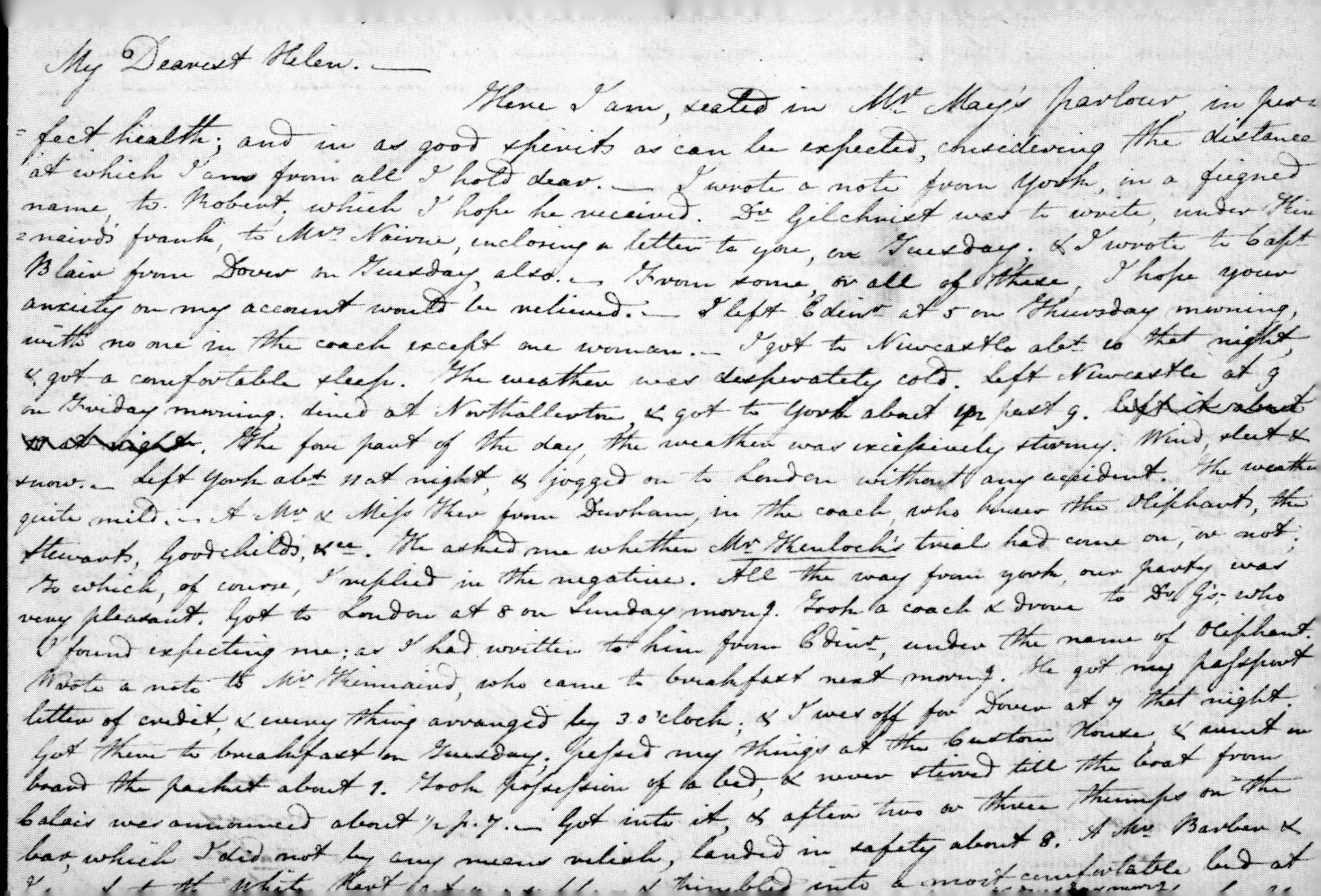

My Dearest Helen. —

PLATE 7
Letter from
'The Outlaw'
in Paris, des-
cribing his
escape from
justice — a
masterly
understatement
— dated 24th
Dec. 1819

PLATE 8
Mrs Kinloch's French passport dated 22 April 1820 'et ces cinq filles', with her
nationality altered from 'dame anglaise' to 'dame ecossaise'

CHAPTER FOURTEEN

A Country House in Strathmore to Let

THE THRILL of achievement in his escape from justice lasted George Kinloch for a few weeks after his arrival in Paris and he wrote to his wife on the last day of the year in a cheerful mood —
I did not suffer at all from my long journey, although I had only three nights in bed out of seven, and only about four hours sleep the night of my departure and that of my arrival here. Thank God, a good constitution and a clear conscience carried me safely through. I felt for nothing, except for the uneasiness which you and the girls must have experienced on my account, and which I sincerely hope is now at an end. I am in perfect health, and as well in other respects as I can be, at such a distance from you, without any object to pursue.
He had settled down in a French boarding-house —
Having seen a French boarding-house advertised, I came yesterday to look at it, and have taken up my abode here for the present. It is in Le Passage des petits Peres behind the north east corner of the Palais Royal, in the most centrical part of Paris and my windows command a view of three streets, the centre one terminating in the Place des Victoires. I think I see you all examining the plan of Paris, to find out my lodging. I have a parlour, respectable enough for an *outlaw*, and a bed closet within it, and a place for my fire-wood. The dinner consists of soup, bouillé, a hash of some kind, fish, a roast, vegetables, apples and chestnuts. The dishes are put down singly before the landlady and a neice

who carve them and send them round to every person. The company is all French except myself, an Englishman and a neat little English woman, whom I took for a girl of eighteen, but who proves to be eight and twenty with a brace of children. Her husband being in bad health, went lately to England, thinking he would be better there. I have the use of the Salon all day and I make them light my fire about nine at night that I may retire to write or read. There are four or five more ladies who dine with us and except the little English woman, I never beheld an uglier set, in all my travels.

He had travelled light and it was therefore necessary to re-stock his wardrobe as economically as possible —

I have been under the necessity of getting a new coat, vest and pantaloons, which I think will serve me till I see you, at any rate, I have bought three night-caps and mean to get three night-shirts, and with these and a new hat, I shall do for a twelve month. I would have been very ill-off in the journey had I not taken George's plaid, which I found most comfortable. I walk about here with my old great coat, sans cérémonie; as the plaid would be rather too conspicuous.

On the first day of the New Year 1820 he wrote again to —

. . . wish you and the bairns a good New Year and many of them happier than this one.

This is a very gay time here. It is the custom to give presents more or less valuable to all the ladies of one's acquaintance. The confectioners have a rare time of it. All their art is displayed in making imitations of everything in sugar. Melons, grapes, apples, peaches, mushrooms, turnips and all kinds of vegetables are imitated so exactly as to deceive the keenest eye. Bales of silk, of cloth, rolls of music, fish, flesh, in short, everything on the earth beneath, or in the waters under it, is imitated to *the life*. The curiosity of the Parisians to see all these things, is so great, that gendarmes are stationed at the principal shops to keep order among the crowd. Besides the confectioners, all the other shops are rigged out in the showiest manner, and certainly in works of taste and fashion, nothing can exceed them.

Then, it is the custom for all *the world* to call upon all their acquaintances during the first week of the year, otherwise you would be scored off their books. This ceremony is easily performed. They call on those whom they really esteem, and to the others, they send their cards by people who make a trade of it, at eight sous for every five cards. All sorts of vehicles are in a state of requisition, and the streets, however dirty, are crowded with pedestrians.

He knew that his wife in her letters would not give all the detailed information which he wanted to hear about what was happening at home, and so he asked her to —

Take one of the large thin sheets of paper and cause Maggy to write in a small hand all the news of everything, however trifling it may appear to you. When you write, you cannot be too particular as to everything within three miles of Kinloch, yourselves and neighbours. The weather, farm operations, wind-mill etc. Mention everything *however trifling* at full length.

Before long there was an indication that it was a strain for him having to live in an assumed name and having to be careful about his movements and friendships —

I don't suppose the *learned* friends would risk to molest me here, but I don't choose to trust them, till I see how the land lies, and at present I defy them to trace me, unless, which is not very likely, they had opened my last letter.

The Government here is about to try the same plan as our *worthies* have adopted lately. They find that the people are too well represented in the chamber of Deputies and they therefore wish to alter the law of elections, so as to diminish the number of electors, or at any rate, to give to those of the higher class, a greater share in them. All whom I have heard upon the subject are decidedly averse to any change at present, and if the Government persists in its foolish plans, there is no saying what the consequences may be. The Bourbons are almost universally disliked, and very little would bring about a revolution similar to that which our 2nd. James caused by his folly. The Bourbons would be chased, and probably the Duke of Orleans appointed to the vacant throne. From all that I can see, they are blindly following the footsteps of our royal bigot, and the same causes will undoubtedly lead to the same effects. How soon, no one can tell. The Minister has not yet developed his projects, but petitions are pouring in from all quarters against any attempt to change the present law. I am told Louis gave a very saucy answer to the Deputies who waited upon him yesterday, namely that they already were informed of his intention to which he was resolved to adhere. That is to say, he is determined to have the law altered. One would think Lord Castlereagh was at his elbow. But leave these weighty matters to those whom it concerns.

He did his best to pass the time, but confessed —

I certainly feel a little lonely at times, but I don't allow myself to be idle. We breakfast at ten, and I then give the little English woman a lesson in French for about an hour. I then sally forth for an hour or two. A French gentleman and I took a walk of three hours, first to see the skaters on the Basin of the canal here, and then to the burying ground of Père la Chaise, which is the pleasantest place of the kind I ever saw. It is very extensive and the grounds finely varied, commands an extensive view of Paris and the surrounding country, and looks like a well laid out English garden, full of monuments. Here surviving friends come to weep over those who are gone before them, and certainly a more agreeable place to mourn in, could not be found.

I have bespoke a clarinet to help to while away the hours.

It was very cold in Paris in this January of 1820 and he wrote again in the middle of the month describing weather conditions both outside and inside the boarding-house —

The Seine has been frozen since the 10th. and some people crossed it on the 12th. I did the same on the 13th. and yesterday there were hundreds upon it, some of them amusing themselves by building a house of ice. On the fish ponds in the Tuilleries, two days ago, the ice was full ten inches thick, and where they had carried it away for their ice houses, the one day, they were skating on it the next. The thermometer was down at seventeen degrees. Would you believe that with all this intense frost, which now lasted a fortnight, the people here don't frost their horses? They at the same time cruelly overload them, so that it is painful to see the poor animals slipping and stumbling at every step. Sometimes they come to a stand-still, and after the whip has been unmercifully applied in vain, three or four passengers take hold of the large wheels, and get them again *under way*. They use their horses very ill.

The cold here has been far greater than any I ever experienced in Scotland, and as the houses are by no means calculated for cold weather, you may suppose they are not by any means so warm as your dining-room. At breakfast, I have the seat next the fire, so that I am pretty comfortable, and as only one or two people remain in the salon in the forenoon, we get room round the fire. As I am always in sometime before dinner, I get myself toasted before the rest arrive, and our dinner does not last above three quarters of an hour, when we return to the Salon, when it is a scramble who shall get near the fire, for I never saw people so totally devoid of all politeness in that respect. When the room *thins*, which it does in about half an hour, we again get near the fire, where I remain reading or conversing till about nine, when I adjourn to my own room. But I must tell you how I am dressed — viz. I have added since I came here, stocking drawers and under-waistcoat with sleeves, and stockings instead of socks. Well, when I go to my room I put on my jacket and great-coat, and a pair of coarse stockings doubled over my shoes. I then spread George's cloak over an armchair so as to cover all my *nether half*, and with my night-cap on, I sit to read or write till a little after twelve, when I go to bed, having previously put on a pair of fleecy socks and my flannel jacket. I have four ply of blankets, and the cloak over all, so that I put the cold pretty much at defiance, but for all that I would be much the better of a certain person to keep my back warm. However, as the Italians say 'Pazienza.' I am certainly better here than in free quarters in the Calton Jail, or on a voyage of discovery, which some of my friends wished me to undertake.

It was difficult to make plans for the future without up to date information from Scotland and he thought of all sorts of alternatives. First he thought of staying permanently abroad and wrote—

If I had power to set free any part of what was my property
I would vest £8,000 – £10,000 in the funds here which
would produce £700 a year on which we could live royally
in St. Germains or Versailles.

He then considered possibility of returning home in disguise —

I have frequently *dreamt* myself at home, disguised. If this
was to be the plan, some house could be taken in a neighbourhood where I was not known, and out of the way, when
I should run little or no risk.

This idea of returning home in disguise put his sorely tried
brother-in-law John Smyth into a fever of agitation, thinking that
George had already created sufficient embarrassment to him
and his firm's business without coming home and risking the
chance of being caught and having to stand trial. He gave his
opinion that it would be some years before they could hope to
have his case re-considered and that George must stay well out
of the way until then.

In the circumstances George Kinloch decided that his wife
and his five daughters had better come out and join him, and
that Kinloch house should be let to a suitable tenant. In spite of
arguments from John Smyth, who wanted to be rid of the
responsibility of the farms as well as the house George Kinloch
was determined to keep the farm in hand and sent home detailed
instructions to the farm manager — Mr. Mustard, to show how
each field should be planted and what stock should be kept. All
the contents of the house were to be sold and then —

I would wish the house to be advertised to be let, furnished
for one, two, or three years. My closet to be reserved for
putting anything you leave into it. Along with the house,
the garden, orchards, and what grass may be wanted but no
land for ploughing; requisite offices, but not all of them.
The sooner it is advertised, the better.

He drafted the advertisement for the newspaper—

Delightful country residence in Strathmore to be let
furnished for one or more years, free of taxes. The Mansion
house of Kinloch with the requisite offices, garden and
orchards. The house is modern and commodious, containing
dining-room, drawing-room, and billiard-room, each 26 by 18,
six bedrooms, bed closets, garret rooms, water closets with

baths, Kitchen, hall, laundry, pantries and other conveniences. In the offices, stabling for twelve horses, coach houses, byres etc. The garden is surrounded with a twelve foot wall, and is remarkably productive and there are two small orchards attached to it. A tenant may have what grass he has occasion for and he may also be supplied with all farm produce at a reasonable rate. He will be entitled to the carriage of a considerable quantity of coals, free of expense. There is likewise a small salmon fishing attached to the property, to which he will have an exclusive right, as well as to the game on the estate. For a sportman it is a most eligible residence.

Post and coach pass within a quarter of a mile of the house, daily.

When it came to the problem of getting the family out to join him, the much-travelled George Kinloch was better informed than any travel agency about the alternative routes from Dundee to Paris, and he wrote on the 29th of February with detailed, although possibly slightly confusing information and instruction about the possible ways of coming—

As to the *time* of your coming out, you must judge for yourself. You cannot come too soon for me. At the same time, as you have your choice of the time, you should take the benefit of the moonlight, by setting out after the first quarter. As to the manner of coming, I don't think you would find it at all pleasant in a merchant vessel from Leith to Havre, as a Merchant ship has no conveniences for ladies, and probably not economical either. I should think your best plan would be to take the after cabin of a Smack to London, where you could stop a few days *in a lodging* which John could take for you. Unless a bottle or two of white wine, and a jar of treacle, you need no stock of provisions in the smack, and I would recommend to you to come by one *the largest* of them. From London, if you can meet with a vessel going to Havre, that will be your best way, as Havre is only fifty-three leagues from this, whereas Calais is seventy. You must get your passport at the French Ambassadors, as to which, John will tell you. *It costs nothing.* If no vessel for Havre, or if the accommodation is not good enough, then you must take any other way that may be thought more expedient; only don't take your places farther than the seaport you are to land at. A few biscuits, apples or oranges are all the provisions you need, for the passage. If you don't come by sea from London, I believe you will find it a good plan to come by the coach to Worthing or Hastings and from thence to Boulogne. There is a packet plies between them, but it sails (I believe) only once a week (Thursday). Perhaps you may find it necessary to take the ordinary route by Dover. By taking the inside to yourselves, I suppose they would allow you to pack six instead of four. As soon as your route from London is fixed, write to me *by two successive posts* mentioning the day you are to set out, and the place you are to land at, so that I may be there to meet you.

On looking at the Almanac, I find it is full moon on the 29th. March so that, if you could be ready to sail on the 26th. or thereabouts you would have the benefit of her ladyship's light all the way.

He started looking about for a house for them to rent, but these were difficult to find and finally he decided to give up the quest until the family arrived.

As none of you understand enough of French to direct French servants I thought you would find yourselves more comfortable to board, for some months, at any rate, as by that means you will have no trouble at all.

It was as well that George Kinloch decided that he would take rooms or a furnished house, as the amount of essential paraphernalia which he found it necessary to ask his wife to bring for him was extensive enough, besides her own and the five daughter's luggage.

I desire you to bring out with you, the two bugle horns, the yellow fiddle, (Hardie's), case of mathematical instruments, and parallel ruler, 3 ft. rule, Courants from the middle of December to middle of January, Walker's dictionary, Buchan's medicine, Cobbet's grammar, Almanac 1820, George's Jacobite songs, Stenhouse's Ready Reckoner, Cartwright's Bill, the copy of Paines Rights of Man. Thompson's songs, Irish Melodies, the best of the pianoforte music with the accompaniments. Byron's poems, Lady

Morgan's France. My light gun I used generally to shoot with, three or four dozen knives, say the balance knives with the black handles and the green ivory ones. You need not bring many forks, as they use only silver ones. A dozen breakfast knives. Calomel, do. pills three grains in each. My razor with the white handle and the separate blades, but not the case. Marking ink, some of Leslie's ink powder. The small scales and weights. A dozen of my best shirts, neckcloths, six white handkerchiefs. The best white waistcoats. Nankeen pantaloons, six best silk handkerchiefs, four pairs best black silk stockings, Do. socks. This is all I recollect at present. *You must not bring anything that is new.*

There were considerable alterations and additions to the list such as a large supply of seeds and plants with their roots wrapped up in damp sog, which must have added to the problem of stowing in the coach where he recommended that 'you should take the inside to yourselves and I suppose that they would allow you to pack six instead of four.'

His obliging five daughters who had never been further away from home than to Edinburgh were given some simple smuggling instructions —

If you could manage to smuggle over the silver forks, I would wish them brought. Each of you could put two of them in each sleeve, with the blunt ends in your gloves at landing, and, as they are not so rude as to shake hands with ladies, there is no risk. You would need to have them in your pockets or reticules before embarking as you might be too sick afterwards to think of them.

While these elaborate arrangements for the journey were being made, George Kinloch had been passing the time as happily as possible. He had been at the Opera at the end of January where—

On Sunday (the better day the better deed), I went to the Opera to see 'Les Danaides,' and where I heard bad music and worse singing. The dancing, to be sure, was beautiful, the scenery *superb*. You must know that the Danaides were fifty young ladies who chose to murder their husbands on the first night of their marriage, and for which deed these same ladies are sent *to hell*. In the last scene which represents this said place, all the art of the theatre is exhausted. Devils of all shapes and sizes, belching flames, and tormenting the guilty misses, flames bursting out from all quarters, thunder and lightning etc. etc. form certainly a sight worth the seeing, *for once.* Indeed at the Grand Opera, as it is called, the eye seems to be the only one of the senses which is consulted.

The Opera was closed after 13th February, the day on which the Duke de Berri had been assassinated there, and he commented on this assassination as follows —

The theatre is never again to be used for that purpose after having been polluted with the blood of a Bourbon.

The ultras would fain have it to be an extensive plot; the fruits of liberalism, but there is not the slightest grounds to suppose that Louvel had any accomplices. He seems to be a man of a strong mind, and determined character, full of love for his country and fancying that by destroying the Bourbons he was doing a real service to his country. He therefore selected de Berri as being the only one of the present family likely to have sons, for you know that in this country, the lassies go for nothing. It is said the Duchess is with child, and, if a young male Bourbon makes his appearance, old Louis flatters himself that all will be well, as if the destinies of a great Nation could nowadays be made to depend upon any individual.

Instead of the Opera he used to go out in the evening to a Café in the Palais Royal —

I get soup, a portion of four different dishes chosen from a list of about forty, a small loaf, and half a bottle of wine for forty sous, and have the additional pleasure all the time, of admiring a lady of six feet four inches high, who presides at the bar. She is young, well proportioned and comely, and therefore nowise terrific. Then, if I chuse to remain picking my teeth, a young lady gives us a Sonata on the piano-forte, with a violin accompaniment. In addition to this I get the newspaper to read, all for my forty sous, and two more to the Garçon. You will allow that this is not very extravagant. Ladies dine there as well as gentlemen, and perhaps some day, I shall introduce some of you to the tall lady, as I am sure it would amuse you.

The diplomatic bag system of correspondence for letters addressed to Mr Douglas Kinnaird, M.P. and Dr. Gilchrist and then forwarded on to Kinloch had not been very reliable so that he got into despair about not hearing when he might be expected to meet the family nor at which port of arrival. However, to see how the arrangements for the journey were progressing with the family in Scotland, it is necessary to return to Mrs Kinloch's diary, and here it must be appreciated that her brief, matter of fact entries covered revolutions in Mrs Kinloch's way of life and domestic routine.

In January, February, and March little out of the ordinary was recorded so that, besides the usual succession of friends and relations coming and going, drinking tea or dining at Arthurstone, Lintrose, Drumkilbo, Parkhill and other houses around, the diary consisted of dates of letters received and written to Mr Kinloch. There were farming facts such as 'Ploughing began on 9th February', or health matters such as on 2nd February when 'Dr. Boyter drew a tooth to me', but, on 22nd February, she entered 'I told the women we were going away.' The decision to go to France had been made and must have come like the end of the world to Helen Porter, Cecilia Carver, Margaret Duncan and the others of the domestic staff for whom Kinloch was their world and their livelihood just as Mrs Kinloch was their employer and banker. Perhaps she may have arranged for some of them to go to Balhary or other neighbour's houses.

On 10th April the entry was — 'Took our places for London,' and on the 13th — 'Left Kinloch at half past eight, dined at Captain Blair's in Dundee and embarked on board "The Perth" at two o'clock'. 'The Perth' was one of the older of the Dundee, Perth and London boats, sixty-nine feet long, one deck, a single mast, and one can only wonder what 'the conveniences for ladies' consisted of.

Mrs Kinloch and her five daughters must have filled most of the berths in the cabin quarters but, as they were each entitled to one 'barrel bulk' of luggage, there would be no difficulty in finding space for the two bugle horns, Hardie's fiddle, and all the garden plants 'wrapped in sog' that were so urgently required in Paris.

The six days passage to London were described in the diary in Mrs Kinloch's usual factual style. She may have particularly noted and remarked on 'Robin Hood Bay', because her husband was at this time signing his letters to her under the pen-name of 'Robin Hood.'

April 14th   All sick but Cecilia and Margaret. Very little wind.
April 15th   A fine wind all night, all better today, and at ten o'clock opposite Whitby, pass Robin Hood Bay and Scarborough.
April 16th. Westerly wind all night and at 10 opposite Cromer, wind fell, waited the tide opposite Yarmouth.
April 17th. Very little progress all night.
April 18th. A thick fog and still very little wind.
April 19th. Clear but still no wind.
April 20th. Arrived at London about 7 at night.

They spent the week of 21st to 27th April in London where, besides drinking tea with Dr. Gilchrist and other people, she had the pleasure of walking to Kensington Gardens which was a good tonic to recuperate from sea-sickness.

On the 22nd the entry was 'Got a passport,' and this Passport for Mrs Smith 'et ces cinq filles' is an interesting document illustrated on plate 8. It will be seen that her designation was altered from 'Dame Anglaise' to 'Dame Ecossaise.'

On the 27th they left London by the Dover coach in the evening. It must have been a tight squeeze with six of them in the inside intended for four, but, after travelling all night, they arrived at Dover at half past seven next morning.

On the 28th they arrived at Calais at mid-day and re-embarked in the coaster to reach Boulogne at nine o'clock in the evening. Whether the silver forks which were to be concealed in the daughters' gloves created any problem is not known but they had all arrived at last in France and on 29th the diary recorded —

'Wrote to Mr. K.'

Four days later 'Mr. K. arrived.'

Was she thankful to hand over responsibility to Mr K.? What recriminations were there about not having started off a

188

month earlier as instructed? But it was all right now, they could relax and follow the star of George Kinloch who told them that — there was no need to hurry off before doing a sight-seeing tour of everything of interest in Boulogne including 'Napoleon's Pillar.' The next day the united family 'took their places,' that is booked in for the Paris coach.

CHAPTER FIFTEEN

Three Years of Outlawry
1820-2

GEORGE KINLOCH soon came to realise that he would have to settle down to the life of an exile abroad for an indefinite length of time and that this was going to be a humdrum way of life. He would have to live under an assumed name, be careful what he talked about, and to whom he spoke besides having to be more than usually careful about the pennies.

The arrival of his family gave him the new interest in taking them round on conducted tours of Paris, but this was entertainment enough for a short holiday only, and did not provide a way of life such as he was accustomed to. He took them to look at the statue of Louis XIV which had just been erected in the Place des Victoires, and commented —

C'est une horreur. La tête du cheval resemble beaucoup plus à celle d'une vache marine (hippopotomus) qu'a celle d'un cheval et quant à Louis le grand, il est habillé en Romain, c'est à dire les cuisses et les bras nûs et la tête assublée d'une grande peruque telle que les Romains n'ont jamais vue, j'en suis sûr.

A letter of 16th May written to his brother-in-law said —

Mrs. Smyth with Ann and Eliza went to the English church on Sunday, and Cec. Helen and I went to the Chapelle Royale at the Tuilleries, where we saw the Count d'Artois and the Duchesse d'Angouleme. Old Louis seldom goes, as he is apt to fall asleep during the service.

Mrs Kinloch may have enjoyed it well enough to begin with, and the brief entries in her diary recorded — 'Walked with Mr. K. and got a bonnet,' 'walked the length of the Boulevards,' 'Mr. K. took us to see the Goblin Tapestries,' 'walked in the Luxemburgh,' 'all at the garden of plants,' 'went to the Louvres,' but it was not her way of life either. She missed her routine, the domestic ploys of doing the flowers, bottling the raspberry wine, ordering her household staff around, and taking cups of tea at the familiar houses. She knew that her own house was empty, that her garden would be going to seed, and that someone else would be winning the prizes at the Coupar-Angus flower show.

In September of 1820 they found a furnished house in the Boulevard des Invalides and Mrs Kinloch 'engaged Henrietta for a servant' so that life became rather more homely and they were able to do a little entertaining. Amongst other Strathmore friends who were living in Paris at that time were Lord and Lady Airlie and regular calls were exchanged. A letter of 13th December 1820 said —

We see the Airlys occasionally. The two little ladies are fine like children, and her Ladyship is in a fair way to add to the family.

Later the diary recorded on 23rd March 1821 that 'Lady Airlie got a daughter, her third'.

The Kinlochs, although outlaws living under the assumed name of Smith, were therefore, not on that account ostracized by their friends and calls were exchanged with the Hallyburtons, and members of the Kinnaird family, besides an increasing circle of new friends.

The same letter of 13th December said —

We also see Sir James Ramsay sometimes. He is deeply smitten with one or all of four sisters, daughters of the lady with whom he boards, so much so, that I should not be at all surprised if he were to make one of them a Baronet's lady; but *don't* mention this as it might cause unnecessary uneasiness.

The daughters took lessons in French and Margaret and Eliza attended the drawing school —

Margaret and Eliza have put themselves to a painting

school here, under Mr. Robert Lefevre, one of the first painters of this place.

His terms are not so extravagent as the Edinburgh ones; as it costs them (for they pay it themselves) only 24 francs a month, and they may remain in the school from daylight till dusk.

There were plenty of new things for the young people to see in Paris, and the diary of 25th June 1820 recorded that 'all but I went to see the balloon.' Another entry said — 'all went and saw the elephant.' A further entry said — 'Mr. K. went to the masked ball,' so that there did not seem to have been any eligible bachelors available to take the daughters out, and perhaps the five sisters together were rather overpowering. To be the daughter of an outlaw cannot have been a good recommendation for marriage.

Throughout the years 1820 and 1821 the scare about a Radical inspired revolution in England and Scotland gradually subsided. Some people may have been ashamed of their unnecessary panic. Lord Cockburn writing retrospectively in his own part in the crisis of December 1819 recollected 'Once more did I prepare to gird on my sword as a Captain in a thing called "The Armed Association," but this battalion was never assembled and in about a fortnight every sane eye saw that the the whole affair was nonsense. Our Tory Colonel Sir James Fergusson of Kilkerran was too much ashamed of it to call us together even to be disbanded.'

The passing of the Six Acts made it too dangerous for any popular movement for Reform to come from the people and it was only the nobility such as Earl Grey and the Duke of Bedford who were able to keep the subject alive. The Duke of Bedford had found himself challenged to a duel by the Duke of Buckingham because of a speech he made on Reform and about which George Kinloch commented — 'I see that a duel fought by the Duke of Bedford against the new made Duke of Buckingham terminated without any ducal blood being shed. Bedford's speech in favour of Reform was very strong and, if his brother nobles would follow his example, the thing would be done soon and quietly.'

In Scotland the Six Acts made it impossible even for a

192

firebrand like Mr Rintoul of the Dundee Newspaper to mention Reform and the politics of his paper became less outspoken.

The unfortunate Gilbert McLeod was the one scapegoat as a result of George Kinloch's speech. This man, the printer in Glasgow, who had been given a short sentence of imprisonment for Contempt of Court for having printed words to the effect that the Jury chosen for the Trial had been 'packed,' was later charged with 'Sedition' because his paper, had printed the text of George Kinloch's speech. He was defended by Mr Jeffrey, the Whig Advocate who had been briefed to act for George Kinloch, who showed in his defence of Macleod that many other newspapers had also printed the Speech, but, in spite of this and of a recommendation by the Jury for leniency, Macleod was convicted and sentenced to five years transportation.

In a letter of March 1820, George Kinloch commented — I see how very merciful the Cormorants have been to poor Macleod and I have not the least doubt that, had we ourselves been there, we should have fared no better. These brutal villains who at present pollute the judgement seat don't consider that, to a man of moral feelings, Botany Bay is worse than death. To a London blackguard, transportation is no punishment at all. It is to him, a party of pleasure. What would it be to you or to me, or to any person in our rank of life, or to any person possessed of moral feelings? Certainly, death would be preferable. These robed miscreants, altho' they dare no longer inflict bodily torture, seem to delight in inflicting torture on the mind, and of the two, the last is undoubtedly far more severe than the former.

In place of the front-page news about the dangers of Radicalism, the newspapers of 1820 were filled with the trouble between George IV and his wife Queen Caroline, who had been married for twenty-five years but had been separated since the first year of marriage. Throughout the summer and autumn of 1820, more than half of the news columns of 'The Scotsman' were occupied with the extraordinary evidence in the House of Lords debate on the Bill of Pains and Penalties to decide whether or not there had been an improper relationship between Queen Caroline and her servant Bergami.

George Kinloch commented about this —

Our gay and youthful King wants to take unto himself a wife and produce, from his own Royal loins, a prince who shall be heir to all his father's virtues. As he is only sixty-two years of age and has always been equally remarkable for sobriety and temperance as for honesty and goodness of heart, I have no doubt that he would succeed in the object dearest to his mind, by blessing us with a long line of Kings with hearts equally Irish and Hanoverian as his own.

The King's popularity sank to rock-bottom when he refused to allow the Queen to attend his Coronation, and to celebrate this occasion and also in an attempt to bolster up his image, it was announced on 27th July 1821 that — 'His Majesty has been pleased, through the Lord Advocate, to extend his Grace and Mercy to fifty-one Radicals accused of High Treason. Those who were in prison have been discharged and those who had absconded are at liberty to return.'

Perhaps George Kinloch was considered to be a special case but, for whatever reason, his name was not on the list of those to be pardoned. He wrote to Thomas Graham, Lord Lynedoch, who had been one of his Tutors during his minority, asking him to intercede, and about this letter he commented —

I am not very sanguine and in fact, after the virulent persecution which poor Hunt has suffered, I could not flatter myself that I was to be made an exception to the general rule; particularly seeing that I do not feel at all disposed either to acknowledge my errors or to promise to refrain from doing 'mon possible' to annoy the rogues in future. Therefore I must be prepared to remain as I am for some time and I am so much of a philosopher as to be very thankful that things are no worse.

Unfortunately Lord Lynedoch was abroad, but eventually he replied in August 1821, saying —

I have but this morning received your letter of the 21st. of June, having just about that time left England on a tour of the Pyrenees.

I regret much not having got it before I left London, as, probably, a personal application to one or two of the Ministers whom I happen to know in some degree of intimacy, (tho' always politically opposing them) might have had a better chance of being attended to than a letter. However, as writing is all that is now in my power I shall lose no time in making the trial — should it fail, you will not be in a worse situation, in being of any use to you.

I expect to be in Paris on my way home about the middle or perhaps towards the end of October. Should your situation remain the same, till then, I should wish much to see you that we might consider of the best means of extricating you from your difficulties.

> I remain, Dear Sir,
>> Faithfully yours, Lynedoch.

This avenue of approach seemed to do no good, and George Kinloch commented — 'As to Lord Lynedoch, it is all my eye and Betty Martin. I never put my trust in Princes, nor in Kings, nor yet in Lords, and I never expect any good from any of them.' He had evidently become very exasperated by this time.

It was discovered through unofficial channels that there would be no consideration of his case by the authorities until Henry Hunt, the hero or villain of the Manchester Massacre, had been released and this was not due before November 1822.

In July 1821 the Kinlochs had moved out of Paris to Chantilly and, throughout this year, Mrs Kinloch's diary became more and more depressed. The principle reason for this depression was the illness of her daughters who had all had a severe attack of measles during the winter and had not made a good recovery, so that two of the daughters returned home in 1821. In the New Year of 1822 they came to the conclusion that Mrs Kinloch might be able to do more to expedite her husband's pardon if she also returned home and started interceding with friends on his behalf. In consequence, on the 27th of April 1822, Mrs Kinloch's diary recorded — 'Cecilia, Margaret, Eliza and I left in the Calais coach.' They arrived in London on 30th April and on the 5th of May 'embarked for Dundee on board "The Perthshire," Captain White, and anchored at seven off Gray's Reach.' 'The Perthshire' was again one of the smallest of the Dundee smacks, and the family had chosen to sail on one of her worst passages. The 6th and 7th were calm days with a light east wind, but on the 8th and 9th it blew up to gale

force from the North East, and on the 10th the diary recorded—
'Wind so high, we had to lie off the Forth all night.' On the 11th
they took shelter in the Firth by daylight and anchored in
Queensferry Roads by 10 o'clock. 'All so tired we intended to
land but were afraid, the sea was so rough.' On the 12th
'remained at anchor all day, wind fallen.' On the 13th they got
as far as Monifieth and landed at Dundee on the 14th taking
nine days for a voyage that usually took five. The Balhary
chaise was sent for them, and Mrs Kinloch probably vowed that
she would never put to sea again, as she never did so.

It was not a happy or encouraging home-coming. They had
all been badly shaken by the voyage. One daughter who was
seriously ill with tuberculosis was only to live for another six
months, and Kinloch House, for which no tenant had been
found, was standing empty, so that the family had to squeeze
into the small farmhouse of Bankhead. The neighbours began
to call as usual and it was difficult for Mrs Kinloch not to feel a
very poor relation as she could no longer keep up the style of
Lady Ashburton, the MacNabbs, the Nairnes, and her other old
friends. She wrote to her husband saying that Mr Ogilvy of
Islabank had visited them and had called Bankhead an uncomfortable house, to which letter George Kinloch replied —
'As to Islabank's idea of your comfortless chateau, let them say
or let them do, its a' ane to me, but there we remain till a
considerable reduction takes place in the debt now owing by
me.' He tried to present a less gloomy picture of their home by
comparing Bankhead with the house which they had occupied
in Paris, and wrote — 'I see you have already had lots of
visitors at your Chateau in which I expect you will find yourselves "no that ill ava" after experiencing the comforts of our
superb logement dans la rue Coquenoud. The view from your
West window is at least as fine as that of the grand salon, as
you will now see the sun without the necessity of getting him
only second-hand from the reflection of a dingy white wall.
Then the chaunting of the mavis and the misle is, in my opinion,
equal, if not superior, to the melodies with which the wine-
inspired Parisians used to charm us on their return from 'hors
les barrières' and the smell of the flowers is preferable to that of
the purling stream which graces the middle of the streets of la

plus belle ville du monde. On the whole, je trouve que vous n'êtes pas bien à plaindre.'

They were badly off at home for transport as the gig had been sold so that her husband suggested a makeshift vehicle which the coachmaker might contrive — 'like the old Windsor chair they had at Balhary. The principle thing is to get a piece of good clean ash for shafts to have some spring, a pair of old carriage wheels from the coachmaker with an oil cloth cover supported on hoops. This would make it wind and water-proof and I see nothing to hinder it to take you to the theatre royal at Meigle or to a ball at Coupar if need be.'

The family was not in a position to attend the festivities in Edinburgh in August 1822 when George IV visited Scotland. Rumour had reached George Kinloch in Chantilly that his daughter Margaret had been presented at Court and had petitioned for her father's release but he knew quite well that this was only a rumour and he wrote to her saying—

Voila des nouvelles que tu ne savais pas, que tu as été presentée a notre grand monarque et que tu lui as presenté une petition pour 'tu sais qui'.

Mrs Kinloch found it difficult to make decisions with all the different advice that she received from her friends, her lawyer brothers, and from her husband still in France who recommended her — 'having been so long accustomed to trust to me for advice, you are diffident in exercising your own judgement but, in your present situation, you must assume more energy and decision.'

Shortly before Mrs Kinloch left Chantilly, her diary recorded with the usual absence of detail — 'Mr. K. hired a room from 1st. May,' and a few days later — 'I went to see the room.' George Kinloch had never attempted to look after himself before, or to do his own cooking, and so, in his first letter after the family departed, he explained how he was getting on with this and said — 'You have spoilt me so much that I don't half like this living alone. I am awakened at four o'clock when the market folks begin to arrive, however, I keep snug till half past seven when I turn out to light my fire et préparer mon déjeuner. I have bought a very nice coffee pot and having now got my establishment into tolerable order, I set the water to boil with the milk along side of it. I then commence my toilet attending, en même temps, to the pots and pans. Finie la toilette, I breakfast in state et après cela arrive le journal.'

As a result of his experiments in domestic routine he had found the value of a plate rack and recommended — 'As I presume you have nothing for dripping plates, I think that it would be worth your while to get a basket made, à la francaise, about 3ft. long by 18 ins. wide, with the sides a little spread. It must be made of peeled willows, and at the bottom the rods should be nearly half an inch asunder.'

He was never short of friends and fortunately there were plenty of people with very little to do, emigrés from their homeland like himself who were living in Chantilly at that time. Amongst these were the Rookes with whom he used to play whist, although he could not stand Mrs Rooke who usually 'fevered' them with her company. 'Diable M'emporte, were she beautiful as the Venus de Medicis, no inducement should make me stay with her, with such an infernal temper as she has.' He and Mr Rooke were made pall-bearers at the funeral of a Spaniard, 'at which the French made a wretched turnout. They clapt a huge taper into Rooke's hands but I declined the honour, however we went through all the rest of the motions, kissed the saucer, sprinkled the Holy Water etc., all very devoutly.'

Amongst his friends were a number of ladies with impressionable daughters who appreciated his kind attentions — 'the evenings of late have been so fine that I could not find in my heart to go and be cooped up at a whist table but preferred one of the nights working in Mme. d'Epinay's garden along with her and Mademoiselle, and the other night walking with Madame Iley and her daughter Marguerite on the Pelouse. 'We had a very pleasant soiree terminated by a kind of "gouter" consisting of milk and fruit with very good ripe apricots.'

With so many ladies about there could not help being some little jealousies and the Rooke's daughter Henrietta was not permitted to go to the D'Epinay's 'because forsooth, the latter has not returned her visit.' 'How we apples swim together?'

The summer entertainments at Chantilly included the 'Fête Dieu' and 'a fine roasting business it was.' 'I am sure that most of the fair demoiselles "baith swat and reekit" and that they would have been much more comfortable if they had "lilted at it in their sarks." They had a band of music enough to make a cat spew sick, no two of the instruments being in tune.' There was also a Sunday in May which had been a great day among the archers who had a wooden pigeon set on the top of a pole. 'The person who succeeded in knocking off the pigeon is declared king for the ensuing year. After we left, a man did succeed in hitting the pigeon and was accordingly declared legitimate monarch of the Archers of Chantilly for the current year. We adjourned to the Rond where we seated ourselves to admire the dancers and swallow a portion of the dust they kicked up.'

The Duke of Orleans and his suite paid a visit to the Château of Chantilly in June. The grounds were open to the public and George Kinloch took Madame de L'Epinay and her daughter along 'pour avoir le plaisir de voir manger tous ces gens là.' He described the scene and the conversation of the crowd in a letter to his daughter Margaret —

Hier, il y a eu une espece de fête champêtre. The grass had been levelled out under six large trees which were hung with lanterns so that the whole suite could dine in the open air. The château and the stables had also been illuminated and it was a beautiful evening but the ducal fête disgusted everyone. The Prince was a in bad temper and, as he went to sit down, finding the spectators too near pushed some of them back himself in a manner pas toute a fait gracieuse. At last, when everyone was seated sadly at the table, surrounded by the Chantilly crowd, I overheard the women making remarks assez grossières some of which the Duke could not help hearing: 'Ah, le voila à coté de sa grosse maitresse. Dieu comme elle mange et comme elle boit. Je parie que le vin et bon. J'en voudrai bien boir un coup moi: et moi au aussi; mais pour elle, elle est trop grosse; il faudrait qu'elle but de vinaigre au lieu du vin pour se maigrir. Ca ne vaut rien de voir boir et manger ces gens là, quand on n'a rien chez soi que du pain bis. Ah, allons nous en.'

By the beginning of October 1822 George Kinloch made up

his mind that there was so little progress being made in pushing his case for pardon that he must return home to find out how the land lay, and 'act accordingly!' Farewell parties were arranged for him and, 'as the Rookes had been so attentive to me, I thought that the best return I could make would be by giving some jolie bagatelle to Henrietta, and I accordingly bought for her a very handsome necklace of small beads with which she was so well pleased that she insisted on putting on a low-breasted frock, in order that she might sport the necklace. I added to it a cake of nice gingerbread.'

He left Chantilly on the 25th October 1822 having been convoyed to the Diligence by Mr Rooke, and others.

I had just before bid adieu to Mme. de L'Epinay and her 'aimable' both of whom seemed a good deal affected at losing one who had certainly contributed to make the last six months pass more agreeably with them, than they would otherwise have done. 'L'aimable' in particular turned very white on the occasion. The day was beautiful, and I took my place aloft enveloped in my tartan plaid, but the sun was so powerful I was glad to lay it aside. All the day time I travelled on the top of the coach, having for companion a sort of French soul doctor, but who had more the appearance of a mender of *soles*. However, he and I did very well together, and our prosperous journey was to be attributed, in some degree, no doubt to his prayers, which he said, or rather read, at least three times a day, the more acceptable to the bon dieu that these were mumbled in Latin. We stopped to dine at Clermont, I still occupying my elevated seat, ate a brace of sandwiches and my dessert consisted of excellent pears and apples, which I bought from an aged Sybil, hard by, and I washed all down with a pennyworth of brandy and water.

About sunset, the old French prêtre and I descended from our exalted station and bundled into the Rotonde, where we did our possible to arrive at the land of Nod, in which I succeeded tolerably well, but the little abbé complained that balmy sleep would not come near him, altho' he tried to woo it in all possible attitudes. It was clear moon light till about one in the morning, and with the aid of it, we got to Amiens about ten. There I took a bouillon, and above it encore another penn'orth o' brandy, total twelve sous. Having again resumed our stations in the Rotonde, we found ourselves about two o'clock at Doulens; after which we proceeded very slowly for sometime, as the night was dark and lamps being a luxury seldom indulged in by the French Conducteurs. About nine we found ourselves at St. Pol, the country having been gradually improving in appearance since daylight. The cottages were a good deal like those in England, and whitened, which, on the outside, at least, gave an appearance of neatness and cleanliness to which my eyes had been for some time strangers. No doubt, a better situation might be found for their *middens*, than just before the doors. About eleven, arrived at Pernes, where we found a good breakfast waiting us, to the which, I did all honour, and moreover enjoyed the superlative luxury of washing myself, a ceremony which my fellow travellers seemed to think wholly unnecessary. The day still most beautiful, and the little abbé and I resumed our stations on the top. The country continued improving as we advanced, there was an agreeable variety of hill and dale, the road was no longer the dull and straight line, tedious as one of Parson Sim's long sermons; but reduced to a reasonable breadth, turned and winded thro' a country, rich, well cultivated and sufficiently wooded, so that the attention was certainly kept alive by the different views which every step presented us. On a hill top, a good way to the right, we saw the town of Cassel, from which it is said, there is one of the finest views in Europe. At twelve, passed thro' Lillers, and at two thro' Airs, a fortified town, in doing which the abbé and I ran the risk of having any brains we are possessed of, knocked out, in passing thro' beneath their damned arched gateways. About four, got to St. Omer, another fortified town, in which our pericraniums were again exposed to great danger, as some of their gates were not above a foot higher than the top of the coach, so that Monsieur l'Abbé and I were obliged to dive down behind the top of the Cabriolet, under pain of being guillotined in a new way, if we did not.

We thought we were to dine at St. Omer, mais pas du tout. The abbé had taken little to breakfast and the gastric juices in his stomach began to give him broad hints that it wished to have something to act upon. Accordingly, I produced the two remaining sandwiches, and gave him one of them, at which he was much delighted but, when on opening it, he found there was beef in it, he drew back his hand as if he had seen a serpent, exclaiming 'mon Dieu, il-y-a de la viande.' It was one of his meagre days, and he was alarmed at the idea of St. Peter slamming the door in his face, for having filled his belly with beef instead of fish, upon a Saturday. What idiots superstition makes us. As I had no apprehensions upon that score, I relieved him of his fears by mangé-ing his share of the beef as well as my own and he thereupon devoured the bread and butter, tho' I don't know how far St. Peter will hold him excused for it, considering that, having been for two days in close contact with a slice of roast beef, it must have imbibed some of the noxious taste and qualities thereof. A remnant of the Clermont pears and apples served us both for dessert and drink, and we proceeded on, smoothly till after sunset, when we again stationed ourselves in the Rotonde till we arrived at Calais a little before nine. Here, the poor abbé discovered that, while he had been intent upon his Latin prayers, the Conducteur had debarrassed him of his sac de nuit, having deposited it and his umbrella safely at Amiens, to wait farther orders. Having settled at the Diligence office, we adjourned to Messieurs Meurice's, where the abbé set himself down to a good supper of fish and vegetables, while I preferred the café au lait. Apres cela, I tumbled into a good bed, and slept soundly till nine next morning.

Sunday, the weather still fine. After breakfast, went down to the pier to see the Lord Melville, and found her to be the finest vessel of her kind I had ever seen. After that dined at the table d'hôte and passed the evening à causer. I persuaded no less than five people to trust themselves to the Melville, instead of going by Dover and they all, afterwards, acknowledged their obligation to me. Monday morning we marched down to the pier, and after paying ten sous for a ladder which we did not want, stepped aboard the first Lord of the Admiralty's namesake, and which, differing totally from it's worthy name-father, is really and truly useful and fit for the work it undertakes. After a good deal of the baggage was on board, the douaniers made their appearance, and insisted upon rummaging all that remained on the quay, to ascertain that there was no treason shut up in it. This very necessary occupation detained us a good while, and procured for the Douaniers lots of polite compliments from all concerned, and at last about twenty minutes past eight, the all powerful steam was allowed to act, the wheels began to revolve, and we sailed majestically out of the harbour of Calais — 'nor cast one longing, lingering look behind.' The weather was superb, and the sun warm as in June; there was hardly any wind, and the sea nearly as still as a mill pond. The tide, to be sure, was against us, mais malgré cela, our steam sent us forward at the rate of, I daresay, ten miles an hour. There was so little up and down motion, that out of about fifty passengers, I don't think more than five or six were sick, and with them it continued only a short time. In short, if we had been so disposed, we might have danced reels or quadreels the whole time, or even country dances, for the after-cabin was large enough for fourteen or fifteen couple. There are no beds on board, but those who incline, may have mattresses to lie down on, on the floor. We passed all the sailing vessels we came up with, as if they had been at anchor, nay, so quick was our motion, that it gave them the appearance of retrograding instead of advancing. We soon came in sight of Ramsgate and Margate and passed the latter about noon. About two, we made the floating light at the Nore, and about four we were abreast of Sheerness and, as towards sunset it began to be cold, I passed the rest of the time in the cabin so I had not the pleasure of seeing Sidmouth's improvement of the landscape, which he has affected by his hanging woods.[1] We arrived at the Tower stairs before nine, having sailed about one hundred and forty miles in twelve hours, without wind and most of the time the tide against us, it being the full of the moon, and the tide consequently strong.

There were so many sacs de nuit to examine, that it was half past nine before we landed, when with my two Abbés and a young Swiss, all of whom I had taken in tow, we adjourned to the Ship Tavern in Water Lane, ate an excellent veal cutlet, drank some capital rum toddy, and then resigned ourselves to the drowsy God. I had my fichues and some of the silk handkerchiefs strapped round my waist, and my fans etc. stowed away in my breeches pocket and boots. All passed, for, tho' they felt the coat pockets of most of the passengers as they stepped into the boat, they touched not mine, contenting themselves with asking me if had I anything about me, to which, of course, I replied in the negative. They examined the Frenchmen nearby as they do in France, for which, no doubt, the darkness was some excuse.

Next morning, after breakfast, we went to the wharf but the luggage was not yet landed. Adjourned therefore to the Alien Office with my convoy, to get their papers en regle and returned to the Custom house and found the search begun. At first, they were damned strict, opening every little parcel, but says I to myself 'lads, you'll soon tire o' this.' Accordingly, I retired to the background, where seated upon a trunk, I waited patiently till after two o'clock when, judging that the principal searcher had quite enough of it, I boldly advanced with my luggage to a deputy, who tipped me the wink, along with a friendly jog of the elbow after which he began his *sham* search with great alacrity. In short, he did it so *cleverly* that I paid for nothing but a parcel of unbound books. After he had thus done his duty, he did not presume to ask anything, but made a very significant gesture, as of one who carries a glass to his mouth (pour boire), to which I made the suitable response in the shape of two shillings, which produced a grin of satisfaction on the *Phiz* of the ancient Briton.

Having thus contributed my share towards the exigencies of the State, I got into a coach, which conveyed me and all my luggage to Giraudier's Hotel, Haymarket. It is chiefly frequented by foreigners and some who wish to eat French dishes, à bon marché. I have been out every day, both before and after dinner for 'I feel not the least alarm' notwithstanding all the nonsense that Patrick Pearson has been frightening you with.

Among other passengers 'Snaigo' [James Keay, a neighbour from Perthshire] and his wife were in the packet, and made up to me very kindly. I told him my situation, and that I would go back to France in a week if matters were not arranged by that time. Mr. John Murray, Advocate was with them and I suppose they told him who I was, and he also made up to me.

Mr Patrick Pearson, the Edinburgh solicitor had written to George Kinloch Junior saying —

I have written to Dr. Gilchrist to dissuade your Father from coming — or if come — to go back, until we have an answer one way or another. Mr. Richardson thinks, with us, that his departure from France will be announced by the police there to our folks at home, and that it is impossible he can arrive in England *incognito*. And he also is quite horrified with the idea that all our solicitude is likely to be upset by a little precipitancy, no doubt most natural in your Father's situation, but which his friends one and all should try to prevent.

Despite all this advice from friends and solicitors the impatient outlaw had returned to London.

---

[1] 'Hanging Woods'. This is again a reference to the men hanging in chains at the approaches to the Port of London.

CHAPTER SIXTEEN

An Outlaw on the Run

G EORGE KINLOCH, still an outlaw, set foot in England again in the same week as Henry Hunt, the controversial personality of Peterloo, was released from prison. Hunt, who was a great showman, came out of Ilchester gaol in the early morning of 30th October 1822 wearing an elegant tartan plaid which he had been given by the Greenock Radicals and a medal hung from a gold chain, a gift from the female Reformers of Leeds. He began his first day of liberty by making a long speech outside the Castle Inn which began with the words — 'I have been confined for two and a half years in yonder dungeon but, let them put me to death if they will, they will never otherwise silence my voice on behalf of the people.' He then entered the Inn and sat down with a large company to a substantial breakfast and told his supporters that imprisonment had not improved his manners and that he was about to begin his old tricks. All this defiance of authority was reported in the newspapers and can have done no good for other suspected leaders of insurrection who were still waiting expectantly for their pardons.

A letter had reached Chantilly just after George Kinloch left for England telling him that Patrick Pearson, his lawyer, had advised that he must not return home on any account while his case was under review by Robert Peel who had succeeded Lord Sidmouth as Home Secretary. George Kinloch was not the least disturbed by this advice when it eventually reached him in London and expressed the opinion that the lawyers were being too 'Waxy nosed,'[1] that is to say too aloof and that 'he did not apprehend the smallest danger.'

The position was that the Lord Advocate of Scotland had committed himself to George Kinloch's lawyers to the extent of saying that 'I have no doubt that Hunt is, in Mr. Peel's view, the obstacle to Mr. Kinloch's pardon and this hint which I have received will be true upon Hunts' release'. George Kinloch, being an incurable optimist, assumed that such a hint meant his pardon would automatically follow Hunt's release but his lawyers had to explain that this was not necessarily the case, and that the matter was not in the hands of the Lord Advocate. Mr. Patrick Pearson wrote saying 'Upon this subject of pledges, the Lord Advocate is necessarily sensitive for Mr. Peel has on various occasions taken the liberty to show that the Lord Advocate is not His Majestie's Government for Scotland.'

November, December and January passed by without any further news of the pardon and during these months George Kinloch, living alone in London, became more and more desperate and as near to losing his sense of humour as at any other time in his life.

A certain bitterness became apparent in his letters due to a combination of disappointments, first that the authorities seemed to have shelved his petition for reprieve for no good reason, secondly that he had returned to England too late to see his daughter Eliza, news of whose death reached him as soon as he arrived in London, and thirdly the general feeling of frustration that he could do nothing for himself except to urge others to work for him.

His first letter to his wife from London said 'As to the base, infernal miscreants who have prevented me from being present to soothe Eliza's last moments, if I hated them before, I hate them ten times more now and the whole faculties of my soul shall be devoted to the destruction of their infamous and oppressive system. Since my poor child is relieved from her sufferings, I have no longer so anxious a desire for my immediate return, tho' God knows, I wish I were with you both for your sakes and mine.'

Occasionally he passed friends in the street whom he knew by sight, such as Mr Keay of Snaigo, whom he had met on board the 'Lord Melville' but he avoided them or as he expressed it 'I shyed them.' He was living at this time at No. 16 Oxendon Street, east from the Haymarket where he had 'a small room at the top of the house, not very splendid but good enough for the use of an old traveller.' Dr Gilchrist, the professor of Oriental languages, who was busily engaged in composing a universal language, was the only friend who knew his address and 'even him I see only occasionally as I dare not go to his house on account of a busy-body servant he has got, whom I take to be no better than he should be'. A letter to his wife said 'Luckily I have got acquainted with some foreigners with whom I pass the evening in a back parlour where we are not intruded on. They are chiefly Piedmontese emigrants obliged to fly their country and consequently their political opinions agree with mine. There is, however, the wide difference in our situation that they are young men without wives or families and consequently cannot feel the irksomeness of their lot so much as I do.'

In writing to his wife about the urgency of pressing his case he said 'I myself do not chuse to apply directly to anyone to use their influence in my favour but you and your brother, if he inclines, should continue to harass all those who you think would take the trouble to apply for me.' The people of influence who were mentioned were Mr Maule, Lord Lauderdale, the Duke of Atholl amongst others and particularly Mr Drummond of Strathallan, the Member of Parliament for Perthshire of whom he said 'I would expect fully as much from him as from any of those who have been applied to'. Although he was not in a position to apply himself he drafted the letter for his wife to write to Mr Drummond and ended, 'There now, take pen, ink and paper and copy the above distinctly, with the points exactly as I have made them.' One point which he made besides emphasizing the hardship which he had suffered and how his offence had been unintentional was that 'the man who is sentenced to a certain term of imprisonment has at least the satisfaction of looking forward to a fixed ending of his punishment, but to me that satisfaction is denied.'

Unfortunately Mr Drummond who was spending the winter at Courbeton in the South of France did not receive Mrs Kinloch's

PLATE 9

The Newtyle end of the 'Kinloch' railway. The building is now used for agricultural purposes

Photograph by Viking Studios, Dundee

The driving wheels were five feet in diameter and the trailing end was carried on a four wheel bogey with three foot wheels. This was the first bogey to be fitted to a railway locomotive in Britain. The weight was about nine and a half tons, and the boiler pressure was 50 lbs. p.s.i.
It cost £700

PLATE 10

The 'Earl of Airlie' the third locomotive to be built in Scotland and constructed in Dundee by Messrs. J. & C. Carmichael came into operation in 1833 letter until late in December and he replied to it early in January saying that although he had very different views about her husband's offence, 'as soon as I return to England, I shall take the earliest opportunity of informing myself upon the subjects in order that my application, when made, may be more effectual.'

In the meantime, George Kinloch was going about London wearing a rather flimsy disguise and calling himself sometimes Mr Smith and sometimes Mr Oliphant. He wrote to his daughter Margaret saying 'Je ne m'expose pas sans necessité et il y a si peu de gens qui me connaissent, que je ne pense pas courir le moindre risque. Avec mon toupet et mes lunettes meme tu ne me reconnaitrais pas.'

He kept himself fit by doing long walks such as 'Saturday last, being a fine day I walked out to Richmond, ten miles, dined there and then went on to Ham two miles further with fine moonlight.' He watched the progress of building on what were then the outskirts of London and commented — 'Yesterday I went as far as Regent's Park, by the new street which leads to Portland Place. It seems to me that this last undertaking will not be very successful because half the houses are empty.'

He went to Drury Lane where he saw 'Rob Roy' with Macready acting 'Rob,' and commented 'Die Vernon was murdered by Miss Gree who sings prettily but whose acting is naught. Some of the Scotch airs were beautifully played and very near "gart me greet" but, upon the whole, I do not think that the piece is well arranged.' He saw 'The School for Scandal' which was 'remarkably well acted,' and 'Othello' with Edmund Kean playing the name part. At Christmas, Drury Lane staged a pantomime called 'The Golden Axe' in which 'Columbine is very pretty and she and Harlequin trippt it neatly on the light fantastic toe. Pantaloon, the clown and Scaramouche were all remarkable for their agility and for their indifference to kicks and cuffs and thumps and bumps which they most liberally bestowed upon one another. It seemed also to be a matter of indifference to them whether they left the stage on their feet or on their hands, on their hips, on their backs, or on their bellies.'

He had been used to buying Radical pamphlets from the shop of Richard Carlile[2] who had been imprisoned for printing seditious literature and, at this time, the bookshop was trying to evade the law by an unusual method. 'I went to Carlile's shop today and I wondered that nobody appeared. Presently a voice asked me what I wanted and, on looking round, I perceived a sort of apparatus in the partition from whence the voice issued. The pamphlet I wanted was then shoved thro' a slit and I was desired to put the money in a tin thing from whence it slid into the concealed place from whence the voice came. It seems they have fallen upon this scheme to puzzle the rascally vice society, as it is impossible to prosecute a voice.'

This winter of 1822/23 was again very cold and the Thames was frozen over on both sides with a lot of floating ice going down. He wrote with gloves on to describe skating on the Serpentine —

I went yesterday to the Serpentine where I was tempted to buy a pair of skates and to try if I still knew how to use them. At first, I felt a little like the Legitimates on their thrones, a little insecure but, by and by, I recovered my footing and became more steady, carrying on à merveille and without gettin' a fa' till, just as I was finishing with a fine outside sweep, my skate happening to come in contact with an unlucky piece of gravel frozen into the ice, I assumed an attitude of complete prostration, both elbows at the same time coming into rather rude contact with the ice. I trudged away home, congratulating myself that it was no worse.'

He was not so lucky when a few days later he was 'crossing St. James Street, my foot slipped and I took full length measure of myself on the ground. I was in the act of buttoning my cloak at the time, so that my hands did not come quick enough to the rally to save "my nez" from a most intimate connection with the pavement or rather with the frozen snow which covered it, so that the claret spurted forthwith. On getting home and admeerin myself in the glass, I found that it had increased to a very respectable size, besides possessing a fine Bardolphian hue, so that I straitway applied to the eau de Cologne.'

By the middle of December, he became so depressed that he felt he must either return home or go back to Chantilly where — 'I should be at liberty to look all the world boldly in the face and not go sneaking about as I am obliged to do here.' He said

'My paramount reason for taking this step is on account of my health which I am convinced would suffer, were I to remain even a few weeks longer in this damned hole. I have a falling off of my appetite and a sluggishness of the bowels which you know is very unusual with me and two days in my own house will put me all to rights.' Contemplating this return home, he had already told his wife to move back into the big house making the excuse that it was for health reasons, but he had to know that the security arrangements at home were all right. 'Then, as to the servants, you could no doubt trust Angus and Ceece Carver as to keeping the secret, but could you trust your other women? They and perhaps Johnny Mill are all who need ever know of the "outlaw" being there. As to coming without being kent, leave that to me, only make shure after I am there. It is a step I would rather avoid but unless Drummond undertakes it and succeeds, I have no immediate hope from the cold-blooded reptiles here.' By the next post his wife replied saying 'I hope in God they will have given you leave to join us but your health is not to be trifled with and I sincerely hope soon once again to embrace you in your own house.' Her reply about the servants had not been satisfactory enough and in his New Year letter he instructed — 'You must ask them distinctly whether they will, if necessary, pledge themselves not to divulge the secret to any human being nor even hint at it in the most distant manner. It should be done with each separately and before two of your daughters. If they solemnly pledge themselves to it, it would be a great satisfaction to me to know that, as far as they were concerned, I could depend on them.'

This letter of 1st January had started by saying 'Many, many happy returns of the day to you and yours. Twice have the villains forced us to keep it separately but, let us hope that in future we shall be independent of them and their atrocious laws made to protect knaves and oppress honest men.'

By the middle of January there seemed to be no progress with the pardon so that, on the 19th he made up his mind to take the risk and return home. The plan was made 'I see by the papers that the West road is very much incumbered with snow so I shall take the York road. I propose to leave this on Tuesday if I can accomplish it, get to York on Wednesday evening and stop there all night. Leave for Newcastle next morning and stop there all Thursday night. Leave Newcastle on Friday morning and get to Edinburgh that night. Stop all Saturday with Wig and Gown man and leave it (Edinburgh) that night by the Mail so as to get to Perth about five on Sunday morning. Leave it immediately, en poste, and stop at the 15 mile stone and then walk on thro' the fields to Headlakehall.' The Wig and Gown man with whom he intended to spend a day was his son George who had a room at Swords Lodging, the corner of Rose Street, the window looking into Hanover Street, up two stairs where he expected to be safe for twenty-four hours. Kinloch, meaning head of the loch or lake, is not difficult to identify with Headlake hall and the 15th mile stone is still standing about a mile short of the Kinloch gates. The letter describing his plan for return went on to say 'My appetite is already improved and I feel every way better since I made up my mind to be away from this smoky hole. You need not be alarmed at the chance of my being frozen on the journey as I am pretty well provided for it. In addition to my great coat and tartan cloak, I have bought a famous camblet cloak with sleeves and cape all lined with baize, also a pair of furred boots for a carriage, and as I have not as yet put on either flannel vest or drawers, I shall have the benefit of them also; so I expect to keep up the radical heat malgré the frost.'

This plan for his return journey home was upset at the last moment because Mrs Kinloch received another letter from Mr Drummond saying that he was passing through Paris at the end of January on his way back to England and that he hoped to meet Mr Kinloch there. This involved operating an elaborate bluff as George Kinloch had to pretend that he was still in France and he wrote a letter to Mr Drummond which was to be posted in Boulogne, pretending that he was staying there.

This difficulty postponed his departure from London for a further month but on Monday the 10th of February he wrote saying:

My Dearest,

I have booked the *blue packet* for Wednesday morning. Gets to Newcastle Thursday at 2 p.m., stops a night there, to Edinburgh on Saturday night, leaves it on Sunday night by the Mail and should get to Perth about five on Monday morning. Now, if you can beg, borrow, hire or steal a Gig, without letting the owner know who or what it is for, Angus might set out on Sunday night, so as to be at Perth about 11 and so have his horse fed and ready to start with the parcel on the arrival of the Mail, and so get home before the folks are stirring on the road. He will inquire for Capt. Smyth at the Mail coach office which I believe is in the George Inn in George Street. Should he not be there, said Captain will proceed in a post chaise. Have been running about all day in a terrible rain and no time to say more.

Hoping to embrace you and the lassies on Monday morning,

Your most affectionate,
Short and Sweet.

This final plan which had been so carefully arranged did not work as smoothly as expected for reasons beyond his control and the last letter from the outlaw on the run explained his unforseen difficulties en route —

Newcastle,
Friday night 14th. Feby. 1823.

My Dearest Helen,

The parcel has got thus far, all safe but it seems the snow to the Northward is still so deep, that no carriage has yet come here from Berwick and I am consequently condemned to remain here till Monday morning, and I expect to get to Edinburgh that night but, as this is not certain, I cannot fix a day for you to send for me to Perth, and if Angus should be gone there, before you receive this, you must recall him. This is bien désagréable, as you may well believe. There was no snow on the other side of York, but it increased as we approached Durham and in the stage before getting to Durham, it was in some parts five or six feet deep on each side of the coach and the fields quite covered with it. I hear that in some places to the Northward, they have been obliged to put up scaffolds and to lift it twice before they can throw it out of the roads. I had no conception of this, and I hope you have not had such a dose of it in the Strath.

Trusting to see you all on Wednesday or Thursday at farthest,
I remain,
Ever yours snowbound.
No coach has come from Berwick since the 1st. of the month.

As Angus with the borrowed gig had been recalled from Perth it can be supposed that the original plan was resorted to and that George Kinloch took the mail-coach from Perth and left it at the fifteenth milestone, pretending that he was on his way to Arthurstone and walked home from there across the fields. The story told by an old wife that she remembered, as a girl, peering out across the fields in the dim light of a freezing dawn and that suddenly out of the mist she saw a tall man striding across the forepark, may therefore have been true. She rushed down-stairs to warn her mistress, and so the outlawed Laird of Kinloch came home.

The entries in Mrs Kinloch's diary of 18th and 19th February 1823 were in her usual laconic style —

18th. Weeding my garden.

and 19th. Mr Kinloch arrived in the morning.

The security arrangements and the secret must have been well kept so that soon after his return a letter was received from Mr Drummond reporting a successful interview with Robert Peel and saying that —

The Secretary of State has consented to recommend to His Majesty to extend his mercy to Mr. Kinloch provided he addresses a Memorial to the King, expressing of his contrition and regret in having offended against the Laws of the country and pledging himself to live quietly and like a loyal and good subject in future.

Although there was the usual stream of visitors coming and going during the months of March, April and May, there is no mention of Mr K. in the diary, so that one must suppose that he was secreted away during these three months, until the 25th of May when Mrs Kinloch recorded —

A letter from George saying that Mr. K's. pardon was arrived.

[1] 'Waxy-nosed.' This refers to the 'make up' commonly used by Advocates, consequently 'off hand' or 'superior'.

[2] Richard Carlile (1790–1843) — Free-thinker, publisher of the 'Black Dwarf', imprisoned many times for publishing seditious pamphlets and advocating freedom of the Press.

CHAPTER SEVENTEEN

Mr K. Went to the Railway Meeting

GEORGE KINLOCH'S FEELINGS on his return to freedom were very different from those of Henry Hunt. He was not and never had been a revolutionary and he did not seek either publicity or limelight. All that he had tried to do was to clear his own conscience by expressing his convictions about the rights of man and, he saw no point in knocking his head against a stone wall. If the country was not ready for Reform, there was nothing more that he could do for the cause. He had done his bit and had got little support from friends or relations. The ten years after his return from exile were spent therefore in comparative peace and quiet and he kept his Radical views to himself.

The cost of his legal defence, the surrender of his bail-bond and the lack of supervision of his farms had seriously affected his financial situation so that the first priority was to get the farms back on to a paying basis and to live economically. All the furniture and contents of Kinloch House had been sold and the re-furnishing had to be done gradually, as opportunity offered, picking up odd bits of furniture at sales here and there wherever good bargains were to be found. Entries in Mrs Kinloch's diary such as 'Got three tent-bedsteads and mattresses,' and 'Got a claw-foot table' showed how progress of the re-furnishing operation proceeded.

George Kinloch collected a little ready cash by selling his Forfar County vote and was liberal with the proceeds, as he wrote to his wife from Dundee in June 1824 —

215

I am happy to say that the vote is at last sold at £525. Tell the girls that, as I am *growing rich* they are to have ten pounds apiece out of the price, to buy bonny wallies with and John will give it them as soon as he receives it. If you would accept any part of it or if you would point out anything you would let me get for you in London, there is no part of it I would dispose of with so much pleasure.

With his own share of this money George Kinloch set off on a return visit to France. On this occasion he was acting as guide, or, as he described it, in the office of Cicerone to his friend Mr Tailyour from Carnoustie, and besides this he had many invitations to visit old friends in London, Paris, and Chantilly. He wrote to his wife on Sunday 27th June 1824, from Old Slaughters, St. Martin's Lane, London, describing the voyage south in 'The Dundee' —

We went on board at Dundee at $\frac{1}{2}$ p. 5 in the evening, and after a great deal of ohioing and hauling and breaking two warping ropes, the Captain found that he had sat too long with his friends, and that he had lost the tide. This, you may believe put us into a most delectable humour, and we abused first the Captain and then the Company till our vocabulary, but not our choler, was exhausted. When we found that our *eloquence* had no effect in moving the vessel thro' the mud, we moved ourselves ashore, and took up our quarters for the night, and again embarked at 6 next morning. Poor Spink was very uneasy at having incurred our displeasure; and I will venture to say he will not soon be so caught again. There was this to be said for him, that it was only his second or third voyage in the Dundee, and a neep tide; while the vessel draws about three feet more water than his former one. He was very attentive to us, and certainly no one could be more anxious or pushing to get on, so that altho' we met in wrath, we parted very good friends, and I would sail with him in preference to any of the others. When we got to the ocean we found a nasty up-and-down sea, with a good deal of wind, almost in our teeth. This prevented us getting on steadily, and opened the biliary ducts of most of the passengers. Our fellow passengers were a Mr. Phillips from Cupar, Fife. I believe a master brewer, there; a very

pleasant young man, and of the *right* way of thinking; a
Scotch baker returning to London; a Cockney tailor or some
such animal; a jolly English farmer of some kind; a smart
young groom, very civil, and who never sat down to meals
till we were done; and a poor little girl going to her uncle,
a baker here. In the steerage we had two friends from the
Circuit, with very ugly bracelets on their ankles, and who
were going to finish their education by a seven year's
attendance in the hulks. It would appear that both of them
had a great desire to know accurately how time went; for
one of them was sentenced for having swindled about a
watch, and the other had appropriated no less than three of
them from his fellow ploughmen. The sentence on both of
them was by far too severe, but Judges must do something
for their salaries. We were out of sight of land, part of
Sunday and the whole of Monday, and on Tuesday morning
we found ourselves in Cromer Bay, just under Holkham,
Mr. Coke's residence. We passed Yarmouth about 4
o'clock, and then stood well out to sea, when the wind
failing us, and the tide against us, we anchored. Got under
way at 5 on Wednesday morning, and rattled on at two
knots an hour to Gravesend, and then steadily up the river
to the Wharf a little before 8. We saw the 'Olive' which
had sailed the tide before us anchor in Yarmouth roads, and
when the breeze rose next morning, we saw her, as Pat
says, just out of sight.

We took up our quarters for the night in the Cock and
Lion, the genteelest hotel in the genteelest part of London —
namely Wapping. I left it after breakfast this morning to
seek for lodgings in this quarter of the town and a pretty
hunting I had before I stumbled upon this house, but we
are very comfortable here.

He met many friends who were to him 'of the right way of
thinking,' including the Hon. Douglas Kinnaird who invited
him to watch the procession to the opening of Parliament from
his house.

To see old *Tunbelly* rolled past his house, on his way to
Westminster. We accordingly did so, and saw the old fat
fellow trundled down the street in his gingerbread coach,

every inch of which, wheels and all, is gilt, and certainly very few misses under twelve years of age would think it otherwise than, as Mathews says, very particular damned beautiful.

He called on Major Cartwright — 'who and Mrs. Cartwright were very glad to see me and I dine with them today.' He met Joseph Hume of whom he said — 'I am much pleased with Hume. He comes up to my expectations,' and again — 'I was much pleased with the opportunity of getting at once pretty well acquainted with Hume.'

He set off to France with Mr Tailyour on 2nd July, as described in a further letter —

I took coach down to the Ship tavern Water Lane, and we very soon adjourned to our beds; but not to sleep soundly, at least as far as I was concerned, for I was obliged to get up and light my candle to go a bug hunting, in which very delectable amusement I was tolerably successful, having killed two brace and a half at three turns; but not till they had made me feel their powers of annoyance. I got up at 4, and after taking off our beards we proceeded in a wherry to the Lord Melville. We began to move at ½ p. 5 and went down the noble river in fine style. There were about 130 passengers and all of them were very much at their ease till after we cleared the south foreland, when, from the appearance to windward, I was aware that a change, not for the better, was about to take place. Accordingly the wind increased and the waves occasioned a great deal more motion than was agreeable to the estomacs of most of the passengers. The sea ran so high as to render all that part of the deck before the mast, or rather chimney, untenable, and on going below, the compound of villanous smells made it impossible for any one not sick, and having the use of their nose, to remain a moment. I therefore made a hasty retreat and took up my quarters in the lee of the chimney, which was the only dry place on deck. The whole of the lee side of the vessel was manned with people in all the various agonies of sea-sickness, and I don't believe there were above ten out of our whole number who did not pay for their temerity in quitting dry land. Mr. T. and I were among the fortunate few who escaped, but neither of us were at all sorry to hear 'land' announced; and about 5 o'clock we entered Calais harbour, and proceeded to Meurice's.

They travelled by coach from Calais to Chantilly and Paris where George Kinloch was to visit many old friends and writing from Rue St. Marc No. 12 on 11th July 1824, he said —

Tailyour is away out by himself to glour at the bonnie wallies in the Palais Royal. He asks you to inform his wife that he will not write until he returns to London.

We dined at Mr May's and drank quant. suff. of his fine wines; after which we adjourned to the Opera, where as usual, we heard a deal of bad music and saw some beautiful dancing, with which T. was delighted, as well as with the scenery and quickness of the changes. After the Opera, we filed off to Tortonis, and ate our ices, con gusto. On the 8th. we went to the Palais de Justice, the Préfecture, la morgue, but nobody in it; Nôtre Dame, and up to the top of it, la halle aux vins, jardin des plantes; fountain of the elephant, and père la chaise. After dinner to Tivoli and once down the mountains, to Montmartre, and ended by *icifying* at Riche's on the Boulevard des Italiens. On the 9th. to Versailles at ½ p. 11, saw the parc, le petit Trianon and the Chateau, and returned to dine at ½ p. 5, and finished by taking our ices at the Café de Paris, Tortonis rival.

Mr Tailyour went home alone and George Kinloch extended his tour abroad by way of Rouen and Le Havre to Southampton and writing from Downton near Salisbury the home of his friend Mr Rooke, he described the return journey.

I left Paris at ½ past 6 on Sunday night, and got to Rouen next morning about 7. Got to Havre at 8 at night, two hours later than we were due. All Havre was in a bushel of confusion, expecting 'the august mother of the darling child on whom repose the hopes and expectations of all France,' at least so said the Mayor's proclamation, altho' I verily believe that the grass would continue to grow, and the grapes to ripen, though the 'darling child' were at the bottom of the sea. However, be that as it may, the 'august mother' was expected on Tuesday, and the Havrians decked out in their best array, went forth in thousands, to meet her.

The town was illuminated, the lamps burned and went out, one by one, but still no Duchess. At length, about $\frac{1}{2}$ past 11, the cannon which had been placed for the purpose, announced to the Havrians that the measure of their happiness was complete, as the august mother of the darling child was actually within their walls; and those who had been foolish enough to wait her arrival, of whom I was one, had the inexpressible satisfaction of seeing — not the Duchess, but the carriage in which her august person was contained. Upon the whole, it was an amusing scene. Next morning I was very glad when ten o'clock came, which was the hour appointed for sailing. Accordingly I went aboard the Camilla, and after the *johndairme* had inspected our passports, and rummaged all the beds to ascertain that we had no smuggled *bodies* aboard, the wheels began to revolve at $\frac{1}{2}$ p. 10, and we soon lost sight of Havre and its illuminations. I went to bed, and slept tolerably, till 6 on Thursday morning, when, on getting up, I found we were within sight of the Isle of Wight, which we coasted along till we came off Portsmouth about 9.

We landed some passengers, breakfasted, and landed at Southampton about a quarter before eleven; having had a most pleasant passage, without any sickness. Passed the ordeal of the Custom house very easily, watches, chains, etc. all safe, including some which Lady Airly entrusted me with.

From Southampton he set out in a 'caravan sort of machine' to Whaddon near Downton where the Rooke family met him in a pony chaise and took him to stay. Knowing George Kinloch's enthusiasm for sight-seeing, the Rookes took him in the gig to see Salisbury Cathedral where they heard a fine organ and also to Stonehenge —

Where the stones at Stonehenge came from, who took the trouble to bring them, how they were brought and put up and for what purpose are questions which have puzzled and will puzzle the brains of poor mortals while the world lasts. Therefore I shall not venture to add my opinion.

He returned to London by the Weymouth coach which passed at half past ten and arrived at Hyde Park Corner at eight o'clock, 'having been driven the last forty miles at the rate of more than ten miles an hour.'

Back home in Scotland the social round at Kinloch returned to normal and the names of all their old friends and many new names from all the big houses in Strathmore appeared in the diary which recorded everyone who came to breakfast, to dinner, to call, or to take tea. Kinloch House became again an open and welcoming house for invited or even accidental guests such as Lady Forbes of Edinglassie, who arrived with two daughters, her son and nephew, when her carriage went on fire after the axle had become overheated and they all stayed for two nights until a repair was effected. One man who became a regular breakfaster was Charles Guthrie, younger of Taybank, an estate near Carnoustie, and in October 1825, the Kinloch daughter Margaret was married to this well-to-do Laird. Mr Guthrie was able to help financially and gave the family the present of a carriage so that the younger generation were able to attend social occasions such as the Perth Races, about which a daughter's letter said —

I forgot to mention how George liked the Perth Races. I believe it is a very stiff assemblage in general.

The Kinlochs were becoming socially acceptable again even in the Murray stronghold of the Perth Races.

By the autumn of 1825, Mr and Mrs Kinloch were both fifty years old which was beyond middle age by the life expectation of the time. Mrs Kinloch was very glad to return to the routine life of her house-keeping, wine making, and to restoring her garden, as her diary showed with the dates of the planting of the mignonette seeds, when the first Jacobite rose was blown, and all the other important records of a keen gardener. George Kinloch, on the other hand, had lost nothing of his youthful energy and enthusiasm for anything new and unusual.

He had never been replaced as one of the land-owner representatives on the Dundee Harbour Board so that, on his return from exile, he began to attend meetings of this Board again, and by doing so he came in contact with the business community of Dundee at a time of great industrial expansion. It was this association with the business people of Dundee which provided him with a new interest and enthusiasm to take the place of his political activities.

The late 1820's were exciting years for anyone with imagination and the Dundee Advertiser kept its readers up to date with a scientific column which described all the new inventions provided by the steam engine. The improvement in sea communications by the steam engine was a feature of the time.

George Kinloch had been greatly impressed by the possibilities of the steamboat as a result of his voyage home from France in the 'Lord Melville,' his passage out again in the same boat, and return to England in 'The Camilla.' He had returned home to find that the steamboat ferries across the estuary of the Tay from Dundee to Fife, whose construction he had approved as a member of the Forfar County Committee before he went into exile, were operating successfully. There was also a new steamboat called the 'Hero' making a daily passage up and down the river Tay from Dundee to Perth where previously the sailing boats had to allow several days for the return passage by this narrow tidal river. There had been some talk about the possibility of constructing a canal through Strathmore to provide an outlet to the sea at Montrose for the linen goods which were spun and woven in the villages and towns of the Isla and Esk river valleys but George Kinloch never supported the idea of a canal. He preferred to explore the possibilities of a railway by the short route through a break in the Sidlaw Hills from Newtyle to link Strathmore with the improving harbour facilities at Dundee.

The Tay ferry boat engines had been constructed by two Dundee brothers, James and Charles Carmichael, who specialised in the construction of stationary engines for the flax-spinning industry. James had an inventive brain and his contribution to industrial progress is best remembered by his invention of 'The fan blast' which produced a revolution in the iron foundries of industrial Lanarkshire. James Carmichael and George Kinloch, who were of the same age, are the two Dundonians whose statues stand a few yards away from one another in Albert Square, Dundee. It is therefore probable that they were friends, although there is no record of any correspondence between them, and it may have been that James Carmichael interested George Kinloch in the possibility of a steam locomotive operating along railway lines.

The first steam locomotive to work successfully on a railway was the 'Rocket' which was built in 1830, so that Dundee was well to the forefront in railway thinking when a meeting was called in February 1825 to consider the feasibility of constructing a railway from Dundee to Newtyle to give an outlet to the sea for the products of the linen mills and the agricultural produce of Strathmore. This meeting, under the chairmanship of George Kinloch, agreed that there was a case for a survey to be made as a result of which an architect by the name of Charles Landale was appointed to make the survey and to report back. A copy of Landale's survey appears in the appendix.

At this date, early 1825, there were no railways in operation with steam locomotives. Owing however to the bad state of the roads, it was being found economical in many parts of the country to lay railway tracks along which the rolling stock was towed by horses. The Stockton and Darlington railway began in this way, as described in an article in 'The Scotsman' of 30th December, 1826, which said —

Railway coaches are now plying regularly on the level part of the road between Darlington and Stockton. These coaches are each drawn by a single horse and yet carry six passengers inside and from fifteen to twenty outside, besides a due proportion of luggage, and run at the rate of ten miles an hour. The above seems an enormous load for one horse to run with and at such a speed; and yet to look at the animal it appears to make scarcely any exertion. It is only occasionally that he gives the vehicle a pull; at other times even ascending the slope from Stockton to Darlington the traces seem to hang quite loose. The coach had no springs of any kind and yet the motion was fully as easy as in any coach on the roads.

This was the conception of a railway against which Charles Landale was invited to make his plan. It involved the construction of three stationary engines to pull the wagons up three steep inclines by ropes and also required a tunnel of over 300 yards long through the Law Hill behind Dundee to bring the

223

line down to sea level. Landale recommended using horses to pull the wagons along the level stretches of track in the first instance, but his report stated that 'in the long term there is reason for believing that machines will work at much less expense than horses.' He knew that no satisfactory locomotives had been produced, but anticipated that it was a mechanical perfection which was sure to come. The Carmichael brothers contracted to produce the three stationary engines for £3,700 and Landale estimated the whole cost not to exceed £26,000.

As a result of this report the necessary capital was subcribed and Landale was instructed to proceed with the work, which started in January, 1826. The largest shareholders were the town of Dundee, the Earl of Airlie, Lord Wharncliff, the Rt. Hon. William Ogilvie and George Kinloch who each subscribed £1000, with George Kinloch acting as Chairman.

George Kinloch and Charles Landale went up to London in April 1826 to pilot the Railway Bill through Parliament and reporting in a letter to his wife on his journey south, he said —

I was like to be a little annoyed on my journey by a bowel complaint which does not at all suit with mail coach travelling; but being a bit of a doctor, I applied to an apothecary at Belford for some Laudanum and peppermint which acted like a charm and enabled me to continue my journey.

There was the usual round of social engagements to attend in London besides piloting the Railway Bill through Parliament, and on 23rd April, he wrote —

On Monday, Landale removed to this house [Reid's hotel 76 St. Martins Lane], and we called on Lord Airly and saw both him and his Lady who seemed to be very near her time, and is looking well. The Bill to restore the Peerages has been introduced.

John of Kilrie [a Kilry Kinloch] came and sat with me till past 12. He expects his regiment to be sent to India and is here trying to exchange into the Cavalry. He is offered a cornetry in the Life Guards for *only* three thousand guineas; or, in the Lancers for one thousand. He waits the decision of his Tutors.

We went to see York House[1] now a building in the stable-

PLATE 11

Commemorative china kindly lent by Dundee Art Gallery and
Museum

Photograph by Viking Studios, Dundee

PLATE 12
Statue, erected in Albert Square, Dundee, on 3rd February 1872, by public subscription, in memory of George Kinloch

Photograph by Viking Studios, Dundee

yard of St. James Palace. It is an immense house all cased with Bath stone. No one can tell where the money comes from tho' I have a shrewd guess that *we*, the *Canaille* have the honour of supplying it. Wyatt's brother Phillip is the architect. We dined with him at Charles Wyatt's.

I dined at Hume's and met no fewer than eight M.P's., namely Sir Robert Wilson, Sir John Newport, Rothiemurcus Monteith, Spring Rice, Maberly, Gurney and Hume.

On the way North he reported again—

Landale and I mean to stop at Darlington to see the Railway and also at Newcastle to see a great many curious things above ground and in the bowels of the earth.

On this journey North he travelled in the mail-coach with John Swinton, a kinsman of Sir Walter Scott, which meeting is reported in Sir Walter Scott's *Journal*[2] —

Coming from Berwickshire in the mail-coach, John Swinton met with a passenger who seemed more like a military man than anything else. They talked on all sorts of subjects at length on politics. Malachi's letters were mentioned, when the stranger observed that they were much more seditious than some expression for which he had three or four years ago been nearly sent to Botany Bay and perceived John Swinton, surprised at the avowal, he added —

'I am Kinloch of Kinloch.'

It can be seen from Mrs Kinloch's diary with her frequent entries — 'Mr K. went to a Railway meeting,' that the supervision of the construction of this railway provided her husband with a great new interest from its first meeting in 1825 until the line eventually opened on the 8th December 1831.

There were many unforseen difficulties and acrimony over the cost, which greatly exceeded the estimate, but without George Kinloch's determination, it might never have been completed. It opened for traffic only three months after the Glasgow to Garnkirk railway which was mainly used for freight. It was well patronised in its early days, and Mrs Kinloch's diary entries show that it paid dividends. Connecting links were provided by a coach proprietor in Blairgowrie who advertised that he ran a coach leaving Blairgowrie at half past six to catch the railway coach at Newtyle at nine a.m., and said that parcels were forwarded carefully and that the fares were moderate. Connections were also supplied by the Defiance Coach from Coupar-Angus which advertised an elegant, light, two horses, safety-coach, which carried four inside and ten outside passengers, constructed in the new improved London fashion.

It will start from Coupar-Angus at a quarter before eight o'clock so as passengers may arrive at Newtyle to be conveyed to Dundee by the first Railway Coach and she will remain there until the arrival of the last Railway Coach from Dundee.

It must have been as exciting for many people as a first flight in an aeroplane and one letter has been found from an unknown traveller 'Cousin Rebecca' to 'Dear Emily' dated the 28th of May 1832 which described her feelings about this new form of transport—

You can't think how delighted I was last week with the ride from Dundee to Newtyle in the Railway Coach. The bustle at taking my seat — by the by, neat ladders should be furnished by which to ascend the coach instead of compelling the ladies to scramble up by long strides and coming off the coach is worse for one's petticoats are entangled, and the inconvenience is so bad as you can't imagine. Well, as I was saying, the bustle, the tolling of the Railway Bell, the sudden movement of sixty human beings by an unseen power upwards like a flock of geese in the air and onwards by a horse at full gallop — the light and shade of the tunnel through the Law — by the by, it's rather dark about the centre; however that depends upon who one happens to be seated beside — the promiscuous mixture of young lassies, young ladies, and crones — dandies, parsons, farmers, merchants, weavers and ploughmen — the varied expression of faces, some merry, some stupid, some sad — the driver Sam lauding the merits of his horse and cracking his whip and his jokes. Dundee and its foul-mouthed chimney stalks fading from our view — flying through a mountainous region, the atmosphere of which is cold as the Arctic regions — the sudden bursting on us of the warm rich Vale of Strathmore — all contributed to my amusement.

After passing through the tunnel, a dandy waved his hand indicating his intention to take a seat — in his hand a fishing rod and in his cheek a cigar. He tript lightly to his seat and, though snug himself, annoyed me with the fumes of his tobacco. A labourer sat behind him with a cutty pipe stuffed with pig-tail. The smoke and smell was almost insufferable and I was almost chocked. I would complain to Mr. Kinloch but he is such an advocate for the liberty of the subject that I have little hope by his means of putting an end to the filthy practice. Little did the dandy know that, but for the nasty cigar, I could have admired him —

Your cousin Rebecca.

As the Glasgow and Garnkirk railway was mainly concerned with freight, 'The Kinloch Railway' may well take the credit of being the first passenger railway in Scotland, and the Railway Station at the Dundee end, has been given credit by 'The Railway Magazine'[3] of being the first Railway Station in Scotland. Some people may call it 'Kinloch's Folly,' as most of it, like General Wade's roads, has now disintegrated into the marsh land, but, nevertheless, in its time it was a triumph of progress and of difficulties overcome.

George Kinloch did not live long enough to see the locomotives operating along it or to develop the new town of Washington, planned as the rail-head town which was to be a collecting centre for the produce of Strathmore. This town of Washington, was to have been a memorial to his hero George Washington, and was one of his dreams which never came true. Like the railway, it was a dream, worth the dreaming by a man with a lively imagination who spent so much of his time thinking how he could help those who were not so well off as himself.

[1] York House — built 1825-27 to the design of Benjamin Wyatt for the Duke of York. The cost of construction was eventually financed by the Duke of Sutherland. This building became The London Museum and is now called 'Lancaster House.' It is used for the entertainment of official guests from overseas.

[2] Sir Walter Scott's Journal, 1825–1832, page 224

[3] Railway Magazine, April 1954, page 78.

CHAPTER EIGHTEEN

Reform has become Respectable

EARL GREY'S WHIG MINISTRY came into office in the autumn of 1830. The King, William IV did not mention Reform in his Address at the opening of Parliament but, before long, such a flood of Petitions from the English and Scottish Boroughs were presented that it became generally accepted that a Bill would be introduced in the Commons to give some measure of reform of the franchise.

The first English Reform Bill which was introduced by Lord John Russell in March, 1831, proposed to disfranchise sixty Rotten Boroughs and to give representation to all the large towns in England. In Scotland the principle change in the Borough representation was that Edinburgh and Glasgow would each return two Members and that Aberdeen, Paisley, Dundee and Leith would be entitled to a Member of their own for the first time.

It was to be nearly two years before the Reform Bill and its Scottish counterpart became law but it rapidly became apparent that no Parliamentary candidate was likely to be successful in a contested election unless he declared himself to be a Reformer. Consequently the doctrine of Reform became respectable, and strange boasts were made by many people who had previously held very contrary views.

In January, 1831, there was a vacancy in the representation of the five Burghs of Dundee, Cupar, Perth, St. Andrews and Forfar, and their choice of a new member fell on Mr Francis Jeffrey, the Whig Advocate who had been briefed to defend

George Kinloch at his trial eleven years earlier. By this time, Mr Jeffrey had been appointed Lord Advocate, and, never having visited Dundee, he was invited as a guest of honour to the town. the 'Dundee Advertiser' did not fail to note that this visit was a great change for Dundee which ever since 1793 had been denounced as a 'hot-bed of sedition' and that the Lord Advocate was coming on this occasion to visit them, not in his character of Public Prosecutor but as a guest to partake of their hospitality. As Lord Advocate he was given full V.I.P. treatment, a gun salute from the shipping in the harbour, a coach and four to meet him at the docks, and a reception and dinner in company with over four hundred people in a banquet hall in Castle Street. Amongst the top-table guests were Mr Kinloch of Kinloch, Mr Hallyburton of Pitcur, Mr James Ivory, Mr Clayhills of Invergowrie and other well-known people.

The hall was described as being brilliantly lighted by gas and so presenting a splendid appearance. Behind the chairman there was a transparency, exhibiting a full-length Britannia, bearing in her right hand a portrait of our gracious Sovereign William the Fourth, and Liberty flying towards her with a wreath. A band of music sat in the gallery amidst a bower of shrubs.

In the course of a long speech after the dinner which started at 5.30 p.m. and did not break up until after midnight — the Lord Advocate said that he had always been in favour of Reform and that the time had now come when those opinions which had long been held by men of intelligence could be expressed with impunity and added that their popular Monarch himself was a Reformer.

George Kinloch may have thought to himself how times had changed to hear such an opinion coming from the Lord Advocate. When it came to his turn to speak, being entrusted with a toast to honour the Press, he restricted himself to few words compared to the other more verbose speakers, but he could not refrain from alluding to the new attitude towards Reform, and said —

Ten years ago, had anyone dared to lift his voice in favour of Reform or to vindicate the people's rights they, like me, would have been sent upon their travels.

It was directly after this dinner that he was tempted into

breaking his political silence and returning to politics. He had been baited into doing so by a letter under the pseudonym of 'Taodunensis' in the 'Dundee Courier' the Tory newspaper, which by this time had a fairly large circulation. This letter described him as an 'ambitious aspirant after popularity,' and said that he was 'bankrupt in reputation and fortune,' and that his political principles were 'inimical to the general good of the country.' He replied as follows in a letter to the rival newspaper 'The Dundee Advertiser,' giving the lie to these scurrilous remarks —

Born into the privileged class and with acres enough to make me independent, I might have lain on my oars and floated calmly down the stream of life, a useful or perhaps a useless country gentleman, regardless of corruption on the one hand or of oppression on the other, but my principles forbade me this inglorious career. Seeing that the happiness of the many was still to be sacrificed to the privileged few and judging that Reform was the only remedy for so monstrous an evil, I was induced to join my feeble voice to that of millions who called for it and proud I am to see that many of those who, erewhile, would have shunned a Reformer as they would a mad dog are now obliged to toss up their caps and shout with the multitude. I continue to be a Radical Reformer although I am neither 'bankrupt in reputation and fortune,' nor 'an ambitious aspirant after popularity' through the medium of 'tumult, anarchy or confusion.' I expect, erelong, the hustings shall be erected at the Cross of Dundee and then, if you think any other candidate better qualified to represent you than I am, I shall bow to your decision for, although a Radical, I am too patriotic to wish to occupy a place for which you shall judge another to be more fit.

As soon as he had made it clear that he was to be a candidate for the Election as Dundee's first Member of Parliament, the Dundee Advertiser gave him their backing and said that they would give him every support. His most serious opponent was Mr D. Charles Guthrie,[1] described as a London merchant, with some business connections in Dundee who started early on to make a door to door canvass of the new electors. The Tory newspaper said that as a merchant and a gentleman of indefatigable industry and perseverance he would commend himself to the great mercantile community of Dundee, but he cannot have been a very glamorous character as the best that one of the correspondents to the 'Courier' could say in support of him was that 'he is unobjectionable in every respect.' The 'Dundee Advertiser' did not agree and asked whether there were any qualities in Mr Guthrie in which Mr Kinloch did not equal or excel him.

In other parts of the country George Kinloch's work for Reform was remembered and at a meeting in Greenock under the chairmanship of Sir John Maxwell, Baronet of Pollok, Mr Kinloch's health was on the list of toasts, and the proposer said:

While I am proud to see the new converts to Reform, so numerous and so highly respectable, raising their voices publicly in behalf of Reform, I am still prouder of those highly-respectable and gifted and excellent individuals who fearlessly came forward and stood in the front of the battle for liberty, at the risk of fortune and personal freedom and I am only sorry to say that few indeed were the number in Scotland. But, there is one who deserves to be noticed, a landed proprietor who came forward and presided at a meeting of the people for the purpose of petitioning for reform, for economy and retrenchment and who was obliged for this offence to fly from his country to escape the prosecution of the Lord Advocate who seemed bent on sending our patriot countryman on a pilgrimage to the land of convicts and of kangaroos. He saw those who lived upon the taxes wallowing on the fat of the land, he saw an agricultural aristocracy imposing a bread tax on a nation of paupers and a myriad of useless placemen, sinecurists and unmerited pensions, a large standing army in times of peace and that the taxes levied upon an exhausted people would soon bring about anarchy. He boldly proclaimed reform, come when it may, and come it shall for a' that. Let us then drain a bumper to the health of the patriot Kinloch of Kinloch who stood forth in the hour of danger at the hazard of fortune and personal freedom.

In London 'The Spectator', now edited by George Kinloch's

old friend R. S. Rintoul, supported his candidature and said—

> We say nothing of the gratitude which is due by Scotland, by the Empire and by the world to such names as Mr Kinloch who by their noble daring opened up that no longer narrow way in which Reform is now marching. We rest not his claims to present support on past deeds, we speak of these but as an earnest of future exertions. We say trust him not because of what he was, but trust him because of what he will be.

In July 1832, the Reform Bill became law after the creation of new Peers to enable it to pass through the House of Lords so that prorogation of Parliament and a new Election was expected before the end of the year. The candidates for the new Dundee seat remained George Kinloch and the London Merchant, Mr D. C. Guthrie, but the 'Dundee Advertiser' fearing that another country gentleman might be sponsored and become a more serious rival said—

> There has been talk by those who object to Mr Kinloch to bring forward another gentleman. The essence of their objection is that Mr Kinloch would represent the people too well and the aristocracy not enough. They do not like him partly because he is beloved by nine-tenths of the people of Dundee including all the working classes and they cannot bear the idea of the latter having anything to do or say with the laws affecting their lives, their labours or their daily bread. Mr. Kinloch's friends should be on the alert.

Fortunately Mr Kinloch's friends were on the alert and told him that Mr Guthrie and his friends were making some impression on the voters by intense canvassing, fulsome promises, and by spreading some damaging rumours about George Kinloch's attitude to the Church. George Kinloch did not approve of individual canvassing and attempting to collect promises of votes, as he thought that this practice might lead to bribery or intimidation, but he agreed to address a large open meeting of his supporters and reply to his critics particularly on the subject of his Sabbatarian views.

At this meeting he said—

> I am not a Reformer of yesterday. I have long been a Reformer and I think that you may be pretty certain that I

will not now abandon my principles when I am floating gaily on the tide instead of struggling against it. It has been asserted against me that I have no regard for the Sabbath because my workers do not observe the 'Fast Days.' My workers, it is true, are allowed to work on the 'Fast Days' and I permit this because I consider that these days are set aside to deprive the poor man of the means to earn his pittance. As to the assertion that I wish the Sabbath abolished, it is a calumny altogether without foundation, although I am of opinion that more might be done on that day for the instruction of the people than is the case at present. I have spent a good many years abroad and whilst there, I respected the institutions of the country whatever they were. In Turkey, I would make my low bow to the Sultan or the Mufti and, in France or Italy, I always conformed to the customs of the country as became a peaceable traveller.

and ended by saying—

I have no selfish ends in view. It is said of a Scotsman that, if nothing else occurs, he will whittle a stick rather than be idle. I too must have a stick to whittle or something else to do for I hate to be idle.

I have endeavoured to discharge my duty as a landlord, a magistrate and even as a doctor for the benefit of my neighbourhood. My object has been to do all the good in my power and use my talents such as they are to the service of my country.

The 'Dundee Advertiser' was confident that George Kinloch had the support of almost the whole of the working class population of Dundee but, with the extension of the vote going only to those who paid a rent of £10 or over, the electorate did not include working-class people. He was still at 'daggers-drawn' with the self-elected town council of Dundee, as can be seen from a letter written to James Saunders, a member of the Guildry in which George Kinloch imagined himself as Dean of Guild with a seat on the Town Council and said — 'I am sure I should be as welcome as the devil at a Presbytery dinner.' The Town Council must have carried a certain amount of weight with the

1600 voters who consisted of the gentry, professional people, merchants and shopkeepers and so, when it came to the week of the polls, the position was by no means certain.

The date on which the election was to be held was the responsibility of the Sheriff of the County who decided that the Dundee election would take place during the week of 19th to 24th December. Nomination day was to be Monday 19th, polling on Wednesday and Thursday, and declaration of the result on Saturday.

Nomination Day was the climax of the election campaign. It was taken to be a public holiday so that all shops were closed and the workmen from the factories began to parade the streets at an early hour with banners, music, and placards. The hustings had been erected at one end of the High Street, and by mid-day the street was packed with thousands of people gathered to hear the Sheriff read out the Writ and later to hear speeches and ask questions from the candidates. The hustings consisted of a large platform, divided down the centre by a railing so that Mr Kinloch and fifty of his friends could occupy one half and Mr Guthrie and his supporters the other half. After the Writ had been read, the proceedings were opened to the candidates and they both in turn attempted to address the crowd. Speeches and questions went on for many hours, but in fact Mr Kinloch's supporters were so vociferous that Mr Guthrie had little opportunity to make himself heard; feelings were running very high, and it needed all of George Kinloch's powerful influence on the crowd to prevent the meeting from becoming a riot.

The polling took place at three polling booths situated at the Steeple Church, Bain's Square, and Mr Russell's Church, at which booths the supervising officers checked in the voters by tallies of ten. At all of these, except the Steeple Church the first days voting went strongly in favour of Kinloch, so that at the end of the day the tallies showed 762 in favour of Kinloch and 259 for Guthrie. Although Mr Guthrie wanted to continue the contest on the following day, his supporters persuaded him that he did not have a chance and that he should give up. The poll books were therefore closed and sealed and sent to Sheriff L'Amy. On the Saturday morning the Sheriff appeared in the

Town Hall of Dundee, opened the seals of the Poll books, and declared Mr Kinloch as the new Member for Dundee.

The custom had been to chair the new Member but George Kinloch asked them to dispense with this honour as he considered that the election was far too serious a matter for frivolity of this sort, and so he was allowed to return home to spend Christmas and New Year with his family. Mrs Kinloch's diary for the last day of the year recorded —

'Snow on the ground. The work people came in and got punch,' so at least a little frivolity was permitted at home at Kinloch.

On the 2nd of January George Kinloch was invited to attend a celebration dinner organised by the electors of Dundee, with his old friend and sponsor William Christie of the Dundee Bank in the chair.

After speeches of congratulation George Kinloch replied — I duly appreciate the greatness of the honour you have conferred upon me and I can assure you that I prize it far beyond any honour which Royalty can bestow, for as our own immortal bard sings:

The King can mak a belted knight
A Marquis, Duke an' a' that
But an honest man's aboon his micht —
Gude faith he manna fa' that!

As you have been pleased to place me in this very honourable situation, I can assure you that no endeavour on my part will be wanting to justify the choice you have made. Again to quote our immortal bard as in the words he has put into the mouth of the great Argyll:

To faction and tyranny equally foe
The good of the land's the sole aim I know.

His speech ended by saying—

Gentlemen, I must mention a curious coincidence which has now occurred.

In December 1819, Sheriff L'Amy, hoping, perhaps, to make my shoulders a stepping stone to a certain bench, to which we know he would have added considerable weight, came over here, poste haste, to examine as to the proceedings at the Magdalen Yard and, in consequence, I was

235

cited to appear before a set of prejudiced judges and a packed jury for the atrocious crime of having said that we need Reform, that cutting of throats was murder and that Castlereagh was a knave and old Sidmouth a fool. My counsel assured me that I had spoken too freely and honestly against myself and that there was no chance for me but to move off. I took the advice, thinking it preferable to visit the hospitable shores of France at my own expense rather than subject my country to the expense of transporting me to Botany Bay. After three years absence, I got leave from that consummate statesman, Sir Robert Peel, to return to my family and my home.

On the 24th. December 1819, I was proclaimed at the Cross of Edinburgh, a rebel and an outlaw.

Now mark the difference!!

On the same day of December 1832, I was by the same Sheriff L'Amy proclaimed the chosen representative of the people of Dundee.

This is passing strange, but it is no less true; and you now see the outlaw of 1819 transformed in 1832 into the representative of this great and flourishing community.

It was indeed 'passing strange' how his political ambition had been achieved at last.

---

[1] D. C. Guthrie — 'The London Merchant' was a Guthrie of Craigie, an estate near Dundee and one of the wealthy Guthrie families of Angus. In 1832 there were Guthries of Guthrie, Guthries of Gagie, Guthries of Taybank and Guthries of Craigie, who were all related.
The Guthries of Craigie were London Merchants to the extent that they had an office there where they had a merchanting business with the Baltic and later with India. They were all powerful Tories and, even at the beginning of the present century, the Radical 'Dundee Advertiser' was forbidden in the house of the Taybank Guthries.

CHAPTER NINETEEN

The First Member of Parliament
for Dundee

G EORGE KINLOCH had suffered several spells of illness during
the last few years. He had missed Harbour Board meetings
and had not been able to be present at the opening of the
railway so that Mrs Kinloch had become alarmed by his
exertions at the time of the election. Nevertheless he was
determined to reach London in good time for the opening of
Parliament on the 1st February, and he set off from home on
the 21st of January as recorded in her diary — 'Mr. Kinloch
left us for Edinburgh on his way to London to attend his duty
in Parliament.'

Never missing an opportunity for novelty in the way of
travel, he decided to go so far by sea from Greenock to Liverpool taking the steamboat 'Manchester' and then travelling
on the railway from Liverpool to Manchester where he would
have his first opportunity of seeing a locomotive 'The Rocket'
in operation. His letter written at two o'clock in the morning
of 28th January 1833 described his journey so far —

My Dear Helen,

Here I am at last, after a very bousterous passage. We
got to the Mersey at 4 last night, but as we drew a good
deal of water, were obliged to wait the tide, and so, did not
get up till one. I was sick, without throwing up, and have
tasted nothing except one peppermint, since Saturday at
6 o'clock. However, I don't feel any inconvenience and am

waiting till it is time to go ashore to get the railway coach at half past six to Manchester; and from thence by the first coach for London where I expect to arrive by ten, eleven, or twelve tomorrow morning, according as we leave Manchester.

I would not have written just now, but as we are in the dock, the lights must be put out. You shall soon hear from me again, so

With kindest love to all,

Ever affectionately yours,

G.K.

He arrived in London two days later and wrote to his wife on the evening of 1st February —

My Dear Helen,

I went down to the House at twelve to-day, and it came to my turn to be sworn in, about one. The Scotch and Irish members turned out very ill, for Wales, Scotland and Ireland were all called at the same time, and only about sixteen answered. I, of course, got a shake of the Speaker's hand, and a gracious bow, and having no more to do there, I went in quest of lodgings, and fixed on one in Parliament Street, that is the street which leads down from the Horse Guards, Whitehall, etc. towards Westminster Hall, from which last it is not above 300 yards distant; so that I shall be very near the *workshop*. It is at a gunsmith's, No. 55 Parliament St. on the third floor, looking to the street — a comfortable parlour and small bedroom within it, at 31/6d. week, and free to quit at a week's notice. A good eating house hard by, and the landlady offered to cook any plain victuals when required.

On coming up the street, I met a young man of the name of Somerville who came up with me from Glasgow, and who has called once or twice for me, so I took him to show him St. James's Park, Bond St., etc. I was the better of Somerville, for last night, in taking off my drawers, I stumbled and gave my weak knee a twist, which has not done it any good. I mean to take the bath tomorrow, which I have not yet had the opportunity of doing.

King Billy is to open the Parliament on Tuesday, with

cream coloured horses, etc. etc. 'Much ado about nothing.'
This is all I have to say at present.

P.S. Tell John Irons to thrash a stack or two of wheat, and
let Carver or Fenton try to sell it. If of good quality,
Douglas will give as much for it as any one. I have either
lost or mislaid my plan of the barn-yard.

Send me a state of the weather, as under.

Toujours a vous,

G.

Weather before 2 o'clock.	*Weather after 2 o'clock.*	
Thermometer morning.	*Thermometer at night.*	
Jany.		

27. 36. South West wind with rain. Windy. Frosty 34
28. 30. Calm, sleet, foggy.   Frosty Clear 27
and so on, for the week.

Mrs Kinloch had written to him fearing that he might be
influenced by the views of some of the extremists of the day such
as Joseph Hume or Cobbett and he replied to this and also
described the opening of Parliament in his letter of the 6th of
February —

My Dearest Helen,

You ought to know me too well to think that I will allow
myself to be led by Hume or Cobbett or any man I have ever
yet met with. I say it in confidence to you, I *feel* that I am
more likely to lead than to be led. I do not form my opinions
rashly, but once formed, I stick to them steadily so long as
I think them right, so you may make yourself quite easy on
that score.

I took possession of my lodging yesterday forenoon, and
find it very comfortable. A parlor with two windows to the
street, and a small bed-room within it with one, also a large
dark closet and a large pantry within the room. The street
is *macaddamed*, so the noise, tho' great, is nothing to what
it would have been with the old pavement.

At a little after twelve yesterday, I went to the House,
and took my seat with Cobbett on my left, and my *friend*
Peel, second from me, on the right. We had prayers, as
usual. Then swearing in members till a little after two, when
the guns announced the approach of King *Bill*. Then came

the Usher of the Black Rod, as fine as a peacock, to summon us to the Lords, and then such a rush as I never witnessed, even at Drury Lane. Well, after a hard struggle, we got into the House of Lords, the side benches of which were filled with ladies in gala dresses, the floor being occupied by Peers in their Robes. Then *Bill* began to read his speech, pretty distinctly, but in somewhat cracked tone, but altho' I strained to the utmost, I could not get even a glimpse of him. He immediately departed and then I stopped a few minutes to admire the ladies and then returned and resumed my seat. Sundry notices of motions were given, and we adjourned till five.

I came home, went and dined at the Cook's shop next door for a *shilling*, including the waiter's penny, and porter, and back to the House, where the speech was read, and Ormelie in full uniform, (I suppose a Depty. Lt's.) moved the address and unfortunately for him, said a good deal too much about Agitators, for which O'Connel paid him home, smartly.

On Monday I accompanied them to the meeting of the National Political Union to which O'Connel likewise came. After the business, they moved thanks to the M.P's., and I had to get up and speechify, which I did very much to the satisfaction of the Meeting. O'Connel followed and was most powerful. Sometimes he convulsed them with laughter and at other times they were all but crying. No wonder he has such command over his countrymen. We were introduced, and he expressed much happiness at seeing me.

Now for home. You may send me two, three, or four bottles of whisky (Dunkeld); a mutton ham, if you have any; a cheese; a couple of pigs of marmalade; red jelly and black, and anything else you think fit; perhaps a small jar of salt butter. If you have a small trunk they will be safest in it, and put a bit of sponge or a little cotton atop of the whisky in the bottles, to prevent it *plunking*.

If you should take a fancy to come up here bye and bye to be my *Housekeeper*, you shall be most welcome. The lodging would hold us both; and I should be the better of you morning and evening.

Kindest love to you all and cheepies as usual,
Always affectionately yours,
G.K.

He wrote again on the 10th of Febuary in a tone of some frustration —

My Dearest Helen,

As to public matters, here we are, after four tedious debates, just where we were. Ministers have provoked it by their abominable speech, and *we* were determined to show them we would not submit to be treated like their slaves under the *old system*, but that we would discuss their measures 'ere we voted either for or against them.

I have taken a hasty dinner, each day, a little after three and been in the House always before four, when the Speaker comes in. Then we have prayers for about eight minutes, and all those who have previously put their names on their seats, and *who are present at prayers* are entitled to retain them for the night. Then goes on the private Bill business, the presenting of petitions, and so forth, till nearly six, when the Speaker calls on the Member who had moved the adjournment to continue the debate; which, on Friday night lasted till past three.

Hume, Wallace and I were in both Minorities and no other Scotch Members but Wallace and myself. To-morrow, the Report is brought up, and then it is moved that the Address be approved of. Upon this, O'Connel is to object to it, and will reply to all the abuse that has been poured upon him during the late debate. Then Cobbett moves an amendment to substitute another address, which Ministers will find it devilish difficult to grapple with.

It was on Mr Cobbett's amendment to the Address in answer to the King's Speech that George Kinloch spoke his first words in the House and these words seem to have astonished the Speaker not a little. Cobbett had been making some very unwelcome remarks which had been continually interrupted by parliamentary coughing and other interjections when George Kinloch rose to his feet and addressed the Speaker saying—

My object, Sir, in rising is merely to recommend those Honourable Gentlemen who so suddenly appear to have

241

been seized with colds and coughs to depart and leave others to discharge that duty, for the performance of which, they were sent to this House.

I call upon you, Sir, to insist on the maintenance of order.

The Speaker explained that new members must get used to such interruptions but he said 'I assure the Hon. Member that I will exert myself to the utmost in maintaining order.'

He wrote home again on the 16th of February —

My Dearest Helen,

I can assure you I do not starve myself. Here is my daily plan. Rise about nine, infuse my tea, shave etc. demolishing two penny rolls. Then letters, all of which that I can answer forthwith, I do. Then out to the Park or elsewhere, having previously gone to the House to ticket my seat. At twenty minutes past three dine at the eating house next door, where the things are very clean and good, and a *plate* of meat, but oftener a plate and a half is as much as I can devour. I then trudge off to the House, so as to be there a little before four, when the Speaker comes in, and then we have prayers, and anyone at prayers can take any seat not then occupied, altho' ticketted.

I have been to-day to 74 Edgeware Road, to let Mr. Sharp the engraver correct the likeness, which will be in the printer's hands by Monday, and from thence I tumbled into an omnibus and rode to the Exchange for 6d. They are long coaches holding fourteen inside, vis a vis. I then walked home, read Earl Grey's *horrible* plan for Ireland, and now write this.

God bless you all, not forgetting the cheepies,

Ever yours,

G.

Earl Grey's horrible plan was the Irish Coercion Bill and George Kinloch gave his views on this Bill in a letter published in the 'Dundee Advertiser'. He said —

For my part, I cannot for the life of me see how additional severity is to effect a cure. Severity has been tried in Ireland without success for six centuries, a long enough period, one would think, to convince any reasonable man of the folly of still persisting in it. Many are of the opinion that a little

242

kindness would be more effectual. I fear that that is not a word to be found in the Stanley vocabulary [Stanley was the mover of the Bill in the Commons]. It would at least have the recommendation of novelty and of cheapness whereas the coercive measures will cost the keeping of an immense military force.

His letter of the following week described a little more social life. He called on Mrs Hallyburton whose husband had rented (from Lord Strathaven) a house at 8 Stanhope Street, looking down on Hyde Park. 'She desired to be most kindly remembered to you all.' He dined at Mr Joseph Hume's house, and having 'cabbed it' was the first to arrive. It was to be a male party and consisted of Sir Henry Parnell about 6 ft. 2 in. and an uncommonly fine-looking handsome man. 'We were almost all M.P's. — Sir John Maxwell and his son, Alderman Wood, Warburton, Shiel, Wallace, Bannerman, Roebuck, Col. Evans, Ewing of Glasgow, two others and myself. O'Connel was to have been with us, but having promised to attend a great meeting in the evening he requested to be excused. We were all pretty much of one mind as to politics. We had a most sumptuous dinner and all kinds of wine and broke up about eleven when Wallace, Ewing and I walked home together.' He had frequent calls from his old friend Mr Rintoul who was at this time editor of 'The Spectator.' Mr Rintoul was in trouble with a charge of libel against him by 'some blockhead of a Lord.'

In spite of these occasional social engagements and going out to the hot baths — 'I went and took my bath in Leicester Square and scrubbed and brushed myself thoroughly,' George Kinloch attended the sittings of Parliament most assiduously although he seldom had an opportunity to take part in a debate.

His final words in Parliament expressed views of which modern Scottish Nationalist enthusiasts would approve. It was during a debate on the second reading of the Royal Burghs (Scotland) Act which had been moved by the Lord Advocate and about which Mr Murray, the Member for Leith, was speaking when an English Member interrupted by saying — 'I really cannot conceive how Honourable Members can thus wish to call the attention of the Government from the much more important subjects which at present demand their attention.'

This was too much for George Kinloch and he spoke out for the Member for Leith saying — 'When any Scotch question is pressed forward upon the attention of the Government or the public, some Honourable Member gets up and says that it is of no importance. Scotland, I can assure the House, has some feeling; and the infamous manner in which the Burghs have been managed has excited a strong feeling in that country. I hope that the Learned Lord will listen to the suggestion of my Honourable Friend, the Member for Leith.'

Besides the arduous routine of attendance in Parliament which his letters described, George Kinloch had become involved in an exhausting correspondence with people and committees from all over the country with those who wanted to express their liberal ideas against the abuses of the times by petition or pamphlet. Those who could not trust their own Members of Parliament to give proper publicity to their wishes felt sure that George Kinloch was the right man to champion their cause.

Pamphlets and letters reached him from such diverse associations as the Cotton Weavers of Bolton-le-moor, the Greenock Puritanical Society for Sunday Observance, the Kirkintilloch Church Reformers, a Shrewsbury Society detailing grievances and unparalleled injustice to the welfare of society, from Birmingham advocating religious liberty and the liberation of the Rev. Robert Taylor who was confined for his opinion upon the Scripture, from the Warwick Political Union against the measure for coercing the Irish, from the Brick and Tile makers of Yorkshire against the excise duty on bricks and tiles, from the Howard Society of Dublin for prison reform and mitigation of the death penalty in Ireland, from the Guildry of Perth in favour of Burgh Reform, amongst many others. There were many letters exhorting him to oppose the Irish coercion Bill and from Paisley, the Renfrewshire Political Union sent him a silver medal, electing him an honorary member and saying that Sir John Maxwell of Pollok was presenting their Petition against the Bill.

From Glasgow he received a proof of the third volume of the Glasgow Reformers Gazette which was dedicated to him:

To

George Kinloch Esq., of Kinloch, M.P.

who

escaped from the tyrants of 1820

and is

now battling, like an honest man, and a patriot, the true
cause of the people in Parliament.

He had, at last, achieved the position to which he had
devoted his life. For the few short months of his Parliamentary
career he had become the champion of the cause of the people.

The first indication that all was not well with him was when
he wrote at the beginning of March saying—

I have a cold in my head but, farther than making me blow
my nose oftener than usual, I suffer no inconvenience from
it. Where I sit in the House, there is a draft of air comes in
from behind which is far from pleasant. I am obliged to sit
with my hat on, as indeed most of the Members do.

The cold developed into a more serious fever and he
confessed to his wife — 'I have been very unwell and I have
kept my bed mostly but I flatter myself the disease is past the
worst. The people are as attentive as possible, but still I miss
you sadly and the bairnies to chatter to me.'

He wrote to the 'Dundee Advertiser' explaining that he had
missed his turn to present a petition from Dundee about
Sabbath observance and said — 'I have not been able to
witness the "palaver" owing to a severe attack of inflammation.
I ascribe my illness to the utter want of sufficient room and
proper accommodation for the members of the House and the
foul heated atmosphere we are compelled to breathe in it.'

On the 13th of March he wrote to his wife—

My Dearest Helen,

I am getting on slowly, but steadily; and if the weather
would only moderate, so as to allow me to go out, I should
soon pick up again. Till it alters, I must keep the house; as
it has been colder these last ten days, than all the preceding
winter here.

Altho' very loth to quit my post, I think I shall, as soon
as the weather changes, ask leave of absence, so as to get
about a month, including the Easter holidays to recruit, and

245

to lay in a stock of health for the summer campaign. I have had petitions sent to me from Kirkaldy, Leith, Glasgow etc. and letters saying, they apply to me because they have lost all confidence in their own Members. This must gall these M.P's. a good deal, but it may perhaps make them more attentive in future.

With cheapies and kindest love, as usual,

Always, affectionately yours,

G.K.

P.S. Any prospect of the locomotives[1] soon being in action?

He got up too soon and attended the House on the 18th in order to present some Petitions but he was unable to accept an invitation from Mr Cobbett to his birthday dinner on the 20th of March. His last letter written on the 23rd of March said that he had not been out again but sent 'Cheapies to the Bairnies and kindest love to you all.'

He died on the 28th in his lodgings in 55, Parliament Street, London, with the sound of the London traffic passing by on the newly macadamised street. It was sad that he could not have survived to come home and see his beloved Strathmore again. His body was brought home by Peter Rooke, his old friend of Chantilly days, in the steamer 'The Queen of Scotland' which now sailed from London to Aberdeen. At Aberdeen his son George met the cortege and brought the coffin home in the Defiance coach to the private burial ground at Kinloch within sight of the Sidlaw Hills and Tullyfergus Braes which he had known so well.

Mrs Kinloch's diary of the 6th April 1833 recorded the last scene —

'My beloved husband laid in our Mother Earth.'

---

[1] The locomotives 'Earl of Airlie' and 'Lord Wharncliffe' built by the Carmichael Brothers came into service in September 1833.

Bibliography

Besides the family letters and papers mentioned under acknowledgments, the following printed papers have been consulted:

Kinloch of that Ilk	by Eve T. Wayne — printed privately in 1922
James Carmichael (1776–1852)	by S. G. E. Lythe in Abertay Historical Society Publication No. 13–1968
Peterloo	by Donald Read, 1958
Major John Cartwright	by F. D. Cartwright, 1826

Other sources of information are recorded by footnote at the end of each chapter.

Index